macromedia® FREEHAND®9

Using FreeHand

macromedia

Trademarks

Afterburner, AppletAce, Attain, Attain Enterprise Learning System, Attain Essentials, Attain Objects for Dreamweaver, Authorware, Authorware Attain, Authorware Interactive Studio, Authorware Star, Authorware Synergy, Backstage, Backstage Designer, Backstage Desktop Studio, Backstage Enterprise Studio, Backstage Internet Studio, Design in Motion, Director, Director Multimedia Studio, Doc Around the Clock, Dreamweaver, Dreamweaver Attain, Drumbeat, Drumbeat 2000, Extreme 3D, Fireworks, Flash, Fontographer, FreeHand, FreeHand Graphics Studio, Generator, Generator Developer's Studio, Generator Dynamic Graphics Server, Knowledge Objects, Knowledge Stream, Knowledge Track, Lingo, Live Effects, Macromedia, Macromedia M Logo & Design, Macromedia Flash, Macromedia Xres, Macromind, Macromind Action, MAGIC, Mediamaker, Object Authoring, Power Applets, Priority Access, Roundtrip HTML, Scriptlets, SoundEdit, ShockRave, Shockmachine, Shockwave, Shockwave Remote, Shockwave Internet Studio, Showcase, Tools to Power Your Ideas, Universal Media, Virtuoso, Web Design 101, Whirlwind and Xtra are trademarks of Macromedia, Inc. and may be registered in the United States or in other jurisdictions including internationally. Other product names, logos, designs, titles, words or phrases mentioned within this publication may be trademarks, servicemarks, or tradenames of Macromedia, Inc. or other entities and may be registered in certain jurisdictions including internationally.

Apple, the Apple Logo, Macintosh, Power Macintosh, Mac OS, and LaserWriter are registered trademarks of Apple Computer, Inc. Adobe, Adobe Type Manager, Illustrator, and Photoshop are trademarks of Adobe Systems Incorporated. CorelDRAW is a registered trademark of Corel Corporation or Corel Corporation Limited in Canada, the United States and/or other countries. Java and all Java-based marks are trademarks or registered trademarks of Sun Microsystems, Inc. in the U.S. and other countries. GIF-LZW is licensed under U.S. Patent No. 4,558,302 and foreign counterparts. This software is based in part on the work of the Independent JPEG Group. The Graphics Interchange Format is Copyright © CompuServe Incorporated. GIF is a Service Mark and the property of CompuServe Incorporated. Portions Copyright © 1988–1992 Sam Leffler. Portions Copyright © 1991, 1992 Silicon Graphics. Images © 1999 PhotoDisc, Inc.

This guide contains links to third-party web sites that are not under the control of Macromedia, and Macromedia is not responsible for the content on any linked site. If you access a third-party web site mentioned in this guide, then you do so at your own risk. Macromedia provides these links only as a convenience, and the inclusion of the link does not imply that Macromedia endorses or accepts any responsibility for the content on those third-party sites.

Apple Disclaimer

APPLE COMPUTER, INC. MAKES NO WARRANTIES, EITHER EXPRESS OR IMPLIED, REGARDING THE ENCLOSED COMPUTER SOFTWARE PACKAGE, ITS MERCHANTABILITY OR ITS FITNESS FOR ANY PARTICULAR PURPOSE. THE EXCLUSION OF IMPLIED WARRANTIES IS NOT PERMITTED BY SOME STATES. THE ABOVE EXCLUSION MAY NOT APPLY TO YOU. THIS WARRANTY PROVIDES YOU WITH SPECIFIC LEGAL RIGHTS. THERE MAY BE OTHER RIGHTS THAT YOU MAY HAVE WHICH VARY FROM STATE TO STATE.

FreeHand was created by Macromedia, Inc. © 1988–1999. All rights reserved. US Patents 5,353,396, 5,361,333, 5,434,959, 5,467,443, 5,500,927, 5,594,855 and 5,623,593. Other patents pending.

This manual may not be copied, photocopied, reproduced, translated, or published in any electronic or machine-readable form in whole or in part without prior written approval of Macromedia, Inc.

FreeHand is produced under the license of DIC to use copyrights of color-data-base derived from sample books. Color Database © Dainippon Ink & Chemicals, Inc. Pantone, Inc. is the copyright owner of PANTONE Color Computer Graphics and Software, licensed to Macromedia, Inc. to distribute for use only in combination with FreeHand. PANTONE Color Computer Graphics and Software shall not be copied onto another diskette or into memory unless as part of the execution of FreeHand. PANTONE® Computer Video simulations used in this product may not match PANTONE-identified solid color standards. Use current PANTONE Color Reference Manuals for accurate color. © Pantone, Inc., 1986, 1988. PANTONE and HEXACHROME are registered trademarks of Pantone, Inc. The Proximity/Merriam-Webster Linguibase® © 1983, 1990 Merriam-Webster, © 1983, 1990. All rights reserved. Proximity Technology Inc. GIF-LZW licensed under U.S. Patent No. 4,558,302 and foreign counterparts. Kodak Digital Science and the DS monogram symbol are trademarks of Eastman Kodak Company and are used with permission. Stone is a trademark of International Typeface Corporation and is used by Stone Type Foundry Inc., under agreement with ITC. © 1991, 1992, 1993 Stone Type Foundry, Inc., Palo Alto, California. Trumatch 4-Color Selector © 1992 Trumatch Inc. Additional fonts supplied by Font Bureau, Inc., Boston, Massachusetts. This software is based in part on the work of the Independent JPEG Group. The Graphics Interchange Format is Copyright © CompuServe Incorporated. GIF is a Service Mark and the property of CompuServe Incorporated. Portions Copyright © 1988–1992 Sam Leffler. Portions Copyright © 1991, 1992 Silicon Graphics.

T/Maker ClickArt License Agreement

First Edition: February 2000
Part number ZFH90M100
Macromedia, Inc.
600 Townsend St.
San Francisco, CA 94103

Acknowledgments

Written by Robin Hunt-Smith, Rocky Angelucci, Stuart Manning, and Randy Varnell.
Edited by Stuart Manning and Monte Williams.
Project management by Monte Williams.
Artwork by John Falcon, Julie Flandorfer, Rocky Angelucci, Delores Highsmith, Robert San Juan, Anna Sturdivant, and Randy Varnell.
Production by Rocky Angelucci.
Special thanks to Kent Dowden, Robert San Juan, and Anna Sturdivant.

CONTENTS

CHAPTER 4
Organizing Your Illustration

CHAPTER 5
Drawing

CHAPTER 7

CHAPTER 8

Printing 213

CHAPTER 1
Getting Started

System requirements

FreeHand runs on both the Macintosh and Windows operating systems. Before you install FreeHand and begin using the application, you need the following equipment:

Macintosh

- System 8.1 or later
- 120 MHz PowerPC processor or higher
- 32 MB of application RAM (64 MB or more recommended)
- 50 MB of available hard disk space (70+ MB or more recommended)
- CD-ROM drive
- Mouse or digitizing tablet
- 800X600 color monitor
- PostScript-compatible printer recommended

Windows

- Windows 95, Windows 98, or Windows NT 4 (with Service Pack 3) or later
- 120 MHz Intel Pentium processor or higher
- 64 MB of system RAM
- 50 MB of available hard disk space (70+ MB or more recommended)
- CD-ROM drive
- Mouse or digitizing tablet
- 800X600 color monitor
- PostScript-compatible printer recommended

Note: To conserve disk space, the FreeHand clipart is not copied to your local hard drive during installation. The clipart is located in the Clipart folder on your FreeHand CD-ROM.

Installing and starting FreeHand

This section describes how to install FreeHand on your hard disk and start the application.

Before you begin, make sure your computer meets the system requirements listed in the System Requirements section. Read the ReadMe document on the FreeHand CD-ROM for late-breaking information.

To install and start FreeHand on a Macintosh:

1 Disable virus-protection extensions and restart your computer.

2 Make sure the FreeHand CD-ROM is in your CD-ROM drive.

3 Double-click to launch the FreeHand installer.

4 Follow the instructions that appear on screen.

   The installation application prompts you to enter required information.

5 After FreeHand is installed, you may be prompted to restart your machine. Double-click the FreeHand icon to launch FreeHand from the Finder.

To install and start FreeHand in Windows:

1 Insert the FreeHand CD-ROM in your CD-ROM drive.

2 Follow the instructions that appear on screen.

3 When FreeHand is installed, launch FreeHand from the Start menu.

   FreeHand will prompt you to enter a serial number.

There are four other ways to install FreeHand in Windows:

- Double-click the installation application, Setup.exe, in the FreeHand folder. Be sure to use the Windows Explorer, not My Computer.

- Click the Install button in the Add/Remove Programs module in the Control Panel and navigate to the Setup.exe application in the FreeHand folder.

- Use the Run command in the Start menu and navigate to the Setup.exe application in the FreeHand folder.

- Select the CD-ROM icon in the Windows Explorer or My Computer, right-click to display the menu, and choose Autoplay.

Note: To disable Autoplay, hold down the Shift key while inserting the FreeHand CD-ROM.

Uninstalling FreeHand

Use the uninstaller to ensure that all FreeHand files are removed from the computer.

To uninstall FreeHand on the Macintosh:

1 Run the installer from the FreeHand CD-ROM and choose Remove from the Options pop-up.

2 Follow the instructions that appear on screen.

The uninstaller removes all FreeHand application files from your computer.

If you used Custom installation to install FreeHand in a different folder than the default location, you must specify the same location when uninstalling.

To uninstall FreeHand in Windows:

1 Choose Start > Settings > Control Panel.

2 Double-click Add/Remove Programs.

3 Select Macromedia FreeHand 9 in the list box.

4 Click the Add/Remove button.

5 Follow the instructions that appear on screen.

The uninstaller will remove all FreeHand program files from your system.

In Windows, manual uninstallation may leave several DLLs and registry database entries.

Resources for learning FreeHand

In addition to the printed *Using FreeHand* manual, there are resources to help you quickly learn how to use FreeHand.

- FreeHand Help

  FreeHand's help, available any time the FreeHand application is active, has expanded to include information on every FreeHand tool, panel, dialog box, and preference.

- Web Links

  Check the web links by choosing Help > Web Links. This launches your browser and takes you to a web page (www.macromedia.com/support/freehand/resources) containing links to helpful FreeHand information.

- Tutorials chapter

  Located in the *Using FreeHand* manual, these tutorials guide you through fundamental and advanced FreeHand features.

- www.macromedia.com

  Macromedia's award-winning web site contains FreeHand tutorials, sample art, and updates.

What's new in FreeHand 9

Integrated environment

Use FreeHand with other applications more smoothly and efficiently than ever.

CorelDRAW—Import Corel DRAW 8 files.

Fireworks—Drag and drop from FreeHand.

Flash—The Flash 3 and Flash 4 SWF export Xtra now supports:

- Clipping paths containing vector paths or image files

- Transparency Lens fills and other Lens fills

- CMYK TIFFs

- Grayscale TIFFs with a resolution greater than 143 dpi

- Exporting selected objects only

Flash Player movies—Export animation that plays at the set frame rate, with the option to play full-screen. Protect a SWF file exported by FreeHand from being imported into another Flash movie.

Flash Anti-alias—Display anti-aliased artwork on the screen, as it will appear when exported to Macromedia Flash SWF format.

Illustrator—Import Adobe Illustrator 7 files with linked images in formats such as GIF, JPEG, PSD, and Targa.

Enhanced bitmap image support—BMP, GIF, JPEG, Photoshop (PSD), and Targa formats can now be linked or embedded in their native formats.

Photoshop

- FreeHand now interacts with Photoshop 5 the same way it does with Photoshop 4.

- FreeHand files exported to Photoshop 5 PSD files (32-bit with alpha channels) retain their layers. FreeHand rasterizes each layer and exports it to a corresponding layer in Photoshop.

GIF—Dither exported GIF files at any of three levels and optimize exported GIFs to create the smallest file with the least number of colors. The new WebSnap Adaptive palette converts each non web-safe color to its nearest web-safe color.

TIFF—Import TIFFs with clipping paths.

PDF—Import documents that contain notes or links to URLs on the web. Export documents that contain notes, envelopes, symbols, or links to URLs on the web, as well as embed fonts, and use PostScript 3 gradients.

Automatic export playback—When exporting a file, choose whether FreeHand automatically opens the file in a selected external application.

Intuitive interface

Xtras and Operations—Xtra Tools and Operations are now on regular toolbars and can be customized like other tools and commands.

Default preferences button—Quickly restore FreeHand preferences to their default settings.

Text tool reverts to Pointer tool preference—The Text tool returns to the Pointer tool after you first create a text block and move the cursor outside the text block. If you prefer that the Text tool remain active as in previous versions of FreeHand, you can change this preference.

Precision illustration

Envelope—Quickly and easily apply envelope transformations to objects or groups directly in the workspace from a new Envelope toolbar.

New selection commands—Exert control over individual components within an illustration by using the new Invert Selection and Subselect commands on the Edit > Select submenu or by using the new Lasso tool in the Toolbox.

Path editing—Directly manipulate path segments without using Bézier control points.

Custom units—Define custom units for precision scale drawing.

Composite path blends—Create blends when one or more of the key paths are composite path blends.

Freehand tool precision control—The Freehand tool allows more precision than ever before when drawing freehand paths.

New Perspective grid—Modify objects using a non-printing array of converging lines to create the appearance of three dimensions.

Bitmap image tracing

◆ Use with RGB and CMYK images.

◆ Trace TIFF images much faster.

◆ Gain greater control of Trace conformity and Noise tolerance by choosing from specific options.

◆ Trace or select contiguous areas of color, and then trace or outline them.

Refined editing and page layout

Copy Special and Paste Special —Copy and paste items to the Clipboard in a file format you specify.

Search for missing links—Reconcile multiple missing links in the same operation.

New text editing shortcuts—Enhanced text navigation and selection commands.

Page tool—Create multipage storyboards with the Page tool. Rearrange, duplicate, or remove a range of pages or scenes. The Page tool places the task of page management directly on the pasteboard.

Dynamic interactivity and Webcentricity

Symbols and instances—Simplify your graphics and improve their editability. An instance is a reference to an original FreeHand object (the symbol). When you modify the symbol, the instances update automatically.

Publish to HTML—Instantly convert your FreeHand document to a web page. Use the HTML Assistant (Macintosh) or HTML Wizard (Windows) to guide you through the process.

CHAPTER 2

Getting Your Bearings

. . . .

Using the document window

FreeHand is an object-oriented drawing application. An object-oriented document is composed of strokes and fills, rather than individual pixels, as in an image-editing application.

Unlike bitmap graphics, an object-oriented drawing's resolution is device-dependent.

This means that the printed resolution of your document depends on the resolution of the output device, not on the resolution of the document itself.

Launching FreeHand displays the document window, your interface to the pasteboard—the area that contains the pages of your document. The 222-by-222-inch pasteboard can hold over 675 letter-sized pages. The buttons, tabbed panels, and toolbars are customizable. See "Using panels" on page 20 and "Customizing toolbars" on page 48.

Using panels

FreeHand panels float on top of the pasteboard and can be placed anywhere on your screen. These customizable tabbed panels can be moved, separated, or combined by dragging their tabs. For example, the Inspector has these panels: Object inspector, Stroke inspector, Fill inspector, Text inspector, and Document inspector. Click a tab to activate a particular panel.

Components of a panel

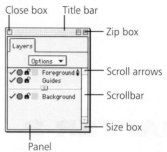

Macintosh

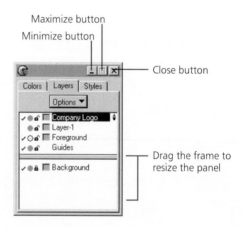

Windows

The following are tabbed panels: Object inspector, Stroke inspector, Fill inspector, Text inspector, Document inspector, Color List, Layers panel, Color Mixer, Styles panel, Symbols panel, Tint panel, and Halftones panel.

Main toolbar contains buttons to activate many common functions.

Text toolbar provides access to the most frequently used text commands.

Page rulers display in the document's unit of measurement.

Object inspector

Stroke inspector

Fill inspector

Text inspector

Document inspector

Info bar provides feedback on selected objects.

Set the page rulers' zero point.

Toolbox contains the drawing and transform tools.

Color Mixer and Tints panel display colors using a variety of color models.

Enter a custom magnification value directly into the entry field.

Inspectors display information and options for objects and text.

Use the Styles panel to create and apply graphic and text styles.

Use the Layers panel to create and modify the layers in your document.

The Color List displays all named colors.

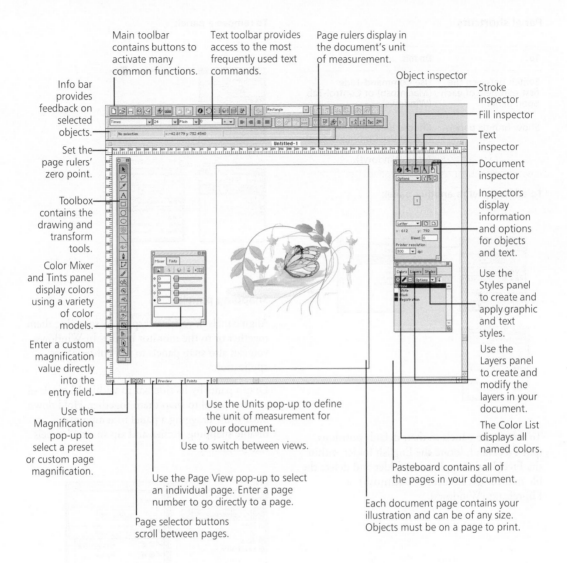

Use the Magnification pop-up to select a preset or custom page magnification.

Use the Units pop-up to define the unit of measurement for your document.

Use to switch between views.

Use the Page View pop-up to select an individual page. Enter a page number to go directly to a page.

Page selector buttons scroll between pages.

Pasteboard contains all of the pages in your document.

Each document page contains your illustration and can be of any size. Objects must be on a page to print.

Panel shortcuts

To	Do this
Switch between the first edit field of each open panel	Use Command-Tilde (Macintosh) or Control-Tab (Windows).
Show or hide panels	Choose View > Panels, use F12, or use Command-Shift-H (Macintosh) or Control-Alt-H (Windows).

To add a panel to another panel:

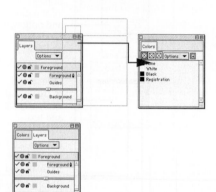

To return the panels to their default positions, quit FreeHand, locate the English folder within the FreeHand 9 application folder and delete the file named "Preferences" (Macintosh) or Fhprefs.txt (Windows).

To remove a panel:

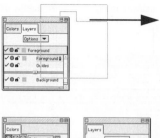

Snapping panels

Align panels in your workspace by snapping them together or to the monitor border. In Windows, you can also snap panels to the border of the application.

Drag a panel by its title bar to within 12 pixels of another panel to snap them together. Hold down Shift while dragging a panel to temporarily disable snapping. Resize and zip snapped panels independently.

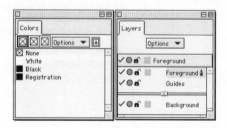

Docking panels

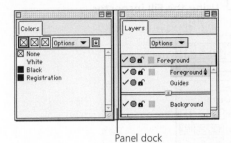

Panel dock

When moving, opening and closing, or zipping and unzipping docked panels, the action affects all docked panels as one unit. Dock one panel either horizontally or vertically to another panel. Resize panels within docked panels.

To	Do this
Dock panels	1. Hold down Control and drag one panel toward another by its title bar. Like snap distance, dragging a panel to within 12 pixels docks them together. 2. Release the mouse button. A panel dock appears to indicate docking.
Undock panels	Click the panel dock between two panels or hold down Control while dragging the title bar of a docked panel away from its adjacent panel.

In Windows, non-tabbed panels do not snap or dock to one another.

Using the inspectors

Virtually every FreeHand drawing task involves at least one inspector.

Use	To
Object	Display the position and dimensions of a selected object. Use Command-I (Macintosh) or Control-I (Windows).
Stroke	Display the stroke attributes of a selected path. Use Command-Option-L (Macintosh) or Control-Alt-L (Windows).
Fill	Display the fill attributes of a selected path. Use Command-Option-F (Macintosh) or Control-Alt-F (Windows).
Text	Display text formatting of selected text. Use Command-T (Macintosh) or Control-T (Windows).
Document	Display thumbnail icons for each page in your document. Use Command-Option-D (Macintosh) or Control-Alt-D (Windows).

Using the Object inspector

The Object inspector displays an object's position and dimensions. For example, with an ellipse selected, the Object inspector displays position (x and y values based on the current page ruler setting) as well as dimensions (height and width in the document's unit of measurement). With a rectangle selected, the Object inspector displays position and dimensions as well as the rectangle's corner radius. Values in the Object inspector are editable. All changes made in the Object inspector's entry fields are reflected in your document as soon as you press Return. The Object inspector provides feedback even with multiple objects selected. This feature is especially useful when selecting a range of text blocks and changing their auto-expansion settings.

 Using the Stroke inspector

The Stroke inspector displays stroke attributes of a selected path. For example, use the Stroke inspector to enter a stroke width and assign a color. The Stroke inspector has settings for five types of strokes: None, Basic, Custom, Pattern, and PostScript. For more information on the concepts of stroke width, cap, join, miter limit, dash setting, and arrowheads, see Chapter 6, "Color, Strokes, and Fills."

 Using the Fill inspector

The Fill inspector defines the type of fill a path contains. For example, use the Fill inspector to change the type of fill or assign a color. The Fill inspector has settings for nine types of fills: None, Basic, Custom, Gradient, Lens, Pattern, PostScript, Textured, and Tiled. Fills are discussed fully in Chapter 6, "Color, Strokes, and Fills."

 Using the Text inspector

The Text inspector has five subpanels:

♦ Character

♦ Paragraph

♦ Spacing

♦ Columns and Rows

♦ Adjust Columns

The Text inspector's five subpanels are explained in Chapter 7, "Text."

Using the Document inspector

The Document inspector contains a miniaturized view of the pasteboard, showing thumbnail icons for each page in your document. With the Pointer tool, move the thumbnails in the inspector, and the corresponding pages move on the pasteboard.

The Document inspector provides three magnification views when manipulating page thumbnails. When magnification is set to the middle or highest levels, all of the pages in the document may not be visible in the Document inspector's pasteboard window. To navigate the pasteboard, hold down the spacebar to switch the cursor to a grabber hand to scroll the pasteboard window. The Document inspector also contains options for adding, duplicating, and removing pages, as well as options to set page size, orientation, bleed, and printer resolution.

Grid size appears in the View menu, and the constrain angle appears in the Modify menu. The Units pop-up appears in the lower-left corner of the document window.

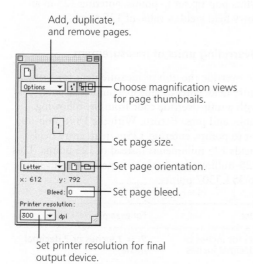

Add, duplicate, and remove pages.

Choose magnification views for page thumbnails.

Set page size.

Set page orientation.

Set page bleed.

Set printer resolution for final output device.

Defining custom page sizes

To add custom page sizes to the Document inspector, choose Edit Pages from the page size pop-up, and define pages in the Edit Pages dialog box. Custom page sizes are based upon the document's current unit of measurement.

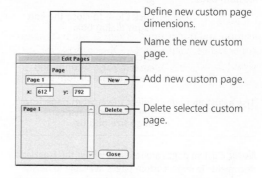

Define new custom page dimensions.

Name the new custom page.

Add new custom page.

Delete selected custom page.

To	Do this
Add a custom page	1. Choose Edit pages from the Document inspector's page size pop-up. 2. Name the new custom page and define dimensions.
Delete a custom page	1. Select a custom page from the Edit Pages dialog box. 2. Click the Delete button. When you delete a custom page preset in the Edit Pages dialog box, custom pages in your document are retained. Their page type changes to Custom in the Document inspector.
Create a custom page using a different unit of measurement than is showing in the Edit Pages dialog box	1. Close the Edit Pages dialog box and change the document's unit of measurement using the Units pop-up in the lower-left corner of the document window. 2. Open the Edit Pages dialog box and create the new custom page.

To	Do this
Modify an existing custom page	Custom pages cannot be modified once added to the Edit Pages dialog box. They must be deleted and recreated.
Accept a new custom page	Press Return. or Click Close to close the Edit Pages dialog box. or Click New to accept current custom page settings and create a new custom page.
Use a custom page	Select the custom page from the Document inspector's page size pop-up.

Note: Custom pages are retained within the FreeHand document. To make custom pages available to newly-created FreeHand documents, add the custom pages to a FreeHand template.

Defining custom units of measurement

Define custom units of measurement based upon FreeHand's default units of measurement. Choose View > Page Rulers > Edit to open the Edit Units dialog box.

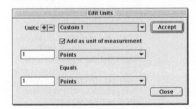

To define a custom unit of measurement:

1 Choose View > Page Rulers > Edit to open the Edit Units dialog box.

2 Create a new custom unit by typing a new name or by clicking the plus (+) sign.

3 Enter numerical values in the text fields and set the units upon which the custom unit of measurement is based.

4 Click the Accept button to save the custom unit of measurement.

To delete a custom unit of measurement:

1 Choose View > Page Rulers > Edit to open the Edit Units dialog box.

2 Select the desired custom unit of measurement from the pop-up.

3 Click the minus (–) sign.

Note: Custom units are retained within the FreeHand document. To make custom units available to newly-created FreeHand documents, add the custom units to a FreeHand template.

Setting units of measurement

To set the unit of measurement for an entire document, choose a measurement from the Units pop-up in the lower-left corner of the document window. This setting affects almost every numerical entry field in the application. With the Units pop-up set to points, entering 125 in an entry field yields a value of 125 points.

Overriding units of measurement

To override the unit of measurement for a single entry field, enter a value in a numerical entry field with a unit-override code from the following table, and press Return. With the Units pop-up set to points, entering 125m in an entry field yields 125 millimeters instead of 125 points. This 125-millimeter value is automatically converted to 354.3307 points.

Use	For example
#i for inches or decimal inches	7i = 7 inches or 7 decimal inches
p# for points	p7 = 7 points
#p for picas	7p = 7 picas

Use	For example
#m for millimeters	7m = 7 millimeters
#c for centimeters	7c = 7 centimeters
#x for pixels	7x = 7 pixels

Numerical entry fields accept mathematical functions. The following mathematical symbols are supported:

◆ + (addition)

◆ - (subtraction)

◆ * (multiplication)

◆ / (division)

To use mathematical equations, create an equation using these symbols. Type this equation in an entry field and press Return. With the Units pop-up set to points, entering "10/2" in an entry field yields a value of 5 points.

To override the unit of measurement using mathematical equations, create an equation using these symbols and any combination of unit overrides. Type this equation into an entry field and press Return. With the Units pop-up set to points, entering "2i + p7" yields a value of 151 points.

Using the toolbars

FreeHand has several toolbars:

◆ Toolbox

◆ Main

◆ Text

◆ Info

◆ Envelope

◆ Xtra Tools

◆ Xtra Operations

◆ Status (Windows)

Although the location and contents of all toolbars are customizable, this chapter describes each tool's default location and contents.

The default location of the Main toolbar, the Text toolbar, and the Envelope toolbar is below the menus and above the active document window.

To show or hide individual toolbars, choose Window > Toolbars. To show or hide all active toolbars, choose View > Toolbars. To show or hide the Toolbox, choose Window > Toolbars > Toolbox.

Toolbox

The Toolbox contains these tools:

Use	To
Pointer tool	Select and drag objects.
Eyedropper tool	Extract a color sample from any object.
Rectangle tool	Draw rectangles and squares.
Ellipse tool	Draw ellipses and circles.
Spiral tool	Draw open spiral-shaped paths.
Freehand tool	Draw freeform and calligraphic paths.

Use	To
Knife tool	Cut a path into two or more paths.
Freeform tool	Push and pull paths.
Reflect tool	Reflect objects.
Skew tool	Skew objects.
Magnify tool	Magnify objects.
Perspective tool	Apply perspective to objects.
Text tool	Create text blocks.
Lasso tool	Select points, objects, and groups within a freeform area.
Polygon tool	Draw polygons and stars.
Line tool	Draw straight lines.

Use	To
Pen tool	Draw paths by anchoring points.
Bezigon tool	Draw paths using automatic curvature.
Rotate tool	Rotate objects.
Scale tool	Resize objects.
Page tool	Add, duplicate, delete, move, and resize pages.
Trace tool	Trace objects.

Main toolbar

Use	To
	Create a new document.
	Open an existing document.
	Save the active document.
	Import a file or object.
	Print the active document.
	Open the Find & Replace Graphics dialog box.
	Open the Align panel.
	Lock the selected objects.
	Unlock the selected objects.
	Open the Object inspector.
	Open the Transform panel.
	Open the Color List.
	Open the Color Mixer.

Use	To
	Open the Layers panel.
	Open the Symbols panel.

ToolTips describe each button's function. Pause the cursor over a button on the toolbars, and a small label appears. This label disappears when you move the cursor away from the button.

Text toolbar

The Text toolbar contains common text commands.

Use	To
AGaramond	Choose a font.
Plain	Choose a character style (Macintosh).
12	Set point size.
0	Set leading.
...	Choose leading options (Macintosh).
B	Apply Bold character style (Windows).
I	Apply Italic character style (Windows).
	Align text left.

Use	To
	Align text center.
	Align text right.
	Fully justify text.
	Flow text inside a path.
	Attach text to a path.
	Detach text from a path.
	Convert selected text to paths.
	Open the Text Editor.
	Check spelling.
	Find and replace text.
	Run text around the selected path.
	Increase leading.
	Decrease leading.

Use	To
	Increase the baseline shift.
	Decrease the baseline shift.

In Windows, the Text toolbar includes buttons for Bold and Italic character styles. Click both Bold and Italic buttons to apply a font's BoldItalic character style, when available. An icon next to the font name indicates whether the font is a TrueType or a PostScript font. The absence of an icon indicates a system font or an unidentifiable font.

Clicking a font name in the Font pop-up in the Text toolbar previews selected text in the chosen font. With no text selected, clicking a font name previews "AaBbCcDd" (Macintosh) or the name of the font (Windows).

Info toolbar

The Info toolbar provides feedback for selected objects, depending on object type and current action. Feedback includes the object type, the position of the cursor, the change in an object's position, the angle, the center of rotation, the radius, and the number of sides. Choose Window > Toolbars > Info to show or hide the Info toolbar.

Envelope toolbar

The Envelope toolbar contains tools to apply envelope transformations to FreeHand objects or groups.

Use	To
	Apply an envelope.
	Save an envelope as a preset.
	Delete a preset.
	Release the envelope, but retain envelope transformations.
	Remove an envelope and all of its modifications to the FreeHand objects.
	Copy an envelope effect as a path to the Clipboard.
	Paste the path on the Clipboard as an envelope onto another object.
	View the envelope grid.

Status toolbar (Windows)

The Status toolbar contains the Magnification pop-up, page selector buttons, Page View pop-up, View pop-up, and Units pop-up. In addition, the Status toolbar displays status messages on the task in progress, the menu command highlighted, or the tool selected. Click the red cancel button in the Status toolbar to cancel an operation in progress.

Setting up your project

Consider your document's design and final output requirements. Decide in advance what settings are best.

Page size

Set the page size in the Document inspector to define the size of your final document. Objects can span multiple printed pages. For more information on setting page size, see "Using the Document inspector" on page 25.

 Page orientation

Page orientation can be portrait (tall) or landscape (wide). Set page orientation in the Document inspector.

Bleed

If a document is to print off the edge of the paper, set a bleed size in the Document inspector and print on paper larger than the page size you specify. Page bleeds are discussed further in Chapter 8, "Printing."

Number of undo's

Use the Edit > Undo command to reverse an action. Enter a value of up to 100 in the General > "Undo's" entry field in the Preferences dialog box.

Number of pages

A single FreeHand document can contain multiple pages, each with its own dimensions, orientation, and bleed size. Add or remove pages in the Document inspector or using the Page tool.

Unit of measurement

Choose from points, picas, inches, decimal inches, millimeters, centimeters, Kyus, pixels, feet, yards, miles, nautical miles, meters, kilometers, ciceros, or didots to display in the rulers, panels, and dialog boxes. Define custom units of measurement as described in "Defining custom units of measurement" on page 26.

Set the unit of measurement in the lower-left corner of the document window. The selected unit of measurement can be overridden in any entry field as explained in "Setting units of measurement" on page 26.

Printer resolution

In the Document inspector, set up FreeHand to recognize the printer resolution for your final output device.

Note: The resolution setting in the Document inspector does not set the resolution on the actual printer.

FreeHand uses the printer resolution value to:

◆ Calculate the number of default steps in a blend. The higher the resolution, the greater the number of steps included in a blend.

◆ Resize bitmap images to match the output device's resolution.

◆ Set the resolution of Gradient fills.

Page rulers

Page rulers use the document's current unit of measurement.

To show or hide page rulers, choose View > Page Rulers, or use Command-Option-M (Macintosh) or Control-Alt-M (Windows). To set the page ruler's zero point, click and drag the zero-point marker from the upper-left corner of the document window to a new location. The zero point represents the intersection of the horizontal and vertical page rulers. To reset the page rulers, double-click the zero-point marker.

Grid

The grid is a non-printing background of horizontal and vertical dotted lines. Choose View > Grid > Show to display the grid. Choose View > Snap to Grid to snap moved objects to the same relative position within the destination grid cell.

Set the desired grid size in the View > Grid > Edit dialog box. To force objects to snap to precise grid intersections rather than relative positions, choose View > Grid > Edit and uncheck the Relative grid option.

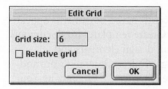

Guides

Guides are non-printing blue guidelines. Use guides to precisely align and place objects. Choose View > Guides > Show to display guides or use the Guides layer in the Layers panel.

To add a guide with the page rulers active, drag from either the horizontal or the vertical page ruler. Choose View > Guides > Edit to display the Guides dialog box and add, delete, and modify guides.

With View > Snap to Guides turned on, objects snap to guides within the value set in the General > "Snap distance" preference.

This cursor	Appears when snapping to
ᐟ	Horizontal guides
ᐟ	Vertical guides

Working with the grid and guides

To	Do this
Show or hide the grid	Choose View > Grid > Show.
Snap objects relative to the grid	1. Choose View > Grid > Edit and check the Relative grid option. 2. Choose View > Snap to Grid or use Command-; (Macintosh).
Snap objects to precise grid intersections	1. Choose View > Grid > Edit and uncheck the Relative grid option. 2. Choose View > Snap to Grid or use Command-; (Macintosh).
Modify the grid	Choose View > Grid > Edit.
Show or hide page rulers	Choose View > Page Rulers or use Command-Option-M (Macintosh) or Control-Alt-M (Windows).
Change unit of measurement	Use Units pop-up.
Show or hide guides	Choose View > Guides > Show.
Snap objects to guides	Choose View > Snap to Guides or use Command-\ (Macintosh) or Control-Alt-G (Windows).
Edit guides	Choose View > Guides > Edit.
Lock guides	Choose View > Guides > Lock Guides or click the padlock in the Guides layer.
Edit snap distance of guides	Enter a value in the General > "Snap Distance" preference entry field.

Editing guides

Choose View > Guides > Edit to display the Guides dialog box and review and edit all the guides.

Use	To
Page	Enter a page number in the entry field or click the next and previous page buttons.
Type	Identify the guide type for each guide on the selected page.
Location	Identify the location for each guide on the selected page.
Release	Turn the selected guide into an object.
Delete (Macintosh) or Remove (Windows)	Delete the selected guide.
Add	Add a new horizontal or vertical guide.
Edit	Set a new location for a horizontal or vertical guide.

See Chapter 4, "Organizing Your Illustration," for more information about turning paths into guides.

Navigating your document

To	Do this
Create a new document	Choose File > New, click the New document button on the Main toolbar, or use Command-N (Macintosh) or Control-N (Windows).
Open an existing document	Choose File > Open, click the Open document button on the Main toolbar, or use Command-O (Macintosh) or Control-O (Windows).

The four most recently saved documents appear in the File menu. Create templates for documents that share common design elements and production settings. To learn how to create and edit templates, see Chapter 4, "Organizing Your Illustration."

Working with pages

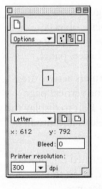

Document inspector and Page tool

To change a page's attributes, activate it in any of these ways:

◆ Display the Document inspector and click a desired page thumbnail.

- Choose a value from the Page View pop-up or enter a value in the entry field. Both are located in the lower-left corner of the document window.

- Click a page selector button.

- Click a page with a tool.

- Choose the Page tool and click a page on the pasteboard.

To arrange pages in the Document inspector:

1 Display the Document inspector.

If necessary, click one of the page magnification buttons to enlarge or reduce the size of the page thumbnails.

2 Using the Pointer tool, click and drag a thumbnail to a new location in the Document inspector's pasteboard window.

Hold down the spacebar to turn your cursor into a grabber hand to scroll the view.

To arrange pages on the pasteboard:

1 Choose the Page tool in the Toolbox.

Choosing the Page tool changes your cursor to the Page tool cursor.

2 Select a page and move it on the pasteboard.

Hold down the Shift key while dragging a page to constrain its movement horizontally or vertically. To duplicate a page, hold down the Option (Macintosh) or Alt (Windows) key while dragging the page. To snap pages to the grid, choose View > Snap to Grid.

To	Do this
Add pages	1. Choose Add Pages from the Document inspector Options pop-up.
	2. Set options in the Add Pages dialog box and click OK.
	or
	Option (Macintosh) or Alt (Windows) double-click the pasteboard using the Page tool and use the Add Pages dialog box to add pages.
Duplicate pages	1. Select a page.
	2. Choose Duplicate from the Document inspector Options pop-up.
	or
	Use the Page tool and Option-drag (Macintosh) or Alt-drag (Windows) a page on the pasteboard.
Modify a specific page	Option double-click (Macintosh) or Alt double-click (Windows) the specific page to open the Modify Page dialog box.

To	Do this
Remove pages	1. Select a page. 2. Choose Remove from the Document inspector Options pop-up. or Use the Page tool to select a page on the pasteboard and press Delete. If the selected page contains objects, FreeHand warns you before deleting the page.
Resize pages	1. Choose the Page tool. 2. Click a page to activate transform handles. 3. Click and drag a corner, top, or side handle. To resize a page proportionately, hold down Shift. To snap pages to the grid while moving them, choose View > Snap to Grid.
Move a page without moving its contents	1. Choose the Page tool and select a page. 2. Hold down Control (Windows) or Command (Macintosh) and drag a page or pages on the pasteboard.
Change page orientation	1. Choose the Page tool and click a page to activate the transform handles. 2. Move the cursor outside the page's transform handles. The cursor changes to the Rotate cursor. 3. Click and drag with the Rotate cursor to change the page orientation.

Setting page magnification

FreeHand supports magnifications ranging from 6 percent to 256 times actual size.

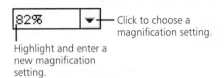

Highlight and enter a new magnification setting.

Click to choose a magnification setting.

To	Do this
Enlarge a page view to the next increment	Choose the Magnify tool and click a page. or Choose an increment from the Magnification pop-up. or Choose View > Magnification to select an increment.
Reduce a page view to the next increment	Choose the Magnify tool, hold down Option (Macintosh) or Alt (Windows), and click a page. or Choose an increment from the Magnification pop-up. or Choose View > Magnification to select an increment.
Zoom to the highest magnification	Choose the Magnify tool, hold down Control (Macintosh) or Shift (Windows), and click a page. or Enter "256 x" in the magnification entry field.
Zoom to the lowest magnification	Choose the Magnify tool, hold down Option-Control (Macintosh) or Shift-Alt (Windows), and click a page. or Choose 6 percent from the Magnification pop-up. or Choose 6 percent from View > Magnification.

To	Do this
Enlarge a selection area	Choose the Magnify tool and drag a selection area. or Enter a value in the magnification entry field in the lower-left corner of the document window.
Reduce a selection area	Choose the Magnify tool, hold down Option (Macintosh) or Alt (Windows), and drag a selection area. or Enter a value in the magnification entry field.

Using magnification shortcuts

To	Use
Change document view to fit the selection	Command-0 (zero) (Macintosh) or Control-0 (zero) (Windows).
Fit view to current page	Command-Shift-W (Macintosh) or Control-Shift-W (Windows).
Fit view to all pages	Command-Option-0 (zero) (Macintosh) or Control-Alt-0 (zero) (Windows).
Set view to 50%	Command-5 (Macintosh) or Control-5 (Windows).
Set view to 100%	Command-1 (Macintosh) or Control-1 (Windows).
Set view to 200%	Command-2 (Macintosh) or Control-2 (Windows).
Set view to 400%	Command-4 (Macintosh) or Control-4 (Windows).
Set view to 800%	Command-8 (Macintosh) or Control-8 (Windows).
Zoom in	Command-Spacebar-click (Macintosh) or Control-Spacebar-click (Windows).
Zoom out	Command-Option-Spacebar-click (Macintosh) or Control-Alt-Spacebar-click (Windows).

Multiple document views

Use multiple views to see a document at different views or magnifications simultaneously. View up to eight windows showing the same document at one time. To close one of the document view windows, click the window's close box. To close all document views, hold down Option and click the close box (Macintosh) or press Control-Shift-F4 (Windows).

To open additional document views:

1 Choose Window > New Window or use Command-Option-N (Macintosh) or Control-Alt-N (Windows).

2 Change the view and magnification of the new windows.

Naming and saving custom views

Name and save the current view's magnification percentage, view mode, and scrollbar positions to recall later. Choose View > Custom > New, type a name in the Name field, and click OK.

Use	To adjust
74% ▾	Magnification percentage.
Fast Preview ▾	View mode.
◁ ▥	Horizontal position.
(vertical scrollbar)	Vertical position.

Choosing View > Custom > New saves these settings to a custom view name. To recall a saved view, choose the view name from the Magnification pop-up or from the View > Custom submenu. In Windows, right-click to open the shortcut menu and choose a custom view from the View submenu.

To define, name, and save a view using the Magnify tool, click the tool, hold down Shift, and click and drag to define a view. The New View dialog box opens after the new view is set.

To edit a named view, adjust view elements to redefine the view, and then choose View > Custom > Edit. Choose a view name from the list in the Edit Views dialog box, then click Redefine. To delete the view, click Delete. To confirm edits and deletions, click OK.

To switch from the current to the previous view, choose View > Custom > Previous or use Command-Option-1 (Macintosh) or Control-Alt-Shift-1 (Windows).

Optimizing document redraw

Choose a view mode from the View pop-up at the lower-left corner of the document window: Preview, Fast Preview, Keyline, Fast Keyline, and Flash Anti-alias. View modes affect a document's on-screen representation, not its object data or print quality. The fast modes optimize redraw by reducing blend steps to 10 and graying text for on-screen point sizes 50 and below.

Switch between Preview and Keyline by choosing View > Preview or using Command-K (Macintosh) or Control-K (Windows). Choose View > Fast Mode or use Command-Shift-K (Macintosh) or Control-Shift-K (Windows) to switch between normal and fast modes. For example, choosing View > Fast Mode when the document is set to Preview switches it to Fast Preview.

Note: To see a path in Keyline mode while the document setting is Preview mode (or vice versa), press and release Option (Macintosh) or Alt (Windows) as you drag the path.

Preview

Fast Preview

Keyline

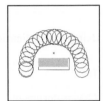

Fast Keyline

Flash anti-alias

Choosing a view mode

Choose	To
Preview	Display the document as it would print.
Fast Preview	Display blends with reduced steps and grayed text.
Keyline	Display only a black hairline stroke, no fill for objects, and X-boxes for EPS images and bitmap images.
Fast Keyline	Display blends with reduced steps and grayed text.

Drawing fundamentals

Selecting objects

Use the Pointer or Lasso tool to select objects.

To	Do this
Select an object	Click with the Pointer tool or 1. Double-click the Pointer tool to open the Pointer tool dialog box. 2. Check the Contact Sensitive Pointer tool option and drag a selection area around any portion of an object's edge.
Select an object with no fill	Click the stroke with the Pointer tool.
Select multiple objects	Drag a selection area around multiple objects or Hold down Shift and click with the Pointer tool or Check the Contact Sensitive Pointer tool option and Shift-drag any portion of each object's edge.
Select all objects on the active page	Use Command-A (Macintosh) or Control-A (Windows) or Choose Edit > Select > All.
Select all objects in a document	Use Command-Shift-A (Macintosh) or Control-Shift-A (Windows) or Choose Edit > Select > All in Document.
Deselect all objects in a document	Press Tab or Choose Edit > Select > None.
Select an object within a composite path, group, blend, or paste inside.	Hold down Option (Macintosh) or Alt (Windows) and click with the Pointer or Lasso tool.

To	Do this
Select all objects within a selected group.	Choose Edit > Select > Subselect.
Select all objects except the currently selected objects.	Choose Edit > Select > Invert Selection.
Select an object underneath another object within a composite path, group, blend, or paste inside.	Hold down Control-Option (Macintosh) or Control-Alt-right click (Windows) and click with the Pointer tool to cycle through selected objects.
Select the composite path, group, blend, or clipping path in which a selected object is contained.	Choose Edit > Select > Superselect.
Select a point within an object	Select the object. Then, drag a selection area around the point or hold down Option (Macintosh) or Alt (Windows) and click with the Pointer tool.
Select multiple points	Hold down Option-Shift (Macintosh) or Alt-Shift (Windows) and click with the Pointer tool.
Select a segment of an object	Select the object. Then, hold down Option (Macintosh) or Alt (Windows) and click with the Pointer tool between the segment's points.
Select multiple segments	Hold down Option-Shift (Macintosh) or Alt-Shift (Windows) and click with the Pointer tool between the segment's points.

Note: Double-clicking an object may display its transformation handles. To learn how to use these handles, see "Using transformation handles" on page 131.

Using the right mouse button (Windows)

Select an object with the right mouse button to display a shortcut menu containing a variety of commands. Such objects include paths, text blocks, bitmap images, EPSs, groups, and blends. Selecting dissimilar objects displays a shortcut menu of common commands.

Selecting an object with the right mouse button displays object-specific options.

To display shortcut menus, right-click in the Document inspector, Color List, Layers panel, Styles panel, Tints panel, Symbols panel, on any color chip, color well, or on a blank area of the document.

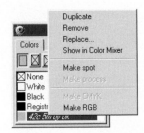

Alternatively, use the right mouse button to magnify an area of your document. Make sure the General > "Right mouse button magnification" preference is checked.

Note: Enabling the "Right mouse button magnification" preference disables Windows shortcut menus.

Using the Lasso tool

The Lasso tool selects points, objects, and groups within a freeform selection area. Click and drag the Lasso tool to define a selection area.

Note: To temporarily switch to the Pointer tool, press Control (Windows) or Command (Macintosh).

Double-click the Lasso tool to open the Lasso tool dialog box, which contains a Contact Sensitive option.

When the Contact Sensitive option is unchecked, the selection area must completely surround a group for it to be selected. The selection area selects the points of objects that lie within the selection area.

When the Contact Sensitive option is checked, the selection area need only encircle a segment of an object or group's edge for the object or group to be selected.

Moving objects

Move selected objects with the Pointer tool, the Transform panel, or the cursor keys.

To move objects with the Pointer tool, click an object or group of objects and drag to a new location. To display a preview of the object, hold down the mouse button for a moment or tap the Option (Macintosh) or Alt (Windows) key before dragging an object. Dragging an object using the right mouse button displays the option to move it or copy it (Windows).

Choose Modify > Transform > Move to move objects in precise increments. Refer to Chapter 5, "Drawing," or FreeHand Help for more information.

Move selected objects with the cursor keys in preset increments. Set the increment in the Modify > Cursor Distance dialog.

The drawing tools

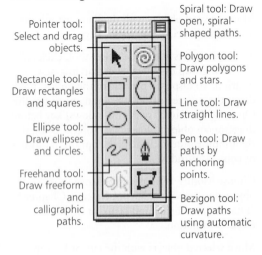

Pointer tool: Select and drag objects.

Rectangle tool: Draw rectangles and squares.

Ellipse tool: Draw ellipses and circles.

Freehand tool: Draw freeform and calligraphic paths.

Spiral tool: Draw open, spiral-shaped paths.

Polygon tool: Draw polygons and stars.

Line tool: Draw straight lines.

Pen tool: Draw paths by anchoring points.

Bezigon tool: Draw paths using automatic curvature.

To use	Do this
Rectangle tool	Choose the Rectangle tool and click and drag on the page. ◆ Hold down Shift and drag to constrain a rectangle to a square. ◆ Hold down Option (Macintosh) or Alt (Windows) and drag to draw a rectangle from its center.
Ellipse tool	Choose the Ellipse tool and click and drag on the page. ◆ Hold down Shift and drag to constrain an ellipse to a circle. ◆ Hold down Option (Macintosh) or Alt (Windows) and drag to draw an ellipse from its center.
Polygon or Star tool	Choose Polygon or Star tool and click and drag on the page. ◆ Hold down Shift and drag to constrain a polygon or a star to 45° increments of the angle entered in Modify > Constrain. ◆ Polygons and stars draw from their centers automatically.

To use	Do this
Spiral tool	Choose the Spiral tool and click and drag on the page. ◆ Hold down Shift to constrain the spiral to 45° increments of the angle entered in Modify > Constrain.
Line tool	Choose the Line tool and click and drag on the page. ◆ Hold down Shift to constrain the line to 45° increments of the angle entered in Modify > Constrain. ◆ Hold down Option (Macintosh) or Alt (Windows) to draw a line from its center.
Freehand tool	Choose the Freehand tool and click and drag on the page.
Pen tool	Choose the Pen tool. ◆ Click to place a corner point. ◆ Click and drag to place a curve point. ◆ Hold down Control and click to place a connector point (Macintosh). ◆ Hold down Alt and click the right mouse button to place a connector point (Windows).
Bezigon tool	Choose the Bezigon tool. Click to place a corner point. ◆ Hold down Option (Macintosh) or Alt (Windows) and click to place a curve point. ◆ Hold down Control and click to place a connector point (Macintosh). ◆ Hold down Alt and click the right mouse button to place a connector point (Windows).

Note: The location and contents of the Toolbox are customizable. For more information on the drawing tools see "Drawing basics" on page 98.

To both constrain a shape and draw from the object's center, hold down Shift-Option (Macintosh) or Shift-Alt (Windows) while using a drawing tool. Double-click any tool with a bracket in its upper-right corner to display the tool options dialog box.

Types of points

Point type describes how the path behaves at that point.

Use	To
Corner point 	Create a corner at the joint of two segments.
Curve point 	Force a smooth connection between two segments.
Connector point 	Connect a straight path to a curved path.

A rectangle is composed of four straight paths connected by corner points.

The connector point connects a straight path to a cur[ved] path.

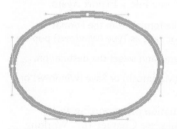

An ellipse is composed of four curved paths connected by curve points.

Importing and exporting

FreeHand can import and export a wide variety of vector (object-oriented) and bitmap graphic formats.

To import a graphic:

1   Choose File > Import or use Command-R (Macintosh) or Control-R (Windows).

2   Select the file you want to import and then click OK.

3   Position the import cursor where you want the upper-left corner of the graphic or text block to appear.

4   Click the mouse button to place the graphic at its default size. Click and drag to scale the graphic.

To export a graphic:

1   Choose File > Export or use Command-Shift-R (Macintosh) or Control-Shift-R (Windows) to display the Export document dialog box.

    To re-export an updated version of the file last exported, choose File > Export Again.

2   Choose the file format from the Format (Macintosh) or Save as Type (Windows) pop-up.

3   Type a file name and select the destination.

4   Click Export (Macintosh) or Save (Windows) or press Return.

For more information on importing and exporting graphics, see Chapter 10, "Working with Other Applications."

Send mail (Windows)

If an MAPI32-compliant electronic mail system is available in your Windows environment, choosing File > Send creates a new outgoing mail message with the active FreeHand document attached. Two options are available when sending an e-mail: include active document and include all open documents.

◆   Choose [File name] to attach the active document.

◆   Choose All Open Documents to attach all currently open documents to your e-mail message.

The document is attached in its current state. If the document is unnamed, it will be attached with the default name.

Customizing your environment

Using preferences

Use FreeHand's extensive preferences to customize your work environment. Choose File > Preferences or press Command-Shift-D (Macintosh) or Control-Shift-D (Windows) to display the Preferences dialog box. See FreeHand Help for a detailed explanation of every preference.

On the Macintosh, click a Category name to display the associated preference options panel.

In Windows, click a tab to display the associated preference options panel.

Use category	To
General	Set the number of undo's and control path editing behavior.
Object	Control path fills and behavior; change default line widths and graphic style behavior.
Text	Control text behavior.
Document	Retain document views and window location; control active page settings and document review upon close.
Import	Control the attributes of imported files; control embedding graphics in EPS and other Clipboard formats.
Export	Control the attributes of exported files; control embedding graphics in EPS and other Clipboard formats.
Spelling	Customize the spelling checker.
Colors	Set guide and grid colors and Color Management options.
Panels	Set panel display options.
Redraw	Switch on and off text effects, activate high-resolution image display, and control Greek type.
Sounds (Macintosh)	Enable and configure snap sounds.

Restoring default preferences

To restore all preferences to their default settings, click the Defaults button at the bottom of the Preferences dialog box.

Customizing cursor key distance

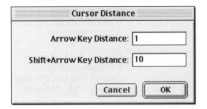

Choose Modify > Cursor Distance and set a value in the Cursor Distance dialog box to specify the distance selected objects move when you press a cursor key on the keyboard. Values are related to the currently selected unit of measure.

To specify the incremental distance selected objects move when you press a cursor key while holding the Shift key, enter a value in the Shift + Arrow key distance field. For more information on units of measurement, see "Setting units of measurement" on page 26.

Customizing shortcuts and toolbars

Use the Customize dialog box to add or change keyboard shortcuts, re-arrange toolbars within FreeHand, and change the buttons on the toolbars.

Customizing shortcuts

Use the Shortcuts panel in the Customize dialog box to change current keyboard shortcuts or to assign shortcuts to commands that have no shortcuts.

Note: To keep all default FreeHand shortcuts intact, click the plus (+) button next to the Keyboard shortcuts setting field and specify a custom shortcut group name before changing any shortcuts. See "Managing shortcut settings" on page 47.

To assign a custom shortcut:

1   Choose File > Customize > Shortcuts.

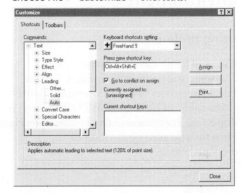

2   Scroll the Commands list and click the triangles (Macintosh) or plus (+) signs (Windows), if necessary, to find the command to which you want to assign a new shortcut.

The Commands list replicates all FreeHand menus, plus some additional features. If the command is not in a FreeHand menu, click Other.

Note: With the exception of the Xtras Manager and the Repeat Xtra command, Xtras are not available for shortcuts.

3   Click the command name.

The command description appears in the Description field. If the command already has a shortcut, it appears in the Current shortcut keys field. A command can have more than one shortcut, although only one appears in the menu.

4   Press Tab or click in the Press new shortcut key field to prepare to assign the shortcut.

5   Press the key or keys that make up the new shortcut sequence.

The shortcut appears in the Press new shortcut key field. If the shortcut is assigned to a command already, the command appears under "Currently assigned to," in the center of the dialog box.

6 Click Assign to assign the new shortcut to the specified command.

Clicking Assign disables any previous assignment for the shortcut. When Go to conflict on assign is checked, the command to which the shortcut had been assigned is highlighted in the Commands field, ready to receive a new shortcut assignment.

7 Continue assigning shortcuts.

8 Save all shortcut assignments in the following ways:

- ◆ Choose a new shortcut group from the Keyboard shortcut setting pop-up. See "Managing shortcut settings" on page 47.

- ◆ Click Close to confirm the new shortcut assignments.

To revert to the previous shortcuts without saving the shortcuts you entered, press Reset.

To remove a shortcut:

1 Perform steps 1 through 3 under "To assign a custom shortcut:" on page 46.

2 Click the shortcut in the Current shortcut keys field.

3 Click Remove.

4 Click Close or choose a new shortcut group to confirm the removal.

Managing shortcut settings

In addition to the default FreeHand shortcut group, FreeHand provides the default shortcut groups for some applications, such as Director, Illustrator, PageMaker, QuarkXpress, and Photoshop.

To view and choose from available shortcut groups, use the Keyboard shortcuts setting pop-up.

When you assign a shortcut, it is queued to be saved in the current group. You can save shortcuts to more than one group before you click Close. However, switching to a new group saves all shortcut assignments to—and removals from— the previous group.

To create your own shortcut group, click the plus (+) button to the left of the Keyboard shortcuts setting field. Enter a unique file name, and then click OK.

To replicate a customized shortcut group on another computer, copy the file from one computer's Settings\Keyboard folder (in the FreeHand 9 English folder) into the same folder on the other computer. The new group's name appears in the Keyboard shortcuts setting pop-up. In Windows, the extension SET is added to the shortcut group file; the extension is dropped from group names in the pop-up.

Printing a shortcut quick-reference card

To print a shortcut quick-reference card, click Print on the Shortcuts panel, and then click Print in the Keyboard Shortcuts dialog box.

Note: For a custom quick-reference card, click Save As. This produces a text file that can be opened in another application capable of converting text to a table and sorting by shortcuts, commands, or descriptions.

Customizing toolbars

The form, location, and contents of all toolbars are customizable. The Status toolbar is customizable only in Windows.

To customize toolbars from the Toolbars dialog box:

1 Choose File > Customize > Toolbars.

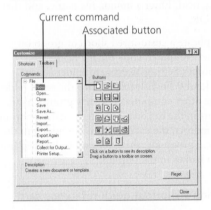

Current command
Associated button

2 Scroll the Commands list and click the triangles (Macintosh) or plus (+) signs (Windows), if necessary, to find the command whose button you want to place on a toolbar.

The Commands list replicates all FreeHand menus, plus some additional features. To locate a command quickly, type the first few letters of the command name. If the command is not on a FreeHand menu, click Other.

3 Click the command to highlight the associated button, or click the button to highlight the command.

4 Drag the button from the dialog box to a specific location on a toolbar and drop it.

Existing buttons move to make room for the new button, if necessary.

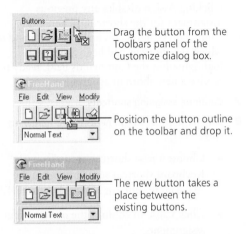

Drag the button from the Toolbars panel of the Customize dialog box.

Position the button outline on the toolbar and drop it.

The new button takes a place between the existing buttons.

To remove the buttons from a toolbar, press and hold, then drag the button away from the toolbar.

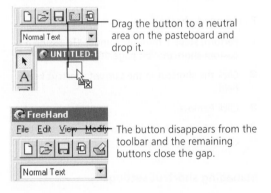

Drag the button to a neutral area on the pasteboard and drop it.

The button disappears from the toolbar and the remaining buttons close the gap.

Customizing toolbars without using the dialog box

To move any button from one toolbar to another, hold down Command (Macintosh) or Alt (Windows) and drag the button to another location on a toolbar.

To remove the buttons from a toolbar, press and hold Command (Macintosh) or Alt (Windows) and drag the button away from the toolbar.

To duplicate a button for placement on more than one toolbar, hold down Option-Command (Macintosh) or Alt-Control (Windows) while dragging the button to the second location.

Note: Disabled buttons cannot be moved or deleted.

To move a toolbar onto the pasteboard:

1 Click and hold a toolbar handle.

Toolbar handle

2 Drag and drop the toolbar onto the pasteboard.

The toolbar becomes a resizable floating toolbar when dropped beyond the toolbar area.

To dock a floating toolbar onto the top or bottom toolbar area:

1 Click and hold the gray area on the floating toolbar.

2 Drag and drop the floating toolbar onto the top, bottom, or side toolbar area.

3 The floating toolbar becomes a regular toolbar when dropped in the area surrounding the pasteboard.

In Windows, when any toolbar is dragged within the toolbar area, the toolbar-arranging cursor is displayed, and the toolbar is highlighted.

Toolbar-arranging cursor

Using defaults

FreeHand's defaults template controls document and object defaults. Document-level defaults affect page size, unit of measurement, printer resolution, and other document settings. Object-level defaults affect objects and text. If you want to use different defaults or add document settings or object settings, create a new FreeHand defaults file.

To create a new defaults template:

1 Choose File > New.

2 Modify the document.

3 Choose File > Save As.

4 Choose the template format from the Formats (Macintosh) or Save as Type (Windows) pop-up.

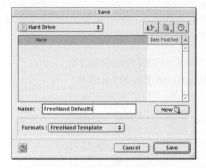

5 Name the file FreeHand Defaults (Macintosh) or Defaults.FT9 (Windows) and save it in the English folder within the FreeHand application folder.

Note: Check the Document > "New document template" preference to make sure that the template file name matches the name entered in this preference.

To apply default settings, check the Object > "Changing object changes defaults" preference to apply current object and text attributes to the next object or text you create. For example, if you draw a rectangle and apply a yellow fill using the Color List or Styles panel, the next closed path you draw will have a yellow fill. Dragging and dropping the color from the Color Mixer does not change the default.

AppleScript (Macintosh)

Install AppleScript and the Script Editor (available from Apple) to automate some of FreeHand's functions, including document manipulation, printing, report generation, and Find & Replace Graphics.

See FreeHand Help or the AppleScript ReadMe for information about using AppleScript.

Working with wizards (Windows)

Use FreeHand's wizards to quickly begin a project and to simplify your workflow. Wizards are interactive screens that guide you through and actually perform a variety of tasks.

To view the wizards, choose Help > Wizards. The Choose a wizard screen offers access to five topics: Welcome, Setup, Screen-based, Stationery, and Publication.

Choosing a wizard

Use	To
Welcome	Create a new document, open the previous document, choose and open a document from a list, open a template on the FreeHand CD-ROM, or launch FreeHand Help. This screen appears when launching FreeHand.
Setup	Create a document based on an illustration style, either freehand or technical. Choose colors, color mode, unit of measurement, page size, and page orientation.
Screen-based	Create a document optimized for creating graphics, either for the Internet or multimedia/image editing. Choose colors and set the size and orientation for on-screen designs.
Stationery	Create documents for common business usage: letterhead stationery, envelopes, and business cards. Choose colors and a standard paper size. You also can browse through a variety of layout ideas.
Publication	Create multipage documents. Choose page size, number of pages, page orientation, colors, unit of measurement, and styles.

Note: With some wizard settings, you can add more than one preset color palette to the Color List.

CHAPTER 3
Tutorials

Tutorial tips

Here are some tips for successful completion of this tutorial.

If you make a mistake, choose Edit > Undo. FreeHand's default number of undo steps is 10. Higher numbers use more computer memory.

To change the number of Undo's:

1 Choose File > Preferences.

2 Click the General tab.

3 Enter a number from 1 to 100 in the Undo's field.

4 Quit and restart FreeHand.

Macromedia manuals and Help use this syntax for choosing a menu command:

Choose Window > Inspectors > Object.

The first word (Window) is the menu name, the second word or phrase (Inspectors) is the menu command, and the third word or phrase (Object) is the submenu command.

The tutorial always assumes that a panel or inspector is closed and asks you to choose it from the Window menu. Check to see whether the panel or inspector is already open before choosing it from the Window menu. If a panel or inspector is already open, choosing it from the Window menu closes it. To open it again, choose it again from the Window menu.

These lessons always use the menu selection method for choosing items. Most menu commands also have shortcut keys, which are listed next to the commands on the menu.

FreeHand basics

This tutorial introduces many of the key features of Macromedia FreeHand and shows you some techniques for creating artwork in FreeHand:

◆ Drawing basic shapes

◆ Changing a path's fill and stroke

◆ Grouping and cloning basic shapes

◆ Arranging objects on a layer

◆ Copying, pasting, and arranging objects

◆ Skewing objects

◆ Creating colors in the Color Mixer

◆ Adding colors to the Color List

◆ Applying colors to objects

◆ Creating and applying tints

◆ Combining objects using Union

◆ Using the Object inspector

◆ Creating and applying a Gradient fill

◆ Using layers

◆ Drawing circles, polygons, and stars

◆ Creating blends

◆ Attaching blends to paths

◆ Attaching text to paths

◆ Pasting imported JPEGs inside paths

◆ Applying Lens transparency fills

◆ Drawing paths using the Pen tool

◆ Creating objects using Punch

◆ Rotating objects using Transform handles

Begin the tutorial

You can complete the tutorial in about an hour. For details about any of the features this tutorial covers, see the index in this user guide.

Install a font

Before you open FreeHand, you must install the Mariage Antique font. The font file is located in FreeHand 9\English\Tutorial.

To learn how to install the font, consult your operating system help or go to http://www.macromedia.com/support/search/ and search for Macromedia TechNote #3648 (Macintosh) or TechNote #3649 (Windows).

Open the tutorial file

During this tutorial, you will complete an illustration of objects on a table.

1   In FreeHand, choose File > Open, and open the file Tutorial_1_Start.fh9 located in the Tutorial folder inside the FreeHand 9 application folder.

2   Choose File > Save As. Name the file My_Work and click Save.

Tutorial_1_Start.fh9, the file in which you will be working, is a six-page FreeHand 9 document:

♦   Page 1 contains the partial illustration that you will complete over the course of the tutorial.

♦   Pages 2 through 5 are worksheets with objects, guides, and visual aids to help you do some of the tasks in the tutorial.

♦   Page 6 contains the completed illustration for reference.

Use the page-turning buttons or the page selection pop-up at the bottom of the FreeHand window to turn pages in a FreeHand document.

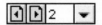

Before you begin working, you can turn to page 6 of Tutorial_1_Start.fh9 to see what you will be creating.

Draw basic shapes

First, you will draw basic shapes and combine them to draw a clock. Then you will copy and paste the clock onto the main illustration.

Draw the round part of the clock.

1   Turn to page 2 of the FreeHand document to begin this activity.

2   Click the Ellipse tool in the Toolbox to choose it.

3   Place the cursor on A under the gray circle labeled 1. Hold down Shift and drag toward B to trace the gray circle.

Holding down Shift constrains the Ellipse tool to draw circles.

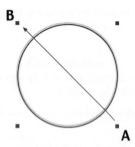

Now draw the rectangular base of the clock.

4 Choose the Rectangle tool.

5 Drag from one corner of the gray rectangle (2) to a diagonal corner to trace the rectangle.

Notice the dots at each corner of the rectangle. These indicate that the path is selected. Generally, clicking on or near a path or group with the Pointer tool selects it. Clicking away from a selected path or group typically deselects it.

Change the fill and stroke of objects

The area inside a path is called the fill. The path itself is called the stroke. You can change or remove a selected object's stroke and fill colors using the Color List.

1 Choose Window > Inspectors > Fill to display the Fill inspector.

2 With the rectangle selected, choose Basic from the fill type pop-up.

3 Click the color well pop-up to display a list of colors stored in the document.

4 Scroll the list to find light blue, then click the color name. The rectangle fill is now blue.

5 Choose Window > Panels > Color List to display the Color List, which displays the same list as the color well pop-up in the Fill inspector.

6 Drag the light blue color chip from the Color List onto the area inside the circle (1) to apply a light blue Basic fill to the circle.

Another way to fill a selected path is to drag a color chip to the Fill selector. Yet another way is to click the Fill selector, then click the color name.

The outline of a path is called the stroke.

7 Click the Stroke selector on the Color List to activate it.

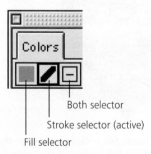

8 Scroll to the top of the Color List to find None.

9 With rectangle 2 still selected, drag the None chip onto the Stroke selector.

The rectangle now has no stroke.

10 Click circle 1 with the Pointer tool to select it.

11 Click None on the Color List.

Since the Stroke selector is now active, clicking a color name assigns that color choice to all selected paths.

Dragging a color chip onto a stroke also changes the stroke color.

The Both selector, the third small square at the top of the Color List, applies a single color choice to both fill and stroke simultaneously.

Group, clone, and arrange objects

You can combine objects as a group and work with them as one object. You can also replicate, or clone, an object or group.

1 Choose the Pointer tool and drag the blue circle onto the clock outline (3). Use the cursor keys to nudge the shape into place.

2 If necessary, hold down Shift and drag a corner handle to resize the circle to fit the outline.

3 Drag rectangle 2 into position below the circle. Resize it to fit the outline.

4 Leaving the rectangle selected, hold down Shift and click the blue circle to add it to the selection.

5 Choose Modify > Group to group the rectangle and circle together, then drag the group onto the left overlapping outline under 4.

6 Leaving the group selected, choose Edit > Clone.

When you clone an object, the clone remains selected.

7 Press the right cursor key repeatedly to move the selected clone onto the other overlapping outline.

8 Leaving the clone selected, drag the dark blue color chip onto the Fill selector. Choose Modify > Arrange > Move Backward.

The clone gives the clock a three-dimensional look.

9 Leaving the clone selected, hold down Shift and click the left edge of the light blue shape and add it to the selection.

10 Choose Modify > Group to group the front and side of the clock.

11 Drag the clock face from the center of the page onto the blue clock.

12 Shift-click to add the clock to the selection and choose Modify > Group to group the clock and face.

Now that the clock is complete, copy and paste it to the main illustration and arrange it on the page.

13 Leaving the clock selected, choose Edit > Copy to copy the clock.

14 Turn to the main illustration on page 1.

15 Choose Edit > Paste to paste the clock to the illustration. Drag it to the area above the glasses using the Pointer tool.

Skew an object

After you draw an object, you can alter, or transform, its shape using the Rotate, Reflect, Scale, and Skew tools in the Toolbox.

1 Choose the Rectangle tool.

2 Draw a teabag-size rectangle in front of the cup.

3 Choose the Skew tool from the toolbox.

4 Place the cursor near the right edge of the rectangle and drag it to skew the rectangle so that it appears to lean against the cup.

Create colors in the Color Mixer

You can mix the basic colors from CMYK (Cyan-Magenta-Yellow-Black), RGB (Red-Green-Blue), or other color models to create specific colors in the Color Mixer. When you create a color you want to use in your illustration, add it to the document Color List.

1 Choose Window > Panels > Color Mixer to open the Color Mixer.

2 Click the CMYK button, then enter C=15, M=35, Y=88, and K=10 in the four fields.

 ← Add to Color List button

3 Click the Add to Color List button. In the dialog box, type teabag to name the color, choose Process, and click Add.

4 Scroll the Color List to find teabag. With the teabag selected, drag the teabag color chip at the bottom of the Color List onto the Both selector.

Now add a white string to the teabag.

5 Choose the Freehand tool. Begin at the top of the teabag and draw a string.

6 Leaving the string selected, drag the White color chip to the Stroke selector and drag the None chip to the Fill selector.

Create tints from a color

Using the Tints panel, you can create tints based on a color.

1 Choose the Pointer tool and select the middle third of the banana.

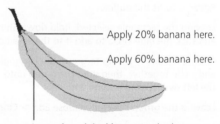

Apply 20% banana here.

Apply 60% banana here.

Leave the original banana color here.

2 Click the Fill selector on the Color List. The fill color name banana is highlighted on the Color List.

3 Choose Window > Panels > Tints to open the Tints panel.

4 Click the Tints panel pop-up, scroll to find banana, and choose it to add it to the Tints panel color well.

5 Click the square between 50 and 70 to create a 60 percent tint of banana.

6 Click the Add to Color List button, and click Add to add the process tint name 60% banana to the Color List.

7 Click the square between 10 and 30 to create a 20 percent tint of banana and add it to the Color List.

8 Drag the 60% banana color chip onto the Fill selector or onto the fill area of the selection. Select the top third of the banana.

9 Drag the 20% banana color chip onto the Fill selector or onto the fill area of the selection.

10 Select the middle section of the banana, and change the stroke to None using the Stroke inspector.

Combine objects using Union

The Union command creates a single object from two or more objects. Unlike objects within a group, objects combined using Union lose their individual identity; their paths form a single path.

This activity creates a pear from two circles and a small line.

1 Turn to page 3 of the FreeHand document to start this activity.

2 Drag the large and small circles onto the gray outline so that they overlap slightly.

3 Shift-click to select both circles.

4 Choose Modify > Combine > Union.

5 Choose Window > Inspectors > Object.

The Object inspector describes characteristics of currently selected objects. Note that the two circles have become a single closed path.

6 Choose Window > Inspectors > Stroke.

The Stroke inspector describes characteristics of a currently selected object's stroke.

7 Select None from the stroke type pop-up to remove the 1-point black stroke from the object.

Apply a Gradient fill

1 Choose Window > Inspectors > Fill.

The Fill inspector describes the fill characteristics of a selected object.

2 Leaving the pear selected, choose Gradient from the fill type pop-up.

3 Choose dark green from the top color pop-up.

4 Choose light green from the bottom color pop-up.

5 Drag the light green color chip to the midpoint of the color ramp.

6 Choose light yellow from the bottom color pop-up.

7 Confirm that the graduated fill button is clicked, Overprint is unchecked, and Linear appears in the Taper pop-up.

8 Turn the angle dial to set the Gradient fill to 130 degrees.

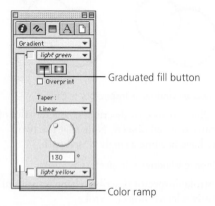

Graduated fill button

Color ramp

9 Drag the drawing of the stem onto the top of the pear.

10 Choose the Lasso tool and drag a selection area around the entire pear.

11 Choose Modify > Group to group the pear parts.

12 Leaving the pear group selected, choose Edit > Copy to copy the pear to the Clipboard.

13 Turn to page 1 of the FreeHand document to return to the main illustration.

14 Choose Edit > Paste to paste the pear onto the picture.

Organize objects

You can organize objects in a FreeHand document into separate layers. Using the Layers panel, you can create new layers, show and hide them, and rearrange their stacking order. You can also rearrange objects within a single layer.

1 Drag the pear onto the empty area under the apple.

2 Choose Window > Panels > Layers to display the Layers panel.

3 Leaving the pear selected, click the layer name Fruit. The pear is now on the Fruit layer.

4 Click the Fruit layer check mark on the Layers panel to hide all objects on that layer.

5 Click again in the check mark column next to the Fruit layer name to show all objects on the Fruit layer.

6 Select the pear again. Choose Modify > Arrange > Send to Back to position the pear under the other fruit.

7 Select the apple, and then choose Modify > Arrange > Send to Back to move the apple behind the pear.

Draw polygons and stars

Using the Polygon tool and the tool options, you can easily draw a range of multi-sided shapes, from triangles to stars with up to 360 points.

1 Turn to page 4 of the FreeHand document to start this activity.

2 Choose the Magnify tool and click once or twice between the shape outlines and the curve. If you magnify too much, choose View > Fit To Page and try again.

3 Choose the Ellipse tool. Hold down Shift-Option (Macintosh) or Shift-Alt (Windows), place the cursor in the middle of the gray circle outline, and drag outward to fit the circle to the outline.

4 Apply a light blue Basic fill and no stroke to the circle.

5 Double-click the Polygon tool to display the Polygon tool dialog box.

6 On the Polygon tool dialog box, enter 5 in the Number of Sides field, choose Polygon, and click OK.

7 Hold down Shift, place the cursor in the middle of the pentagon outline and drag outward to fit the outline.

8 Apply a Basic red fill and no stroke to the polygon.

9 Double-click the Polygon tool again.

10 In the Polygon tool dialog box, choose Star and Automatic and click OK.

11 Hold down Shift, place the star cursor in the middle of the star outline, and drag outward to fit the outline.

12 Apply a yellow Basic fill and no stroke to the star.

Create a blend on a path

1 Choose the Pointer tool.

2 Select the blue circle, then hold down Shift and add the red pentagon and the yellow star to the selection.

3 Choose Modify > Combine > Blend.

4 Choose Window > Inspectors > Object to display the Object inspector.

5 Type 30 in the Number of steps field and press Enter.

6 Hold down Shift and click the curve to add it to the selection.

7 Choose Modify > Combine > Join Blend To Path.

8 Experiment with the blend on a path by typing other values in the Number of steps field.

Attach text to a path

1 Choose View > Fit To Page, then use the Magnification tool for the next activity as needed.

2 Select the text on the bottom half of page 4.

3 Hold down Shift and click the curve to add it to the selection.

4 Choose Text > Attach To Path to attach the text to the path.

5 In the Object inspector, choose Vertical from the Orientation pop-up.

6 Click the fourth inspector tab to display the Text inspector.

7 Type 4% em in the Range Kerning field and press Enter.

Group the text and the blend

1 Choose View > Fit To Page.

2 Drag the blend on a path down to place it just above the text on a path.

3 Hold down Shift and add the text on a path to the selection.

4 Choose Modify > Group. Choose Edit > Copy to copy the logo.

5 Turn to page 1 of the FreeHand document and click Edit > Paste to paste it onto the picture. Drag the logo onto the top area of the newspaper.

6 Leaving the logo selected, click the layer name Newspaper on the Layers panel to move the logo to that layer.

7 Hold down Shift and drag a corner handle to resize as needed.

Create a paste inside

You can place a picture inside a FreeHand object so that the object temporarily crops the picture to the shape of the object, like a picture frame. This is known as a paste inside or clipping path.

1 On the Layers panel, click the layer name Newspaper to make it the active layer.

2 Choose File > Import. Navigate to the Tutorial folder on the FreeHand application folder, choose swat.jpg, and click Open.

3 Position the import cursor above the top-left corner of the blank picture area on the newspaper.

4 Click and drag the cursor down and to the right so that the outline slightly overlaps the blank picture area, then release the mouse button.

5 Select the image and choose Window > Panels > Transform.

6 Click the Rotate button. Type 10 in the Rotation angle field and click Apply (Macintosh) or Rotate (Windows).

The picture is now correctly oriented for its place in the main illustration.

7 Leaving the picture selected, choose Edit > Cut. Select the blank picture area. Choose Edit > Paste Inside.

Apply a Lens fill and Transparency fill

FreeHand has six types of lens fills: Magnify, Transparency, Invert, Lighten, Darken, and Grayscale. Each alters the appearance of objects under its centerpoint. First, create lenses for the eyeglasses.

1 Select the circle in the pasteboard area to the right of the glasses on page 1.

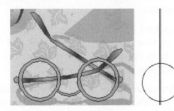

2 Choose Window > Inspectors > Fill to display the Fill inspector. Choose Lens from the Fill Type pop-up.

3 Choose Magnify from the Lens Type pop-up and enter 2 in the magnification field.

4 Choose Edit > Clone to create an identical circle on top of the selected circle.

5 Use the Pointer tool to drag each lens onto the eyeglasses in the picture. Use the cursor keys to position the lenses.

Now create a transparency lens to draw tea in the cup.

6 Click the inside of the cup to select the ellipse forming the cup rim.

7 Choose Edit > Clone to clone it. Apply a teabag-colored Transparency Lens fill to it.

8 On the Fill inspector, adjust the Opacity percentage to make the tea appear as strong or as weak as you like it.

9 Leaving the tea ellipse selected, press the down cursor key repeatedly to place the tea surface lower than the cup rim.

Punch out a portion of an object

1 Turn to page 5 of the FreeHand document to start this activity.

2 Choose the Magnification tool and click the gray outline A to magnify it to about 200 percent.

3 In the Stroke inspector, set a basic black stroke. In the Fill inspector, set a fill of None. Click the layer name Cup Front to set it as the active layer.

4 Choose the Bezigon tool. Hold down Shift and click on the gray path at point 1.

5 Hold down Option (Macintosh) or Alt (Windows) and click a point on the gray outline at each arrow, from 1 to 10.

For now, do not be concerned that the path you are drawing does not precisely follow the gray outline.

6 After point 10, click on top of point 1 again to close the path.

When you position the cursor over the first point again, a small black square indicates that clicking will close the path.

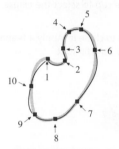

As you can see, the object you drew does not quite match the gray outline. You can adjust the shape of the path using point handles.

7 The segment between point 6 and point 7 needs to be adjusted. Using the Pointer tool, click point 6 to reveal a set of point handles.

8 Using the Pointer tool, drag the handle protruding downward from point 6 toward point 6 to adjust the adjacent path segment to match the gray outline.

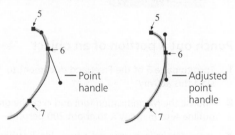

9 Adjust the path segments between point 9 and point 1 to fit the gray outline using the handles for points 9, 10, and 11.

10 When the path is complete, choose View > Fit To Page to view the whole page so that objects A through D are visible.

11 Using the Pointer tool, drag shapes A and B onto the gray outline C. Select shape A and choose Modify > Arrange > Bring To Front, in preparation for using Punch.

12 Hold down Shift and click to add shape B to the selection.

13 Choose Modify > Combine > Punch.

14 Choose Window > Inspectors > Fill to display the Fill inspector.

15 Choose Gradient from the fill type pop-up. Choose dark blue from the top color well and light blue from the bottom color well. Set the Gradient angle at 340 degrees.

16 Click the Stroke inspector tab to open the Stroke inspector, and choose None from the stroke type pop-up.

17 Using the Pointer tool, select the yellow and blue highlight object D. Choose Modify > Arrange > Bring to Front.

18 Drag the highlight onto the top curve of the handle.

If you move only a point on the highlight object by mistake, choose Edit > Undo, magnify the object, and try again. Use the cursor keys to position it on the handle.

19 Choose the Lasso tool and draw a selection area around the entire handle.

20 Choose Modify > Group, and then choose Edit > Copy.

21 Turn to page 1 of the FreeHand document and paste the handle onto the picture. Use the Pointer tool and the cursor keys to attach it to the right side of the cup.

Use the Transform handles

1 Choose the Pointer tool and double-click the spoon to display the transform handles.

If the transform handles do not appear, choose File > Preferences, click the General category, check Double-click enables transform handles, and click OK.

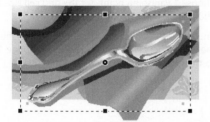

2 Place the cursor just beyond any corner handle so that the rotate cursor appears.

3 Drag the rotate cursor clockwise to rotate the spoon about 90 degrees.

4 On the Layers panel, click the check mark next to the layer name Spoon Shadow to hide the shadow.

5 Place the cursor in the area bounded by the transform handles, but not directly on any handle, so that the move cursor appears.

6 Drag the spoon to place it into the cup.

7 Leaving the spoon selected, click the layer name Cup Inside on the Layers panel.

8 Leaving the spoon selected, choose Modify > Arrange > Move Backward so the spoon appears to be in the tea.

New features

This tutorial introduces some of the features that are new to FreeHand 9, including perspective grid and transform and copy, as well as enhancements to envelope and the Trace tool.

Get started

You can complete the tutorial in about a half-hour. This tutorial assumes you are generally proficient with FreeHand. If you are new to FreeHand, taking the FreeHand basics tutorial is recommended. For details about any of the features this tutorial covers, see the index in this user guide.

Open the tutorial file

In this tutorial, you will complete a landscape illustration.

1   In FreeHand, choose File > Open, and open the file tutorial_2_start.fh9 located in the Tutorial folder inside the FreeHand 9 application folder.

2   Choose File > Save As. Name the file My_Work_2 and click Save.

Tutorial_2_start.fh9, the file in which you will be working, is a three-page FreeHand 9 document:

◆   Page 1 contains the scene on which you will create the illustration over the course of the tutorial.

◆   Page 2 contains the items you will use to create the illustration.

◆   Page 3 contains the completed illustration for reference.

Use the page-turning buttons or the page selection pop-up at the bottom of the FreeHand window to turn pages in a FreeHand document. Before you begin working, you can turn to page 3 to see what you will be creating.

Define the perspective grid

You are going to create a three-dimensional scene using FreeHand's perspective grid. By snapping objects to the perspective grid, you can orient them in relation to a vanishing point.

You can create custom grids with one, two, or three vanishing points to use in any FreeHand document. In this tutorial, we will create a perspective grid with one vanishing point.

1   Turn to page 1 of the FreeHand document to begin the tutorial.

2   Choose View > Perspective Grid > Define Grids to open the Define Grids dialog box.

3   Double-click the word Grid 1 and type Yard to rename the grid.

4   Choose 1 vanishing point, set the grid cell size to 108 points, and click OK.

5   Choose View > Perspective Grid > Show to show the grid. If necessary, click anywhere on page 1 so the grid will appear on page 1.

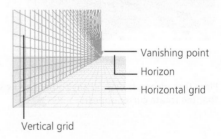

Vanishing point
Horizon
Horizontal grid
Vertical grid

6   Choose the Perspective tool.

7 Position the Perspective tool cursor near the horizon line, which is the top border of the horizontal grid. To avoid inadvertently moving objects, you can position the cursor off the page.

8 When the cursor changes to a horizontal line with a triangle under it, hold down the mouse button and drag the horizon line to the top of the green yard.

The point at which the vertical grid meets the horizon of the horizontal grid is the vanishing point.

9 Double-click the vanishing point, where the vertical grid meets the horizon. The vertical grid is hidden. A small triangle represents the vanishing point.

Vanishing point

10 Drag the vanishing point to the middle of the fence section.

11 Double-click the vanishing point again to display the vertical grid.

12 Position the cursor along the outer edge of the vertical grid, and then drag the grid edge to the left edge of the page.

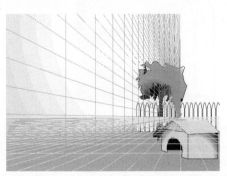

Attach an object to the perspective grid

Now you will build a fence on the perspective grid to create a three-dimensional yard scene.

1 Turn to page 2 of the FreeHand document, select the white fence picket, and then choose Edit > Copy.

2 Turn to page 1 of the FreeHand document, and then choose Edit > Paste.

3 Using the Perspective tool, drag the picket to the area near the lower-left corner of page 1 of the FreeHand document.

4 While holding down the mouse button press the left cursor key. The picket changes into an X-box attached to the vertical grid.

5 Drag the X-box to align the bottom of the X-box to the bottom of the vertical grid and to the left edge of the page.

The perspective grid has distorted the picket so that it is abnormally wide and short. You can use shortcut keys to adjust its size on the grid.

6 While holding down the mouse button on the picket, press the 3 key about 18 times to make the picket more narrow.

7 While holding down the mouse button on the picket, press the 6 key about 20 times.

The picket should be roughly the same shape as the original picket on page 2 and about 4 vertical grid cells tall. If necessary, reposition the picket into the corner of the page.

Create copies along the perspective grid

Now that the picket is the right size and in the right position on the grid, you will complete the fence by making copies of the picket that are also attached to the grid.

1 Hold down Option-Shift (Macintosh) or Alt-Shift (Windows). Using the Perspective tool, drag to the right from the original picket and position the picket copy next to the original, leaving a small space between the pickets.

Holding down Shift constrains the copies to the same orientation on the grid as the original picket.

2 Repeat the previous step about 20 times to complete the fence, releasing the mouse button after you make each copy.

3 If you need to adjust the spacing of the pickets, click a picket with the Perspective tool, hold down Shift, and press the left and right cursor keys.

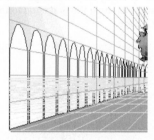

When you attached the pickets to the perspective grid, they became envelopes instead of objects. To convert a picket into an object while retaining perspective, you can choose View > Perspective Grid > Release with Perspective.

4 Choose View > Perspective Grid > Show to hide the perspective grid and view the illustration.

Transform copies and use an envelope preset

FreeHand's transform and copy feature applies a transformation to a copy of a selected object, then applies the same transformation to the copy, for as many copies as you specify.

First you will create a grove by copying a single tree and resizing the copies simultaneously.

1 On the Layers panel, click the padlock icon next to the layer name Scene to unlock it.

Objects on a locked layer cannot be selected.

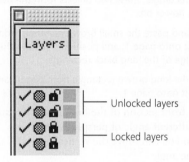

Unlocked layers

Locked layers

2 Select the tree.

3 Double-click the Scale tool to open the Transform panel.

4 Uncheck the Uniform option, and then enter 95 in the x field, 110 in the y field, and 4 in the Copies field, and then click Apply.

Four copies of the tree are created, and each has been incrementally transformed.

5 Using the Pointer tool, drag each tree over to the left half of the page, arranging them as a grove behind the fence.

6 Click the padlock icon next to the layer name Scene to lock the layer again.

Next you will create decorative shapes using a preset envelope, and then distribute copies.

7 Turn to page 2 of the FreeHand document and select the spiral shape.

8 On the Envelope toolbar, choose 4 Point Star from the Preset Envelope pop-up.

9 Choose Modify > Envelope > Create or click the Create Envelope button. An envelope shaped like a four-point star forces the spiral to conform to the envelope shape.

10 Drag the design onto the small brown rectangle on page 2 in the FreeHand document.

11 Choose Edit > Clone, and then move the cloned design to the left side of the long brown rectangle.

12 Leaving the clone selected, choose Window > Panels > Transform to open the Transform panel. If necessary, click the Move button on the Transform panel.

13 Enter 65 points in the x field, 0 in the y field, 3 in the Copies field, and click Move. Four equally spaced copies of the design are distributed across the long brown rectangle.

14 Select the four designs and the long brown rectangle and choose Modify > Group to group the objects. In the same way, group the single design and the small brown rectangle.

Put the flower box in perspective

The perspective grid is useful when creating a box or a building with a three-dimensional look. For example, the doghouse in the scene was created using a perspective grid.

Now that you have decorated the pieces of the flower box on page 2 of the FreeHand document, you can put the box together using the perspective grid.

1 Copy the long black rectangle on page 2, and then paste it onto page 1.

2 Choose View > Perspective Grid > Show to display the perspective grid.

3 Using the Perspective tool, select the long black rectangle and press the left cursor key to attach it to the perspective grid.

4 Drag the box to the area on the left side of the picture, and position it against the fence, aligning the bottom of the box with the bottom of the fence.

5 Copy the small black rectangle from page 2 and paste it on page 1 next to the right edge of the long black rectangle. If necessary, use the Scale tool to resize it to match the edge of the long black rectangle. these two objects form the back of the flower box.

6 Copy and paste the small brown rectangle from page 2 onto page 1, and position it next to the left edge of the long black rectangle.

7 Copy the long brown rectangle from page 2 and paste it onto page 1.

The long front section of the flower box needs a slightly different angle of perspective to look correct, so you can move the vertical grid to change the angle.

8 Using the Perspective tool, drag the left side of the vertical grid to the right, aligning it with the right edge of the small brown rectangle.

Move the vertical grid to here.

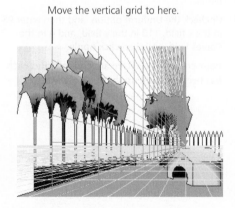

9 While holding down the Perspective tool on the long brown rectangle, press the left cursor key to attach it to the perspective grid.

10 Position the brown rectangle to form the front of the flower box.

11 If necessary, hold the Perspective tool on the rectangle, and press a number key from 1 to 6 to adjust the rectangle so that the box fits together.

Remember, keys 1 and 2 shrink and expand both dimensions of an object on the grid; keys 3 and 4 adjust the width; keys 5 and 6 adjust the height.

12 Using the Pointer tool, shift-select the long and short brown rectangles and choose Modify > Group.

Grouping objects moves the group to the front of the stacking order on a layer.

13 Copy and paste the grouped flowers from page 2 onto page 1. Drag them onto the flower box.

14 Leaving the flowers selected, choose Modify > Arrange > Move Backward to put the flowers inside the flower box.

15 Choose View > Perspective Grid > Show to hide the perspective grid and view the illustration.

Trace a JPEG

The yard scene is almost complete. You will now add a dog to the grass area in the foreground.

With FreeHand's Trace tool you can create many kinds of objects based on all or part of an imported image. In this section, you will use the Trace tool to create a path that outlines an object within an image, and then draw a vector version of the image by tracing details in the image.

1 Choose File > Import, navigate to the Images folder within the Tutorial folder in the FreeHand 9 application folder, and then choose the file named dog.jpg.

2 Position the import cursor in the green grass area on page 1 click to import the image.

First, you will draw an object shaped like the dog, then use that object to mask the dog image, creating a paste inside.

3 Double-click the Trace tool to open the Trace tool dialog box.

4 Choose Outer Edge from the Path Conversion pop-up, move Trace Conformity, Noise Tolerance, and Wand Color Tolerance sliders to the middle, and click OK.

5 Using the Trace tool, drag a selection area around the entire dog, but inside the black border of the image, to create a path in the shape of the dog.

6 Using the Pointer tool, select the dog image, and then choose Edit > Cut.

7 Select the dog-shaped path object, and then choose Edit > Paste Inside.

8 Leaving the dog-shaped path object selected, open the Stroke inspector and choose None from the Stroke type pop-up.

9 With the dog-shaped path object still selected, choose the Scale tool, hold down Shift, and drag the tool until the dog is the size you want it to be.

The image in the paste inside is linked. If you do not want a linked image in your file, you can use the Trace tool to convert the dog image into a vector path drawing.

10 Reapply a Basic stroke to the paste inside so you will be able to see the path object after releasing the image from the paste inside.

11 Choose Edit > Cut Contents to release the dog image from the paste inside.

12 Drag the dog image across the page to reveal the path object that defined the paste inside, select the path, and press Delete.

13 Double-click the Trace tool to open the Trace Tool dialog box.

14 Choose Outline from the Path Conversion pop-up and click OK.

15 Using the Trace tool, draw a selection area around the entire dog, but inside the black border. The result is a vector drawing of the dog.

16 Leaving the vector version of the dog selected, choose Modify > Group.

17 Drag the dog into position in the scene. Using the Pointer tool, hold down Shift to constrain proportions and drag a corner handle to resize the dog.

18 Select the original image of the dog and press Delete.

19 To complete the scene, copy and paste the blue butterfly from page 2 onto the fence area on the left side of the page.

4

CHAPTER 4
Organizing Your Illustration

Organizing your illustration is time well spent. The more complex your illustration, the more you benefit from organizing it with templates, layers, groups, object styles, paragraph styles, and symbols.

Templates—Use them as defaults for creating new documents to avoid recreating frequently used design elements and production settings.

Layers—Edit and manage complex illustrations with many overlapping objects in manageable portions. Categorize related objects, and turn off layers to print objects selectively. Merge layers to combine related objects.

Groups—Freeze two or more objects in relation to one another. Move or transform multiple objects together.

Object styles—Quickly apply the same formatting to multiple objects and globally edit graphic attributes.

Paragraph styles—Apply and modify text formatting.

Symbols—Manage multiple instances of a graphic from one central location.

Using templates

To work more efficiently and avoid design inconsistencies, create templates for documents that share common design elements and production settings.

A template's settings and attributes are defaults for creating other documents. Save a document as a template when you want to create new documents with the same objects, settings, colors, and object and paragraph styles. For example, to create a series of designs that have the same page size and layout, save the first one as a template and then use it to create the rest in the series.

A template file saves what is in a FreeHand document, including the following:

◆ Guides

◆ Layer information

◆ Object styles

◆ Paragraph styles

◆ Symbols

◆ Custom colors

◆ Custom page sizes

◆ Custom units of measurement

When opening a template, an untitled copy the template appears. Use the untitled copy to create or replace an existing template. You can also designate a template as your default for new documents.

To save a document as a template:

1 Choose File > Save As.

2 Enter a name for your template file in the Save (Macintosh) or Save Document (Windows) dialog box.

3 Choose FreeHand Template from the Format (Macintosh) or Save as type (Windows) pop-up.

4 Choose a destination and click Save. In Windows, an FT9 extension is added to the file name.

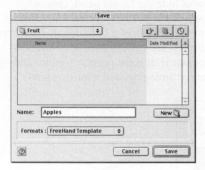

Macintosh Save dialog box

Windows Save Document dialog box

To edit a FreeHand template:

1 Open the template, make changes, and then choose File > Save.

2 Save the newly revised document as a template with the same name and location.

3 FreeHand prompts you to replace the original template file. Click Replace and the new template replaces the old one.

To set a template as the default for new documents:

1 Open and edit a template.

To edit the default template, choose File > New and edit the untitled copy.

2 Choose File > Save, and name the file.

Name the file FreeHand Defaults (Macintosh) or Defaults.ft9 (Windows). To use a template file with a different name, type the file name in the Document > "New document template" preference.

3 Save the template in the English folder within the same folder as the FreeHand application.

The next time you choose File > New, an untitled copy of your new default template appears.

To convert any FreeHand file into a template without opening it (Macintosh):

1 Select the file in the Finder.

2 Choose File > Get info and check the Stationery pad checkbox.

To convert a template into a FreeHand document, uncheck the Stationery pad checkbox.

Simplifying a complex illustration using layers

Layers divide an illustration into discrete planes, as though the different components of the illustration were drawn on separate tracing paper overlays. Every object in an illustration resides on a layer. Only objects on visible, unlocked layers are editable. Create all layers before you draw or add individual layers as you need them. Merge layers to combine similar objects.

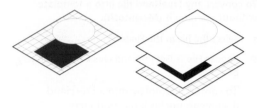

Objects on a checked layer are visible.

A layer in Preview mode displays objects as they will print.

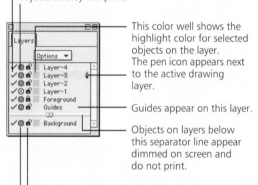

This color well shows the highlight color for selected objects on the layer. The pen icon appears next to the active drawing layer.

Guides appear on this layer.

Objects on layers below this separator line appear dimmed on screen and do not print.

Objects on a locked layer cannot be moved.

A layer in Keyline mode displays outlines of objects.

Navigating the Layers panel

To show or hide the Layers panel, choose Window > Panels > Layers, or use Command-6 (Macintosh) or Control-6 (Windows). The Layers panel displays the current state of all layers in your document. It is the primary tool for adding, duplicating, arranging, and removing layers.

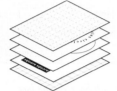

To control how objects on a layer appear, use the check mark, padlock, color well, and Preview/Keyline icons beside the layer name. Hide or lock layers to avoid accidentally moving or deleting objects. Work in Preview mode to see objects as they will print. Choose Keyline mode to view only the outlines of objects on a layer and to speed redraw. Use the color well to assign a highlight color, which distinguishes objects on one layer from those on another when the General > Smoother Editing preference is checked.

Choose Edit > Select > None to deselect all objects, then click the layer name to choose a layer to be the active layer. A pen icon appears next to the active layer. The next object you draw appears on this layer. Deselecting all objects prevents inadvertently moving objects to the new active layer. To prevent selected objects from moving to the active layer, you can also uncheck the Panels > "Clicking a layer name moves selected object" preference. For more information on moving objects between layers, see "Moving objects and reordering layers" on page 77.

To rename a layer, double-click the layer name, type a new name, and press Return to accept the name.

Moving objects and reordering layers

Change the way objects overlay one another in your document by moving objects from one layer to another, or by rearranging the order of the layers. Designate layers as non-printing by dragging them below the separator line, or by dragging the separator line.

The Panels > "Clicking a layer name moves selected object" preference controls how objects are moved between layers. With this preference checked, clicking a layer name moves selected objects to the clicked layer. Unchecking this preference prevents this behavior.

To move an object to another layer with the Clicking a layer name preference checked:

1 Select an object.

    The object's layer name appears highlighted on the Layers panel.

2 Choose the destination layer by clicking the destination layer name.

To move an object to another layer with the Clicking a layer name preference unchecked:

1 Select an object.

2 Choose the destination layer by clicking the destination layer name.

3 Choose Move objects to current layer from the Layers panel Options pop-up menu.

Note: Alternatively, you can move selected objects to another layer by Control clicking (Macintosh) or right-clicking (Windows) and choosing "Move selection to this layer" from the pop-up.

To move one layer in front of or behind another layer:

1 Choose Edit > Select > None or press Tab to deselect all objects in the document.

2 On the Layers panel, click the name of the layer you want to move.

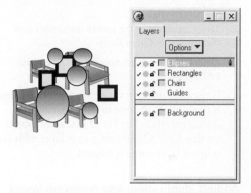

3 Drag the layer name to a new position, either above or below another layer name.

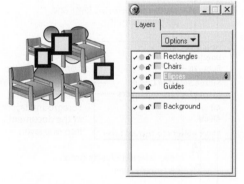

To merge specific layers:

1 Select discontiguous layers by Command-clicking (Macintosh) or Control-clicking (Windows) or select a range of layers by Shift-clicking.

2 Choose Merge Selected Layers from the Layers panel Options pop-up.

    Objects on merged layers retain their stacking order relative to one another.

To merge all Foreground layers

Choose Merge Foreground Layers from the Layers panel options pop-up.

To copy layer information to another document:

1 Check the General > "Remember layer info" preference.

2 Select an object in the source document and choose Edit > Cut or Copy.

3 Open the destination document and choose Edit > Paste.

If the layer name in the destination document is the same as the one in the original document, then FreeHand places the object on that layer. Otherwise, a new layer with the original layer name is created.

Adding, duplicating, and removing layers

Add a new layer.

Copy the contents of the selected layer onto a new layer.

Delete the selected layer and all objects on it.

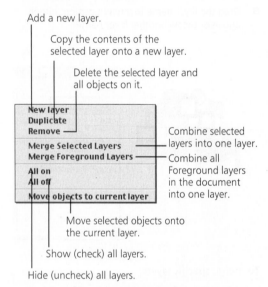

Combine selected layers into one layer.

Combine all Foreground layers in the document into one layer.

Move selected objects onto the current layer.

Show (check) all layers.

Hide (uncheck) all layers.

Options pop-up on the Layers panel

To	Do this
Add a new layer	Choose New from the Options pop-up.
Combine selected layers into a single layer	1. Select layers. 2. Choose Merge Selected Layers from the Options pop-up.
Combine all Foreground layers into a single layer	Choose Merge Foreground Layers from the Options pop-up.
Duplicate a layer and all objects on it	Click a layer name and choose Duplicate from the Options pop-up.
Remove a layer and all objects on it	Click a layer name and choose Remove from the Options pop-up.
Remove several layers and all objects on them	1. Hold down Command (Macintosh) or Control (Windows) and click the layer names. To remove contiguous layers, hold down Shift and click the multiple layer names. 2. Choose Remove from the Options pop-up.

Note: The Guides layer is unaffected by merge commands.

Turning on and turning off layers

To		Do this
Turn on a layer	Rivers / Topography	Click to the left of the unchecked layer name.
Turn off a layer	Rivers / Topography	Click the check mark to the left of the checked layer name.
Turn on a range of layers		Click in the space to the left of an unchecked layer name and drag to select a range of contiguous layers. All selected layers are checked.
Turn off a range of layers		Click the check mark to the left of a checked layer name and drag to select a contiguous range of layers. All selected layers are unchecked.
Turn on all layers		Choose All on from the Options pop-up, or
		Hold down Option (Macintosh) or Control (Windows) and click in the space to the left of an unchecked layer name.
Turn off all layers		Choose All off from the Options pop-up, or
		Hold down Option (Macintosh) or Control (Windows) and click to the left of a checked layer name.

Turning off a layer hides all objects on that layer, but does not remove them from the document. Turning on a layer shows all objects on that layer. If the active layer is turned off, then newly created
objects are not visible until the layer is turned on again.

Note: To print all foreground layers when layers are turned off, choose File > Output Options, and check Include invisible layers.

Hiding selected objects from view

To hide specific objects, select them and then choose View > Hide Selection.

Using Hide Selection hides all selected objects. Hidden objects print as if they are visible. Locked objects remain locked when hidden. Guides cannot be hidden using Hide Selection.

To show all hidden objects, choose View > Show All. Hidden objects reappear when the file is closed and reopened.

Note: Show All does not show a hidden layer.

Locking and unlocking layers

To		Do this
Lock a layer	Rivers / Topography	Click the open padlock to the left of the layer name.
Unlock a layer	Rivers / Topography	Click the closed padlock to the left of the layer name.
Lock a range of layers		Click the open padlock to the left of a layer name and drag to select a contiguous range of layers. All selected layers are locked.
Unlock a range of layers		Click the closed padlock to the left of a layer name and drag to select a contiguous range of layers. All selected layers are unlocked.
Lock all layers		Hold down Option (Macintosh) or Control (Windows) and click an unlocked padlock.
Unlock all layers		Hold down Option (Macintosh) or Control (Windows) and click a locked padlock.

Viewing layers in Preview or Keyline mode

To	Do this
View a layer in Preview mode	Click the hollow Keyline icon.
View a layer in Keyline mode	Click the filled Preview icon.
View a range of layers in Preview mode	Click a hollow Keyline icon and drag to select a contiguous range of layers. All selected layers are switched to Preview mode.
View a range of layers in Keyline mode	Click a filled Preview icon and drag to select a contiguous range of layers. All selected layers are switched to Keyline mode.
View all layers in Preview mode	Hold down Option (Macintosh) or Control (Windows) and click a Keyline icon.
View all layers in Keyline mode	Hold down Option (Macintosh) or Control (Windows) and click a Preview icon.

Guides

To view guides, turn on the check mark at the far left of the Guides layer name. To hide the guides, turn off the layer. To view the guides in black, set the drawing mode to Keyline for the Guides layer. To view them in the guide color chosen in the Colors > "Guide color" preference, set the viewing mode to Preview.

To turn an object into a guide, select the object and click the Guides layer. The object displays in the guide color. To turn a guide into an object, double-click the guide and click Release in the Guides dialog box. The object returns to its original layer.

For more information about guides and the Guides layer, see Chapter 2, "Getting Your Bearings," and FreeHand Help.

Using highlight colors to distinguish objects on different layers

With the General > "Smoother editing" preference checked, highlight colors for each layer can distinguish objects on one layer from those on another. The editable color wells on the Layers panel display the highlight color of a particular layer.

With the General > "Highlight selected paths" preference checked, the layer highlight color appears as a one-point line on top of selected, ungrouped paths. View and edit highlighted paths on any layer without bringing them to the front of your illustration. The highlight color does not affect the color of the object.

To assign a highlight color, check the General > "Smoother editing" preference and drop a color chip from any color well onto the color well next to the layer name. FreeHand now uses the new color to highlight all selected items on that layer.

To highlight selected objects, handles, and points, but not draw a highlight line on top of paths, uncheck the General > "Smoother editing" > "Highlight selected paths" preference.

Uncheck "Smoother editing" to eliminate all highlight colors. Although the Smoother editing preference uses more RAM, this feature also provides other drawing enhancements in addition to highlight color.

Note: For better results on Macintosh, leave Smoother editing turned on. In Windows, Smoother editing may reduce performance.

To assign a highlight color, drag a color chip from any color well onto the color well next to the layer name.

Working with objects on a single layer

Arranging objects on the same layer

To	Do this
Move an object forward on the same layer	Select the object and choose Modify > Arrange > Move Forward.
Move an object to the front of a layer	Select the object and choose Modify > Arrange > Bring to Front.
Move an object backward on the same layer	Select the object and choose Modify > Arrange > Move Backward.
Move an object to the back of a layer	Select the object and choose Modify > Arrange > Send to Back.

To	Do this
Paste an object behind a selected object on the same layer	1. Select the object and choose Edit > Cut or Copy. 2. Select the object behind which you want to paste. 3. Choose Edit > Paste Behind.

To	Do this
Paste an object in front of a selected object on the same layer	1. Select the object and choose Edit > Cut or Copy. 2. Select the object in front of which you want to paste. 3. Choose Edit > Paste in Front.

Use the Arrange commands to change the stacking order of objects. However, you may not see a change in the stacking order if the objects are not overlapping. Pasting an object behind or in front of an object within a group or a clipping path integrates the pasted object into the group or the clipping path. Clipping paths are paths into which other objects are pasted. To learn how to create clipping paths, also known as paste insides, see "Working with clipping paths" on page 115.

To hide selected objects on a layer without turning off the layer, select one or more objects and choose View > Hide Selection. See "Hiding selected objects from view" on page 79.

To select all objects on a single layer in a multilayer document:

◆ Hold down Option (Macintosh) or Alt (Windows) and click on a layer name.

For more information on selection commands see "Selecting objects" on page 39.

Grouping objects

Grouping two or more objects freezes their positions and stacking order relative to one another, so you can manipulate them as a single object. Objects within a group retain their individual characteristics, unless you modify the entire group.

To	Do this
Group objects	1. Select multiple objects. 2. Choose Modify > Group, or use Command-G (Macintosh) or Control-G (Windows). After grouping, click any object in the group to select the entire group. Grouping objects on different layers moves these objects to the current drawing layer but retains their relative stacking order.
Ungroup objects	1. Select the group. 2. Choose Modify > Ungroup, or use Command-U (Macintosh) or Control-U (Windows). Ungrouping objects with the General > "Remember layer info" preference checked returns these objects to their original layers.

Subselecting within a group

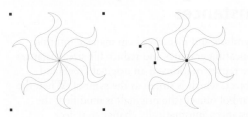

Grouped object   *Component subselected*

To work with individual objects within a group, either ungroup the objects or subselect only the objects you want to modify. Modifying attributes of a subselected object changes only the subselected object and not the rest of the group. Subselected objects cannot be moved to other layers or grouped with other groups.

To	Do this
Subselect one object within a group	Hold down Option (Macintosh) or Alt (Windows) and select the object.
Subselect two or more objects within a group	Hold down Shift-Option (Macintosh) or Shift-Alt (Windows) and select the objects.
Select all objects within a selected group	Choose Edit > Select > Subselect.
Subselect one object behind another object within a group	Hold down Control-Option and click the object (Macintosh) or hold down Control-Alt and right-click the object (Windows).
Deselect a subselected object	Press Tab or click the document outside the group.
Select all objects except the currently selected objects.	Choose Edit > Select > Invert Selection.
Select the group containing a subselected object	Choose Edit > Select > Superselect, or press Tilde (~).

Working with nested objects

Nested objects are objects in groups within larger groups. Manipulate them just as you would any other group.

To nest an object within an existing group:

1   Select an object and a group.

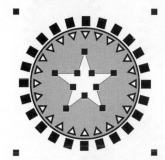

2   Choose Modify > Group or use Command-G (Macintosh) or Control-G (Windows).

Use Group up to 20 times in succession to nest objects within a group, or to combine groups within a larger group. A nested object is an object within a group. Although the actual nesting limit is 28, certain objects such as inline graphics and paste insides may have nested objects within them and therefore may account for more than one nest.

Note: Multiple nested groups can significantly increase printing time and complexity.

To subselect a nested group:

1   Hold down Option (Macintosh) or Alt (Windows) and select an object within the nested group.

2   Choose Edit > Select > Superselect or press Tilde (~) until you have selected the nested group you want.

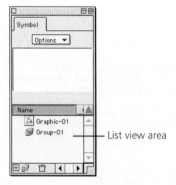

Working with symbols and instances

Symbols and instances help manage multiple repeating graphics and reduce file size. Instances are representations of an original FreeHand object, which is stored as the symbol. When the symbol object (the original) is modified, the instances automatically change to reflect modifications to the symbol.

Store symbols in the Symbols panel for reuse throughout a document. Import and export symbols for use in other FreeHand documents.

To open the Symbols panel, click the button on the Main toolbar or choose Window > Panels > Symbols.

Creating a symbol

Create a symbol from any object, text, or group by selecting an object and using any of these methods:

♦   Drag and drop the object onto the List view area of the Symbols panel.

♦   Choose Modify > Symbol > Convert to symbol.

Creating a new symbol automatically adds the symbol to the Symbols panel.

You can duplicate or clone a symbol by choosing Options > Duplicate from the Symbols panel. Doing so adds the duplicate symbol to the Symbols panel.

To preview a symbol, choose Options > Preview from the Symbols panel.

Creating an instance

Create an instance using any of these methods:

- Drag and drop a symbol from the Symbols panel.

- Copy and paste, duplicate, or clone an instance.

Modifying a symbol

Modify a symbol to automatically modify all associated instances.

To modify a symbol:

1 Drag and drop a symbol from the Symbols panel.

2 Choose Modify > Symbol > Release Instance.

3 Modify the object.

4 Drag the object onto its original name to replace the original symbol with the modified object.

5 Click Replace to confirm the replacement.

All instances tied to that symbol update automatically.

Working with symbols, instances, and the Symbols panel

To	Do this
Create a symbol	Select an object, group, or text and drag and drop it onto the List view area of the Symbols panel, or Choose Modify > Symbol > Convert to symbol.
Create an instance	Drag a symbol from the Symbols panel and drop it into the document, or Copy and paste an instance, or Duplicate an instance, or Clone an instance.
Delete an instance	Select the instance, then press Delete.
Delete a symbol and all associated instances	Choose Options > Remove and confirm in the resulting dialog box to delete all instances.
Break the link between an instance and its symbol	1. Select the instance. 2. Choose Modify > Symbol > Release Instance.
Open the Symbols panel	Choose Window > Panels > Symbols.
Delete a symbol from the Symbols panel	1. Select the symbol. 2. Choose Options > Remove from the Symbols panel.
Import symbols	1. Choose Options > Import from the Symbols panel. 2. In the Open dialog box, navigate to the file to import and click OK.
Export symbols	1. Choose Options > Export from the Symbols panel. 2. In the Save As dialog box, navigate to the folder in which to export the symbols and click OK.

Using styles

Use styles to maintain visual consistency and to simplify formatting. Modify object styles and paragraph styles to quickly change graphics and text throughout your document. You can create and save styles to use as part of a template.

Object styles—Use object styles to format graphics with preset stroke, fill, color, and halftone attributes. These attributes are available in the Stroke inspector, the Fill inspector, or the Halftones panel. Object styles are available in the Styles panel.

Paragraph styles—Format individual paragraphs or entire text blocks. Options include font, color, style, size, justification, text effects, tabs, margins, spacing, range kerning, baseline shift, hanging punctuation, and paragraph rules. These attributes are available in the Text menu, the Text inspector, and the Text toolbar. Paragraph styles are available in the Styles panel and the Text Character inspector.

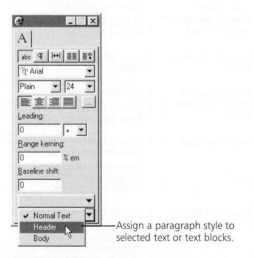

Assign a paragraph style to selected text or text blocks.

Text Character inspector

Navigating the Styles panel

To show or hide the Styles panel, choose Window > Panels > Styles or use Command-3 (Macintosh) or Control-3 (Windows). The Styles panel displays the current object styles and paragraph styles in your document. It is the primary tool for adding, duplicating, removing, and modifying object and paragraph styles. Choose available commands from the Options pop-up. Click a style name and choose Edit from this pop-up to set specific attributes.

Choose from two viewing options available in the Options pop-up on the Styles panel: Show names or Hide names. When Show names is selected, styles are listed by name, with either the graphic or text icon shown. When Hide names is selected, styles are represented using previews that reflect the styles' attributes.

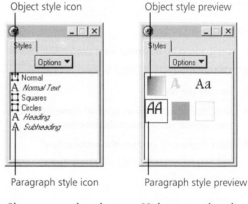

Object style icon   Object style preview

Paragraph style icon   Paragraph style preview

Show names selected   *Hide names selected*

Managing styles

Applying a style

To apply a style	Do this
To selected objects or text	1. Select one or more objects, paragraphs, or text blocks. 2. Click a style name in the Styles panel to apply the style's attributes to the object or text.
Using drag and drop	Drag and drop a style from the Styles panel to an object or text.
Using the paragraph styles pop-up in the Text Character inspector	1. Select one or more paragraphs or text blocks. 2. Choose a style name to apply the style's attributes to the text.
From one object to another using Copy Attributes and Paste Attributes	1. Select the source object. 2. Choose Edit > Copy Attributes or use Command-Shift-Option-C (Macintosh) or Control-Shift-Alt-C (Windows). 3. Select the destination object and choose Edit > Paste Attributes or use Command-Shift-Option-V (Macintosh) or Control-Shift-Alt-V (Windows).

Drag and drop a style to apply it to a paragraph of text.

By default, applying a paragraph style changes an individual paragraph's attributes. To affect an entire text block, choose the Text > "Dragging a paragraph style changes" > "Entire text container" preference. To learn how to prevent changing text effects, paragraph rules, hanging punctuation, tabs, or margins when applying a new style, see "Keeping previously applied paragraph attributes" on page 89.

See FreeHand Help for additional information regarding the Object > "New graphic styles" preference and the Text > "Build paragraph based on" preference.

Adding, duplicating, and removing styles

Options pop-up on the Styles panel

To	Do this
Add a new style	1. Choose Edit > Select > None to deselect objects. 2. Set object or text attributes. 3. Choose New from the Options pop-up.
Add a new style based on a selection	1. Select an object or text. 2. Choose New from the Options pop-up.
Duplicate a style	1. Choose Edit > Select > None to deselect objects. 2. Click a style name on the Styles panel. 3. Choose Duplicate from the Options pop-up.
Remove a style	1. Choose Edit > Select > None to deselect objects. 2. Click a style name on the Styles panel. 3. Choose Remove from the Options pop-up.
Remove all unused styles	Choose Remove unused from the Options pop-up.

Note: To rename a style, double-click the style name, type a new name, and press Return.

Importing and exporting styles

Use the Styles panel's Options pop-up to import and export styles. Export styles to transfer to other illustrations, distribute to other users, or store for future use.

To export styles:

1 Choose Window > Panels > Styles to display the Styles panel.

2 Choose Export from the Options pop-up.

3 Using the Export dialog box, choose styles for export.

4 Choose a destination—type a file name for the exported style library, and click Export.

FreeHand has many preset object styles that can enhance your illustrations. These preset styles are located in the Styles panel's Options pop-up.

To import styles:

1 Choose Window > Panels > Styles to display the Styles panel.

2 Choose Import from the Options pop-up.

3 Click the name of the styles library or FreeHand document containing the desired styles, and click Import.

Modifying styles

To edit an object style:

1 Click an object style name in the Styles panel.

2 Choose Edit from the Options pop-up to display the Edit Style dialog box.

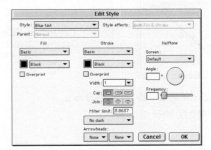

3 Change any attribute and click OK to save your style.

You can modify any stroke, fill, color, or halftone attribute in the Edit Style dialog box.

To edit a paragraph style:

1 Click a paragraph style name on the Styles panel.

2 Choose Edit from the Options pop-up to display the Edit Style dialog box.

3 Change any attribute and click OK to save your style.

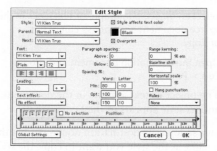

To regain the settings present before modifying a paragraph style in the Edit Style dialog box, choose Restore Original Values from the Global Settings pop-up. Choose Restore Program Defaults to regain the default settings.

Keeping previously applied paragraph attributes

When creating a new style or modifying an existing style, disable attributes in the Edit Style dialog box. This prevents modifying them when applying the style to text that already has the attributes you want.

To disable	Do this
Font	Choose No selection from the Font pop-up.
Style	Choose No selection from the Style pop-up.
Point size	Leave the field blank.

To disable	Do this
Justification	Click the blank button to the right of the justified button.
Leading	Choose No selection from the Leading pop-up.
Text effect	Choose No selection from the Text effect pop-up.
Color	Uncheck Style affects text color.
Paragraph spacing	Leave the fields blank.
Spacing %	Leave the fields blank.
Range kerning	Leave the field blank.
Baseline shift	Leave the field blank.
Horizontal scale	Leave the field blank.
Hang punctuation	Click the Hang punctuation checkbox until a hyphen [-] (Macintosh) or a dimmed check mark (Windows) appears.
Rules	Choose No selection from the Rules pop-up.
Tabs and margins	Check the No selection checkbox on the text ruler.
All settings	Choose No selection from the Global Settings pop-up.

Each click of the Hang punctuation checkbox changes its status. An empty checkbox indicates that hanging punctuation is turned off. An X (Macintosh) or a check mark (Windows) indicates that the option is turned on. A hyphen (Macintosh) or a dimmed check mark (Windows) indicates No selection.

Note: Unlike choosing No selection, choosing None in the Rules pop-up removes all paragraph rules in paragraphs to which the style is applied, and choosing No effect in the Text effect pop-up removes all text effects.

Overriding styles

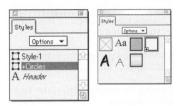

To	Do this
Override a style	1. Select an object, paragraph, or text block. 2. Change any stroke, fill, color, halftone, or text attribute. When you select the object or text, the overridden style appears highlighted with a "+" in front of it.
Redefine a style based on a selected object or text	1. Select an object and apply the desired attributes. 2. Choose Redefine from the Options pop-up in the Styles panel. 3. In the Redefine style dialog box, click the name of the style you are redefining, and click OK. The style now assumes the attributes of the selected object or text.
Remove a style override	1. Select an object, paragraph, or text block with an overridden style. 2. Click its style name. The original style applies to the object or text, removing any override.

To base one style on another style:

1 Choose Edit > Select > None to deselect all objects.

2 Click the style name for the child or dependent style.

3 Choose Set Parent from the Options pop-up to display the Set Parent dialog box.

4 Choose another style to be the parent or source style, and click OK.

Use Set Parent from the Options pop-up to base variations of a style on another style. The resulting style, called the child style, depends on the attributes of its source style, called the parent style. When you edit a parent style, the attributes shared by the child style also change. Attributes unique to the child style do not change.

If you remove a child style from an object or text, the parent style becomes the active style, but the object or text retains all of its attributes.

To copy style information to another document:

1 Select an object, paragraph, or text block in the source document and choose Edit > Cut or Copy.

2 Open the destination document and choose Edit > Paste.

The object or text appears in the document, and its style appears in the Styles panel.

When a style in the destination document has the same name as the style you want to copy, the style is overridden but not redefined.

Use the Import and Export commands to transfer styles between documents. See "Importing and exporting styles" on page 88.

CHAPTER 5
Drawing

Vector drawing

When drawing in FreeHand, paths are the basic elements of your graphic designs. Generated mathematically within FreeHand, a path consists of at least two points. Each point connects one or more line segments, either straight or curved.

Because of the way it generates lines on screen, FreeHand is classified as a vector drawing application. Vector applications produce resolution-independent graphics, which appear crisp and smooth regardless of the level of on-screen magnification. A vector graphic always appears at your computer's maximum screen resolution, no matter how closely you zoom in to see its details.

In contrast, by displaying a matrix of pixels on screen, bitmap image applications produce resolution-dependent graphics. When viewed from afar, these pixels form a continuous graphic, but as you zoom in, the graphic becomes increasingly granulated as you begin to see individual pixels.

Bitmap image applications are best used for computerized painting and texturizing, as well as for editing continuous-tone graphics such as photographs. Whether vector or bitmap, each application has its unique strengths. To learn how other applications work with FreeHand, see Chapter 10, "Working with Other Applications."

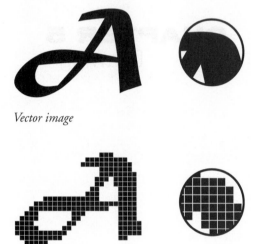

Vector image

Bitmap image

Path characteristics

Vector graphics consist of paths, which consist of points and path segments. A path segment, either straight or curved, is the element spanning two points. Paths have a variety of characteristics:

- Path status (open or closed)
- Stroke and fill attributes
- Direction

Types of paths

- **Open**—An open path is one where the beginning point and the ending point do not connect.

Open paths

- **Closed**—Although it may have overlapping path segments, a path is not closed until the beginning and ending points are the same.

Closed paths

Stroke and fill attributes

Color, the primary attribute for both strokes and fills, enables you to distinguish other visible attributes of open and closed paths. Without color, paths would not appear on screen or in print.

- A stroke consists of the attributes applied to a path's line segments. To display and print fills contained in open paths, check the Object > "Show fill for new open paths" preference before creating the path.

- A fill consists of the attributes applied to the area within the border of a closed path. Closed paths always print both strokes and fills.

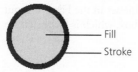

The Stroke, Fill, and Both selectors in the Color List indicate the color applied to paths. To learn how to apply strokes and fills to paths, see Chapter 6, "Color, Strokes, and Fills."

Direction

When drawing a path, the order in which you place points establishes path direction. Think of path direction as either clockwise or counterclockwise. The initial path direction of FreeHand's preset shapes—ellipses, rectangles, and polygons—is clockwise.

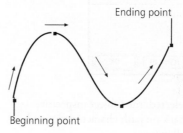

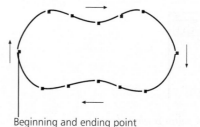

Beginning and ending point

Path direction determines which handle adjusts a given path segment and to which path end an arrowhead applies. Path direction is also important when you bind text to a path, blend paths, or fill composite paths created from two paths with different directions.

To change the path direction of any path once drawn, use the Reverse Direction path operation. Choose Modify > Alter Path > Reverse Direction, choose Xtras > Cleanup > Reverse Direction, or click the Reverse Direction button on the Xtra Operations toolbar.

Selecting paths

Using the Pointer tool, select paths just as you would any other object: either click the path or drag a selection area around the path. Hold down Shift when clicking paths to select more than one.

To select paths without dragging around the entire path, double-click the Pointer tool in the Toolbox and check the Contact Sensitive tool preference. With this preference checked, dragging around a portion of the path selects the entire path.

With a path selected, the Object inspector provides feedback on path characteristics and displays the following:

A path of 4 points is selected.

◆ **Object type**—A path is an object. When your selection includes more than one object, the Object inspector tells you the number of objects selected.

◆ **Number of points**—FreeHand's limit of 32,000 points per path lets you import very complex files from other sources. Depending upon your output, you may want to monitor the number of points in a selected path. Increasing the number of points increases the file size, slows redraw, and slows printing. The fewer points a path has, the easier it is to modify, display, and print. Use Xtras > Cleanup > Simplify to decrease the number of points in a path. Use Find & Replace Graphics to selectively simplify paths in an entire document. For more information on Find & Replace Graphics, see page 137.

◆ **Even/odd fill**—With Even/odd fill checked, overlapping portions of closed paths are transparent.

◆ **Closed**—Check Closed to automatically connect the endpoints of a selected, open path. Uncheck Closed to remove the last path segment from a selected, closed path.

◆ **Flatness**—On a PostScript output device, a curve consists of a series of tiny line segments. Flatness gauges the size of the line segments comprising a path—the lower the flatness value, the smaller the line segments and the smoother the path. If your output device generates PostScript error messages, assign a higher flatness value. Printed objects will appear more blocky, but the document will print faster.

Use this option only when you want to assign different flatness values to individual paths. The flatness value set in the Object inspector overrides the value set in the File > Output Options dialog box, which is for the entire document.

Selecting path segments

A segment is a section between two points on a path.

To select a segment:

1 Using the Pointer tool, click the path to select it.

2 Hold down Option (Macintosh) or Alt (Windows) and click the segment anywhere between its two end points.

   To select multiple segments, hold down Option-Shift (Macintosh) or Alt-Shift (Windows) and click each segment anywhere between end points.

Point characteristics

Points not only determine path direction but also the shape and position of adjacent path segments. Providing the framework for vector graphics, corner, curve, and connector points are useful tools to create and edit paths. Most of the points you create will be corner or curve points.

Type of point	Function	Handle behavior
Corner `⌐`	Creates hinges between adjacent path segments	Corner point handles are retracted and move independently. Therefore, it is possible to adjust adjacent path segments, either straight or curved, one at a time.

Type of point	Function	Handle behavior
Curve `↝`	Maintains smooth, winding transitions through a point between adjacent curves	By default, curve point handles extend. They move around a point in tandem, affecting adjacent path segments at the same time.
Connector `→`	Maintains smooth transitions between a straight path segment and a curved one or between two curves meeting at a sharp angle	When a connector point is preceded by or followed by a curve, handles extend. The position of the points on either side of a connector point limits the movement of its handles.

Selecting points

Using the Pointer tool, click individual points to select them, or drag a selection area around either an entire path or a portion of it to select points. Hold down Shift when clicking points to select more than one. Selected points appear hollow rather than solid.

With a point selected, the Object inspector provides feedback of point characteristics, in addition to the path information shown in "Selecting paths" on page 94.

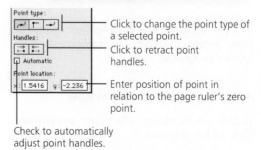

Click to change the point type of a selected point.

Click to retract point handles.

Enter position of point in relation to the page ruler's zero point.

Check to automatically adjust point handles.

- **Point type**—Use the Pointer, Lasso, Pen, or Bezigon tools to select a point. With a point selected, one of three point buttons is selected. To change the point type, select a point and click a different point button.

- **Handles**—To retract handles and adjust the path shape, select a point and click the button corresponding to its point handle.

- **Automatic**—This setting positions the point handles of a selected point with respect to the position of the preceding and following points. Select the desired points and then check Automatic. Manually adjusting or retracting a point handle turns off Automatic.

  The Automatic setting is useful when you want to drag a selected point so that the curvature of the path segments before and after the point automatically adjust.

- **Point location**—The Point location entry fields display the x and y coordinates of the point in the document unit of measurement. The displayed point location is relative to the zero point defined on the active page.

Viewing paths with highlight color

Check the General > "Smoother Editing" > "Highlight selected paths" preference to view the non-printing highlight color of paths. With "Highlight selected paths" checked, a line of the designated highlight color appears on top of the selected path. With "Highlight selected paths" unchecked, only the points of the selected path appear in the highlight color.

This line is selected with the "Highlight selected paths" preference checked. The highlight color appears on top of the path.

Hiding selected objects from view

To hide specific objects, select them and choose View > Hide Selection.

Using Hide Selection hides all selected objects. Hidden objects print as if they are visible. Locked objects remain locked when hidden. Guides cannot be hidden using Hide Selection.

To show all hidden objects as selected objects, choose View > Show All.

Note: Choosing Show All does not show hidden layers.

Selecting a path with the right mouse button (Windows)

Commands from a variety of menus appear in the Path shortcut menu. To display path commands, select one or more paths with the right mouse button.

Choosing shortcut commands for paths (Windows)

Choose	To
Edit	Display the Edit menu showing commands applicable to the path.
Text	Create a new text block that flows either along or inside the path.
Curve, Corner, or Connector	Change the point type of a selected point.
Path	Change the status of the path to either Open or Closed.
Tools	Choose one of the applicable Toolbox tools.
Xtras	Choose a command from the Xtras menu.
Select	Choose a selection command.
View	Choose a magnification view for the active page.
Export Object	Export one or more selected objects.
Print Object	Print one or more selected objects.
Arrange	Move the path or object by choosing: Bring to Front, Move Forward, Move Backward, or Send to Back.
Lock or Unlock	Lock or unlock the path's position. Locked paths cannot be transformed, cut, or deleted.
Group or Ungroup	Group or ungroup objects.
Properties	Display the Object inspector to view path or point options.

Toolbox tools for drawing paths

Use	To
Pointer tool Shortcut key: 0 (zero) or V	Select paths and other objects on screen. Although the Pointer tool is not a drawing tool, it is essential for selection and placement of objects.
Lasso tool Shortcut key: L	Select points, objects, and groups within a freeform selection area.
Rectangle tool Shortcut key: 1 or R	Draw rectangles and squares.
Polygon tool Shortcut key: 2 or G	Draw polygons and stars.
Ellipse tool Shortcut key: 3 or E	Draw ellipses and circles.
Spiral tool	Draw open spiral-shaped paths.
Line tool Shortcut key: 4 or N	Draw straight lines.

Use	To
Freehand tool Shortcut key: 5 or Y	Draw freeform paths. Choose from three options: Freehand, Variable stroke, and Calligraphic pen.
Pen tool Shortcut key: 6 or P	Draw by placing points. Use the Pen tool to anchor points and manipulate point handles as you draw.
Knife tool Shortcut key: 7 or K	Cut a path into two or more paths.
Bezigon tool Shortcut key: 8 or B	Draw by placing points. Use the Bezigon tool to reposition a point before releasing the mouse button to place it. Point handles adjust to adjacent path segments.
Freeform tool Shortcut key: 9 or F	Edit a path within a specified area. Choose from two options: Push/Pull, or Reshape Area.
Trace tool	Trace both imported and native graphics and text to yield editable paths.

To momentarily switch back to the Pointer tool while drawing, hold down Command (Macintosh) or Control (Windows). This is useful when you need to quickly select an object while using a drawing tool.

Double-click any tool button with a bracket in its upper-right corner to display tool options.

Drawing basics

In FreeHand, there are three ways to draw:

- ◆ To draw paths by dragging, use the Rectangle, Polygon, Line, Ellipse, Spiral, or Freehand tool. FreeHand automatically places the appropriate type of point.

- ◆ To draw paths by placing points, use either the Pen or Bezigon tool. Choose the types of points to place as you draw.

- ◆ To create paths by tracing another object, use the Trace tool. FreeHand traces text, bitmap images, or vector graphics to yield editable paths.

Drawing by dragging

To draw using a basic shape tool:

1 Select one of the shape tools: Rectangle, Polygon, Ellipse, Spiral, or Line.

2 Hold down the mouse button to start a path, drag to draw, and release the mouse button to end the path.

To constrain a shape, hold down Shift while dragging.

Use Shift with	To constrain shapes to
Rectangle tool	Squares
Ellipse tool	Circles
Spiral tool	Angles at increments of 45°
Polygon tool	Angles at increments of 45°
Line tool	Angles at increments of 45°

To draw a rectangle, an ellipse, or a line from its center, hold down Option (Macintosh) or Alt (Windows) and drag the respective tool. The Polygon tool automatically draws from the center. By default, the Spiral tool automatically draws from the center. Double-click the Spiral tool to change its defaults.

The center cursor

To both constrain a shape and draw it from its center, hold down Shift-Option (Macintosh) or Shift-Alt (Windows) while using a drawing tool.

When drawn, rectangles and ellipses are initially grouped. When selected, a rectangle and an ellipse are labeled as such in the Object inspector. Choose Command-U (Macintosh) or Control-U (Windows) to ungroup them and manipulate individual points. If ungrouped they are no longer editable as rectangles or ellipses.

The corner radius value determines the curvature of the corners of your rectangle.

To assign a value	Do this
Before drawing a rectangle	1. Double-click the Rectangle tool to display the Rectangle Tool dialog box.
	2. Enter a numerical value or use the slider to adjust the corner radius, click OK, and then draw the rectangle.
	A value of zero yields standard, 90° corners.
After drawing a rectangle	Select the rectangle and then enter a numerical value in the Corner radius entry field in the Object inspector. Press Return. The shape of the rectangle changes.

Creating polygons and stars

To	Do this
Set the number of sides for polygons and stars	1. Double-click the Polygon tool to display the Polygon Tool dialog box.
	2. Choose either the Polygon or Star option.
	3. Choose a value ranging from 3 to 20 using the Number of Sides slider or enter a value up to 360 in the entry field.
Set the angle of star points	1. Choose the Star option to create a star and set the Number of Sides. Star options appear.
	2. Click the Automatic option or move the acute/obtuse slider to set the star shape.
	With Automatic selected, stars are drawn to preset star shapes. Moving the acute/obtuse slider changes Automatic to Manual.

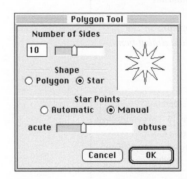

Automatic　　　*Acute*　　　*Obtuse*

Using the Freehand tool

With the Freehand tool, draw freeform paths following the direction of your hand movements. The three modes of operation for this tool are Freehand, Variable stroke, and Calligraphic pen.

To draw a path using the Freehand tool:

1 Double-click the Freehand tool to display the Freehand Tool dialog box.

2 Click one of three options in the dialog box: Freehand, Variable stroke, or Calligraphic pen. Click OK.

3 Hold down the mouse button to start a path, drag to draw, and release the mouse button to end the path.

4 Hold down Option (Macintosh) or Alt (Windows) to draw a straight line with the Freehand tool.

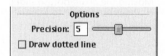

Freehand options in the Freehand Tool dialog box.

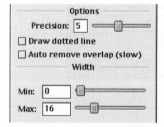

Variable stroke options in the Freehand Tool dialog box.

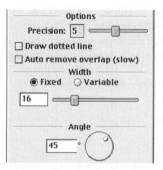

Calligraphic pen options in the Freehand Tool dialog box.

Use the Precision slider to control how closely the Freehand tool duplicates your mouse movements. Lower values create fewer control points and use less RAM. In addition to using less RAM, paths with fewer points generally make printing faster. Higher values tell FreeHand to match your hand movements as closely as possible to the paths on screen. To speed up path creation, check Draw dotted line. With this checked, FreeHand displays fragmented paths as you draw; the actual path appears when you release the mouse button.

Using the Variable stroke tool and the Calligraphic pen

Depending upon the width settings, the Variable stroke tool and the Calligraphic pen tool draw closed paths with stroke and fill attributes. Width refers to the distance between the centerline of the strokes opposite each other. Verify that the Color List displays the stroke and fill attributes of your choice.

To draw paths of varying widths:

1 Click the Variable option in the Freehand Tool dialog box.

For the Calligraphic pen only, click the Fixed option to set calligraphic paths to a constant width.

2 Set minimum and maximum widths for your path, and then start drawing.

3 As you draw, increase and decrease path width in one of the following ways:

- ◆ To decrease path width, use the left cursor key, the numeral 1 key, or the open bracket key.

- ◆ To increase path width, use the right cursor key, the numeral 2 key, or the close bracket key.

Note: The open and close bracket keys apply only to the Macintosh.

Each time you press a key, the width changes by one-eighth of the width range as defined in the Variable stroke tool settings or the Calligraphic pen settings.

When using a pressure-sensitive tablet, the width of the path segments increase or decrease according to the amount of pressure applied. When switching from the Wacom pressure-sensitive pen to its eraser, FreeHand switches from a drawing tool to the Knife tool.

To automatically remove overlap from paths as you draw, check Auto remove overlap, which maintains the path's original shape while removing unnecessary path segments. Auto remove overlap yields composite paths.

Auto remove overlap unchecked

Auto remove overlap checked

Note that checking Auto remove overlap may slow redraw. Therefore, you may first draw the path and remove overlap later. Select the finished path and then choose Modify > Alter Path > Remove Overlap, choose Xtras > Cleanup > Remove Overlap, or click the Remove Overlap button on the Xtra Operations toolbar.

To set the angle of the Calligraphic pen, enter a degree value in the Angle entry field or move the circular Angle dial to a location representing an angle from 0° to 360°. The angle set corresponds to the angle of the Calligraphic pen tip. Choose no stroke and a Basic fill to most closely approach a real calligraphy pen.

To erase as you draw using the Freehand tool, continue to hold down the mouse button, press Command (Macintosh) or Control (Windows), and trace backwards—opposite to the path's original direction. Release the modifier key to continue drawing.

Drawing by placing points

The Pen tool and the Bezigon tool

The fundamental difference between the Pen tool and the Bezigon tool is the way each places points:

- ◆ Use the Pen tool to place anchored points and interactively manipulate handles to adjust path shape. To move the position of the point and the point handles simultaneously, hold down Command (Macintosh) or Control (Windows) as you place a point.

- ◆ Use the Bezigon tool to create and then freely move a point before placing it; FreeHand adjusts handles and path shape in reference to the position of the point.

When it is important for you to control the shape of the path regardless of point position, use the Pen tool. When you want FreeHand to predict the curve for you, use the automatic curvature of the Bezigon tool.

Use the Pen tool to interactively move point handles.

Use the Bezigon tool to create paths that automatically curve.

Use the Pen tool to	Do this
Place a corner point	Click.
	As you place a corner point, hold down Option (Macintosh) or Alt (Windows) and drag to extend a handle as you place it. This handle affects the next path segment.
Place a curve point	Click and drag.
	Curve point handles extend automatically. Since the Pen tool anchors points in place, use the point handles to adjust path shape.
	Press Command (Macintosh) or Control (Windows) while dragging to move the curve point to a new location.
Place a connector point	Hold down Control and click (Macintosh).
	Hold down Alt and right-click (Windows).
	Dragging as you place a connector point extends a handle. This handle affects the next path segment.
Continue a path from its last point	Select the last point on the path and click with the Pen tool to continue the path.

To place a path segment at a sharp angle to a preceding curve, place a curve point and leave it selected. With the Pen tool, click the point to retract its outgoing handle. Place the next point wherever you wish.

Placing a path segment at a sharp angle.

Use the Bezigon tool to	Do this
Place a corner point	Click. With the Bezigon tool, you cannot extend handles until after the point is placed.
Place a curve point	Hold down Option (Macintosh) or Alt (Windows) and click. Curve point handles extend automatically. Both the handles and the preceding and following curves adjust as you position the point. Releasing the mouse anchors the point in place.
Place a connector point	Hold down Control, click, and drag (Macintosh). Hold down Alt and the right mouse button and drag (Windows).

Inserting and deleting points

To insert a corner, curve, or connector point into the middle of a path, click the path with the Pen tool or the Bezigon tool. For example, with the Pen tool, click and drag to insert a curve point and extend its handles. Reshape adjacent path segments. With the Bezigon tool, insert a curve point and reshape the path using automatic curvature.

For information about manipulating a path or path segments, see "Path manipulation" on page 105.

Repositioning points

Reposition points in paths using any of three methods:

◆ With the Pointer tool or the Bezigon tool, select an endpoint or a point in the middle of a path and move it. Release the mouse button to place the point.

◆ With the Pen tool, select an endpoint or a middle point. Hold down Command (Macintosh) or Control (Windows) and drag the point to a new place. Release the mouse button. Using either method, point handles and path segments adjust automatically.

◆ With the Freeform tool, reshape a path or an area containing paths. Points are added, deleted, or changed accordingly.

To reposition two or more points at a time, use the Pointer or Lasso tool to select a point and then hold down Shift to select more points, or drag a selection area around a portion of the path. Use the Pointer tool to click one of the selected points and drag to reshape the path. Point handles and path segments adjust automatically as you move the point.

Closing paths

To close a path manually with the Pointer, Pen, or Bezigon tool, select an endpoint and drag it to the other endpoint. When the cursor turns into a black square, release the mouse button to close the path. To close a path automatically, select a path, display the Object inspector, and check Closed. In Windows, right-click the path to open the Path shortcut menu and choose Path > Closed.

As you draw a path with the Pen or Bezigon tool, double-click as you place the last point to end the path or press Tab to deselect the path. Click in a new place to start another path.

Path cursors

As you draw and edit paths, cursors confirm the operation you are performing.

This cursor	Indicates
$+$	Using a tool (other than Freeform). This is the standard crosshair cursor.
$+_{\square}$	Placing the first path point of a new path when using either the Pen or Bezigon tool.
$+_{\blacksquare}$	Closing a path when one endpoint is on top of the other.
$+_{\wedge}$	Inserting a point into the middle of a path.
$+_{\bullet}$	Placing the cursor over the endpoint of a path drawn with the Freehand tool. Continue drawing from this endpoint rather than beginning a new path.

Basic point handle manipulation

To extend point handles manually, select a corner, curve, or connector point. First hold down Option (Macintosh) or Alt (Windows). Then, using the Pointer tool, click and drag handles, one at a time, from the selected point. The first handle you extend curves the path segment following the point. The second handle you extend curves the path segment preceding the point.

Note: If you click a point before you hold down Option (Macintosh) or Alt (Windows) when extending point handles manually, dragging will clone the path rather than extend point handles unless you release the modifier key before releasing the mouse button.

To extend point handles using the Object inspector, select a curve point with handles retracted. Use either Command-I (Macintosh) or Control-I (Windows) to display the Object inspector. Check Automatic to adjust point handles and adjacent path segments to best conform to the existing path. Therefore, the curve point handles do not necessarily return to the position in which they were first placed. Checking Automatic does not extend the handles of corner or connector points.

To retract point handles automatically, select a point with handles extended and display the Object inspector. For curve points, click the left and right point handle buttons. For corner and connector points, check Automatic; FreeHand automatically adjusts the adjacent path segments.

To retract point handles manually, select a corner, curve, or connector point with handles extended. With the Pointer tool, click and drag the end of each handle into the point.

Adjust the curvature and the angle of path segments by manipulating point handles. The range and direction of handle movement varies for each type of point. In FreeHand, point handles are slender with small point knobs. If you wish to use larger handles, uncheck the General > "Smaller handles" preference.

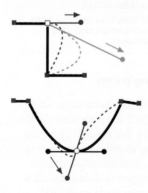

The farther you drag a handle away from a corner, curve, or connector point, the more pronounced the curve becomes.

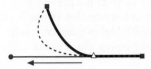

For information about manipulating a path or path segments, see "Path manipulation.".

Constraining path segments as you place points

To	Do this
Place a corner point at the constrain angle	Hold down Shift and click the Pen tool or Bezigon tool.
Place a curve point at the constrain angle	Hold down Shift and click and drag the Pen tool. Hold down Shift-Option (Macintosh) or Shift-Alt (Windows) and click the Bezigon tool.
Place a connector point at the constrain angle	Hold down Control-Shift and click the Pen tool or Bezigon tool (Macintosh), or hold down Shift-Alt and right-click (Windows).

The Modify > Constrain command affects editing points, creating objects such as rectangles and ellipses, and constraining angles using Shift. When holding down Shift as you place a point, the angle set in the Constrain dialog box determines the angle of a newly placed point measured from the axis of the previously placed point.

When the constrain value is 0 (zero), holding down Shift constrains objects to 0°, 45°, 90°, etc. Changing the constrain angle to 10°, for example, changes constrain lines to 10°, 55°, 100°, and so on.

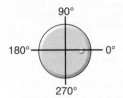

Path manipulation

Edit paths, path segments, and points by selecting and manipulating them.

To	Do this
Select an entire path	Click a path.
Select a segment of a path	1. Click a path. 2. Hold down Option (Macintosh) or Alt (Windows), and click a path segment.
Select a point on a path	1. Click a path. 2. Click on a point or drag select a point.
Select multiple paths, segments, or points	Hold down Shift while selecting paths, segments, or points.
Clone a path while editing	Hold down Option (Macintosh) or Alt (Windows) while dragging a path or point.

To	Do this
Use Bend-O-Matic	Hold down Option (Macintosh) or Alt (Windows) while dragging a path segment. (Automatically adjust Bézier handles to the new position of a path segment).
Delete a path, segment, or point	Select a path, segment or point and press Delete. *Note:* Deleting one or more segments from a path leaves one or more open paths.

Editing paths using the Freeform tool

For greater control and flexibility when changing the shape of a path, use the Freeform tool to push or pull any part of the path. Unlike Bend-O-Matic, the Freeform tool automatically adds points, deletes points, or changes point type along the path as you edit the path. The Reshape Area feature reshapes a path within an area. Double-click the Freeform tool in the Toolbox to display the Freeform tool dialog box.

Push/Pull—Check to display settings for the Freeform tool's push and pull features.

Reshape Area—Check to display settings for the Freeform tool's reshape feature.

Size—To set the diameter of the push cursor, type a number from 1 to 1000 pixels or use the slider.

Precision—To set the accuracy of the push cursor, enter a number from 1 to 10 or use the slider. Lower numbers result in less precision (fewer points added to the path); higher numbers result in more precision (more points added to the path).

Bend—Choose one of two bend methods in the pop-up.

◆ To pull a segment between two points on a selected path, choose Between Points.

◆ To pull a segment of a specific length with the pull cursor as the centerpoint, choose By Length.

Length—When bending By Length, enter a segment length from 1 to 1000 pixels or use the slider.

Size (Pressure)—Check to activate a drawing tablet's pressure-sensitive size adjustment capability.

Length (Pressure)—Check to activate a drawing tablet's pressure-sensitive length adjustment capability.

The cursor changes to reflect the current Freeform tool feature.

This cursor	Indicates
	The Freeform tool is active. Click and hold on a selected path to activate the pull cursor. Click and hold away from the selected path to activate the push cursor.
	The pull cursor is active, and By Length is set, if on a selected path. Pull the path to reshape the path. This cursor also indicates no path is selected. Use the Freeform cursor to select a path.
	The pull cursor is active and Between Points is set. Pull the path to reshape the path.

This cursor	Indicates
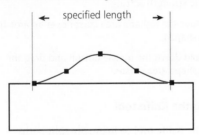	The push cursor is active; push the selected path with the adjustable outer circle to reshape the path.
	The reshape area cursor is active; pull the path inside a specified radius and with a specified gravitational strength.

Note: To deselect a path, press Tab.

To pull a path segment of a specified length:

1 Double-click the Freeform tool in the Toolbox to display the Freeform Tool dialog box.

2 Choose the Push/Pull option.

3 Choose By Length in the Bend pop-up.

4 Specify the length of the path segment to be pulled in the Length field or use the slider, and then click OK.

5 Point to the selected path, press and hold the mouse button, and drag the path.

Pull: By Length

To pull a path segment between two points:

1 Double-click the Freeform tool in the Toolbox to display the Freeform Tool dialog box.

2 Choose the Push/Pull option.

3 Select Between Points in the Bend pop-up, and then click OK.

4 Move the cursor onto the selected path, click and hold the mouse, and drag the path.

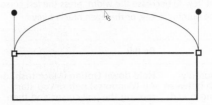

Pull: Between Points

To push a path segment:

1 Double-click the Freeform tool in the Toolbox to display the Freeform Tool dialog box.

2 Choose the Push/Pull option.

3 Type the size (diameter) of the push cursor from 1 to 1000 pixels or use the slider.

4 Type the precision from 1 to 10 or use the slider, and then click OK.

5 Move the cursor away from the path and click and hold the mouse button.

The push cursor appears. If the pull cursor appears instead, select the path.

6 Drag the push cursor along the path.

The outer circle pushes the path.

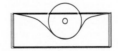 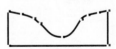

Push set at 50   *Curve after being pushed*

Note: To increase the width of the push cursor, press the right cursor key, the number 2 key, or the close bracket key. To decrease the width, press the left cursor key, the number 1 key, or the open bracket key.

To	Do this
Temporarily switch between By Length and Between Points	Hold down Option (Macintosh) or Alt (Windows) before you start moving the pull cursor and then drag the cursor.
Clone the path you are changing and leave the original path	Hold down Option (Macintosh) or Alt (Windows) after you start moving the cursor.
Constrain push cursor direction to 45° increments	Hold down Shift while using the Freeform tool to push a path.
Temporarily switch to the Pointer tool	Hold down Command (Macintosh) or Control (Windows).

Freeform Reshape Area

Choose Reshape Area in the Freeform Tool dialog box to display the Freeform Reshape dialog box.

With Reshape Area chosen, the Freeform tool button in the Toolbox changes to indicate that Reshape Area mode is active.

Freeform toolbar button in Reshape Area mode

To reshape an area of a drawing:

1 Double-click the Freeform tool in the Toolbox to display the Freeform Tool dialog box.

2 Check the Reshape Area option.

3 Type the size (diameter) of the reshaping circle from 1 to 1000 pixels or use the slider.

4 Type the strength of the reshaping circle from 1 to 100 percent, and click OK.

With the General > "Smoother editing" preference checked, the distance between the red inner circle and the outer circle represents the strength setting.

5 Move the reshape area cursor over an area to be reshaped.

6 Hold down the mouse button and drag the reshape area cursor.

Using the Knife tool

Use the Knife tool to manually split paths yielding either open or closed paths. Select a path and drag the Knife tool across the path.

- **Freehand**—Use to cut along a freeform path. With the Freehand option selected, hold down Option (Macintosh) or Alt (Windows) to cut a straight line.

- **Straight**—Use to cut along a straight line.

- **Width**—Set the width of the Knife tool's path. The higher the value, the wider the cut; the width is best seen when cutting a filled path with Close cut paths checked.

- **Close cut paths**—With Close cut paths checked, both the stroke and the fill are retained. With Close cut paths unchecked, only the stroke of a filled path is retained. FreeHand adds endpoints at the intersection of the Knife tool and your path.

Unchecked   *Checked*

- **Tight fit**—Create a cut that closely follows the path of your hand movements.

With the General > "Smoother Editing" preference unchecked, the new points resulting from a cut path may not be visible.

Note: When switching from the Wacom pressure-sensitive pen to its eraser, FreeHand switches from a drawing tool to the Knife tool.

Replicating an existing path

Create copies of existing paths by duplicating or cloning.

Duplicating

To duplicate an object, select the path and choose Edit > Duplicate or use Command-D (Macintosh) or Control-D (Windows). A copy of the path appears offset from the original. Holding down Option (Macintosh) or Alt (Windows) when dragging an object also copies it.

Cloning

To clone an object, select the path and choose Edit > Clone or use Command-= (Macintosh) or Control-Shift-C (Windows). A copy of the path appears on top of the original. Use Clone when you want to maintain the original path's position. For example, to copy a path and scale the resulting path so that the centers of both objects match, use Clone.

Power-duplicating

Using power-duplication, you can repeatedly move, scale, rotate, reflect, or skew copies of an object. Combine more than one kind of transformation, but use each kind of transformation only once.

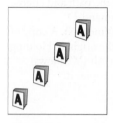

Moving

Moving and scaling

Moving, scaling, and rotating

To power-duplicate, select an object, choose Edit > Duplicate or Edit > Clone, transform the object, and then choose Edit > Duplicate again. Do not deselect the transformed copy before duplicating it. Choosing Edit > Duplicate with the most recent copy selected applies the transformation to the next copy.

To learn how to transform an object, see "Modifying shape and position" on page 130. Experiment by using the Mirror Xtra tool to create rotated and reflected copies of an original object.

Drawing by automatically tracing

 To trace a graphic, click the Trace tool in the Toolbox and drag a selection area around the object to trace. Hold down Shift to constrain the Trace tool's selection area to a square.

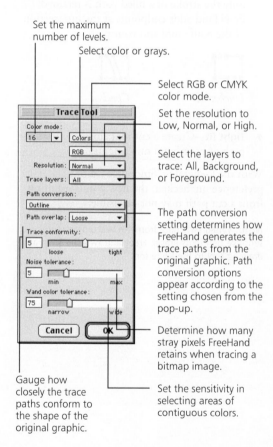

Set the maximum number of levels.

Select color or grays.

Select RGB or CMYK color mode.

Set the resolution to Low, Normal, or High.

Select the layers to trace: All, Background, or Foreground.

The path conversion setting determines how FreeHand generates the trace paths from the original graphic. Path conversion options appear according to the setting chosen from the pop-up.

Determine how many stray pixels FreeHand retains when tracing a bitmap image.

Set the sensitivity in selecting areas of contiguous colors.

Gauge how closely the trace paths conform to the shape of the original graphic.

The original default settings for the Trace tool provide good results when tracing bitmap and vector graphics using a reasonable amount of RAM. See "Considering resolution and memory allocation" on page 111.

The Trace tool traces any objects appearing on screen: bitmap images, text, or native graphics. The Trace tool traces graphics according to the settings in the Trace Tool dialog box. In addition, the Trace tool samples areas of contiguous color based upon settings in the Trace tool Options dialog box. Double-click the Trace tool in the Toolbox to display trace settings. Because the Trace tool's settings are saved to the FreeHand Preferences file when you quit FreeHand, it is a good practice to confirm the dialog box settings before tracing objects.

Choosing a color mode

To set the color mode of your resulting trace, choose either Colors or Grays and choose either RGB or CMYK from the Color mode pop-ups in the Trace Tool dialog box. Whether your original graphic is bitmap or vector, use the Trace tool to convert a graphic in any of the following ways:

◆ From color to color

◆ From grayscale to grayscale

◆ From color to grayscale

For example, if you wish to trace a color TIFF in grayscale, choose Grays from the Color mode pop-up. In the resulting vector graphic, gray values are substituted for the original color pixels in the TIFF. To trace an RGB TIFF and define the resultant image using the CMYK color model, choose CMYK from the Color mode pop-up.

Note: Use the Name All Colors Xtra to place colors from imported or traced graphics into the Color List. Choose Xtras > Colors > Name All Colors.

Choosing the number of colors

FreeHand internally identifies the frequency of each color in a graphic and then averages all color values evenly within the number of colors set in the Color mode pop-up (up to 256). Since the colors available determine how true of a match your trace is to the original graphic, choose a high value when tracing graphics with subtle color variations. Otherwise, you may lose these variations in your trace.

If the graphic goes beyond the limit you specify, FreeHand automatically converts the excess values to the closest values of the colors selected in the graphic. In the Color mode pop-up, either enter a color value limit in the entry field or choose from the pop-up. Settings higher than 16 require more RAM.

Considering resolution and memory allocation

When scanning images to be traced in FreeHand, we recommend a resolution of 300 to 600 dots per inch. Scanning images at a resolution higher than 600 dots per inch results in too many points. When tracing graphics, choose High, Normal, or Low resolution in the Resolution pop-up to determine the degree of detail in the resulting trace. A setting of High will capture more detail than a setting of Normal, and a setting of Normal more than a setting of Low. However, there are two advantages of using Normal or Low. One is that conversion time is less than when using the High setting. The other is that the Low setting requires less RAM than the Normal setting and Normal less than High.

FreeHand must perform an intense operation when tracing high-resolution TIFFs. Therefore, you may need to allocate more RAM to FreeHand on the Macintosh. When the amount of system RAM limits your ability to trace a high-resolution graphic and you cannot allocate more RAM, FreeHand uses the lowest allowable resolution setting.

Choosing trace layers

With the Trace layers pop-up, designate traceable layers: All, Foreground, or Background. FreeHand traces all paths on the layers designated.

Choosing the way FreeHand creates trace paths

Trace paths can be either open or closed. FreeHand converts your graphics into paths according to the settings in the Path conversion pop-up.

The Path conversion pop-up consists of four choices: Outline, Centerline, Center/Outline, and Outer edge. These settings determine the placement of strokes in the resulting trace paths.

- **Outline**—FreeHand traces along the outside border of the graphic elements. The resulting trace objects are closed, filled paths.

  Choosing Outline displays the Path Overlap pop-up.

  - Choose None when tracing logos, line art, and text.

  - Choose Loose to make trace objects overlap each other to prevent light leaks. Checking this option is most suitable when tracing continuous-tone images such as scans of photographs, paintings, and rendered graphics.

  - Choose Tight for more precise color tracing.

- **Centerline**—FreeHand traces at the center of the graphic strokes. This option is best suited for tracing line-intensive graphics that have almost no filled areas, such as technical drawings and schematics.

Choosing Centerline displays the Uniform lines checkbox.

- Checking Uniform lines yields a trace object with a consistent stroke width of one point throughout, even though the original graphic contains lines of varying widths.

- With Uniform lines unchecked, FreeHand generates open paths with varying stroke widths.

- **Centerline/Outline**—Choose this to use a combination of both Outline and Centerline methods. FreeHand evaluates the original graphic and decides what attributes to give each trace path based on the Open paths below option.

  Enter a value from 2 to 10 pixels in the Open paths below entry field. The default value is 3 pixels. The Trace tool uses this value to determine which paths are drawn as open paths. For example, using the default setting of 3, FreeHand draws an open, stroked path for any item in the graphic that is less than 3 pixels wide.

- **Outer edge**—FreeHand traces only the outer contours of the graphic, providing an accurate clipping path so that the original graphic can be pasted inside.

Setting trace conformity

Use the Trace conformity slider or entry field, with values ranging from 0 to 10, to define how closely the resulting paths conform to the curved and straight lines of the original graphic. A setting of 10 produces resulting paths that closely conform to the original graphic, but it increases the number of points in the trace paths. A setting of 0 has the least amount of conformity to the original graphic and has fewer points, resulting in a smaller converted graphic file. This setting is useful to create traces that are less precise versions of the original graphic.

Setting noise tolerance

With the Noise tolerance slider or entry field, FreeHand eliminates stray pixels, or noise, most frequently found in bad scans or original graphics of poor quality. The higher the setting, the more FreeHand ignores noise. In contrast, a minimum setting makes FreeHand keep as much file information as possible.

Setting Wand color tolerance

Use the Wand color tolerance slider in the Trace Tool dialog box to set the sensitivity in selecting areas of contiguous colors. Use a low number to select a narrower range of color and brightness values. Values range from 0 to 255.

To trace a contiguous area of color:

1 Click the Trace tool in the Toolbox.

2 Click an area of color to be selected.

- ◆ To add to the current selection, hold down Shift and click additional areas.

- ◆ To subtract from the current selection, hold down Shift and click a selected area.

- ◆ To deselect all areas, press the Tab key.

3 After selecting all areas, click any selected area with the Trace wand to open the Wand Options dialog box.

- ◆ Choose Trace Selection to trace the selected areas using the settings in the Trace Tool Options dialog box.

- ◆ Choose Convert Selection Edge to trace only the edges of the selected areas.

- ◆ Press Option (Macintosh) or Alt (Windows) when clicking the selected areas to bypass the Wand Options dialog box and trace the selected areas using the current settings.

Working with complex objects

Groups

Grouping two or more objects freezes their positions and stacking order relative to one another, so you can manipulate them as a single object. Objects within a group retain stroke, and fill attributes. Apply path operation, transformation, and distortion commands to an entire group.

Ungrouped, selected   *Grouped, selected*

When you transform groups, stroke widths stay proportional if "Strokes" is checked in the Scale subpanel of the Transform panel. Check Transform as Unit in the Object inspector to transform stroke widths to show perspective. When these objects are ungrouped, the stroke width reverts to its undistorted state.

Composite paths

Joining two or more closed paths creates a composite path, which acts as a single path. Stroke and fill attributes of the object farthest back are applied to every object within the composite path. Union, Remove Overlap, Expand Stroke, Punch, and Convert to Paths can be used to create composite paths.

To create a composite path:

1 Select two or more closed paths.

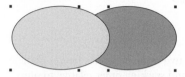

2 Choose Modify > Join or use Command-J (Macintosh) or Control-J (Windows).

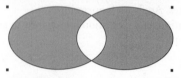

To edit a path within a composite path:

1 Select a composite path.

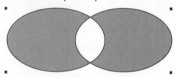

2 Hold down Option (Macintosh) or Alt (Windows) to subselect a path within the composite path.

Hold down Shift while subselecting to subselect more than one path.

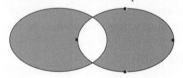

To split a composite path:

1 Select a composite path.

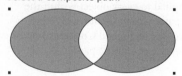

2 Choose Modify > Split or use Command-Shift-J (Macintosh) or Control-Shift-J (Windows).

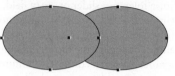

To remove transparent sections of a composite path:

1 Select a composite path.

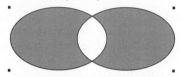

2 Display the Object inspector and uncheck Even/odd fill.

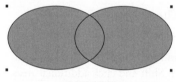

☐ Even/odd fill

Working with path direction

◆ **Even/odd fills**—With a composite path selected and Even/odd fill checked in the Object inspector, overlapping subpaths of a composite path alternate between filled and transparent. With Even/odd fill unchecked, these overlapping sections are filled or transparent based on the winding of the fill.

◆ **Winding fills**—Closed paths have one of two directions: clockwise or counterclockwise. When a clockwise path meets a counterclockwise path, these paths yield a transparent, overlapping section in a composite path. When two closed paths of the same direction overlap, these paths yield a filled, overlapping section. If your composite path's winding fill does not behave as expected, then try Modify > Alter Path > Correct Direction or subselect a path and apply Modify > Alter Path > Reverse Direction.

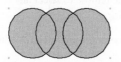

Fills based on Even/odd fill—Paths are filled and transparent regardless of direction.

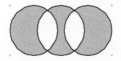

Fills based on winding—All paths are of the same direction in this example, so overlapping sections are filled.

To apply Correct Direction:

1 Select a composite path.

2 Choose Modify > Alter Path > Correct Direction, Xtras > Cleanup > Correct Direction, or click the Correct Direction button on the Xtra Operations toolbar.

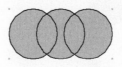

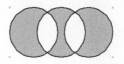

In addition to composite paths, path direction is important when working with arrowheads, blends, or text or blends attached to paths, and when exporting paths.

Since some applications, such as Adobe Illustrator, base fills on winding, use the winding method to fill composite paths for use in another application. Before exporting, choose Modify > Alter Path > Remove Overlap to a composite path with even/odd fill to reconstruct the composite path such that no path overlaps. This yields an accurate screen representation of your original path, although paths themselves are in discrete sections.

Working with clipping paths

Fill a closed path with any objects: vector graphics, text, or bitmap images. These paths are called clipping paths, and the items they contain are called contents or paste insides. To use composite paths as clipping paths, create the composite path before pasting inside. When transforming a clipping path, the contents are transformed when Contents is checked in the Transform panel.

To create a clipping path (using Paste Inside):

1 Select an object to use as the contents.

2 Position the object as you want it to appear in the clipping path.

3 Choose Edit > Cut.

4 Select the clipping path.

5 Choose Edit > Paste Inside.

Only the contents within the clipping path are visible. The current fill appears in areas not covered by the contents.

To modify the clipping path, select it and modify it. Adjusting the path shows or hides portions of the contents.

To edit contents:

1 Select the clipping path.

2 Select its contents.

- ◆ Subselect the contents to edit them.

- ◆ Double-click the handle to select all contents for editing.

Once items in the contents are selected, edit as usual.

3 With the Pointer tool, drag the handle to reposition the contents.

Contents extending beyond the clipping path are hidden, not deleted.

To remove contents from a clipping path:

1 Select the clipping path.

2 Choose Edit > Cut Contents.

To add additional contents to a clipping path:

1 Select an object or objects.

2 Choose Edit > Cut.

3 Choose Edit > Paste Inside.

The new elements appear in front of the original contents.

Modifying objects

Creating new paths from existing paths

Use	To
Union	Combine two or more closed paths into a single path enclosing the entire area of the original paths. Stroke and fill attributes of the object farthest back are applied to the resulting path.
Divide	Cut selected paths into sections defined by areas of overlap. Use open paths, closed paths, or a combination. Stroke and fill attributes of the topmost path are applied to the areas common to all selected paths.
Intersect	Create a path enclosing the area common to all selected, closed paths. Stroke and fill attributes of the object farthest back are applied to the resulting path.
Punch	Remove portions of selected, closed paths below the topmost, closed path. Stroke and fill attributes remain unchanged.
Crop	Remove portions of selected, closed paths outside the area of the topmost, closed path. Stroke and fill attributes remain unchanged.
Transparency	Create a new path from the area common to two or more closed paths containing Basic fills. Using the color information from the fills of the original paths, an intermediate color giving the appearance of transparency is created. To make the topmost path appear more transparent, enter a value greater than 50 in the Transparency dialog box. Values less than 50 make the topmost object appear more opaque.
Blend	Create a transition between two or more paths, with respect to shape, stroke, and fill.

Apply Blend, Union, Divide, Intersect, Punch, Crop, or Transparency to selected objects in any of the following ways:

◆ Choose Window > Toolbars > Xtra Operations and choose the appropriate operation from the Xtra Operations toolbar.

◆ Choose Modify > Combine and choose the appropriate command from the Combine submenu.

◆ Choose Xtras > Path Operations and choose the appropriate command from the Path Operations submenu.

Applying Union, Divide, Intersect, Punch, or Crop to objects may yield a composite path, which consists of individual paths joined together.

With the Object > "Path operations consume original paths" preference checked, original paths are deleted when using any path operation. Uncheck this preference to retain original paths automatically. To retain original paths for a single path operation without changing the default setting, hold down Shift while applying a path operation.

Applying Divide discards segments of open paths outside areas of overlap regardless of whether the "Path operations consume original paths" preference is checked. However, Divide discards closed paths depending upon the preference setting.

Note: For a complete discussion of blends, see "Working with blends" on page 120.

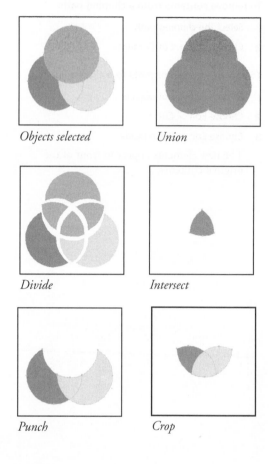

Objects selected   *Union*

Divide   *Intersect*

Punch   *Crop*

Maintaining fills and contents when using Divide

To yield composite paths that maintain these fills across individual paths, hold down Option (Macintosh) or Alt (Windows) when applying Divide to paths with Gradient fills. To subselect a path within a composite path, hold down Option (Macintosh) or Alt (Windows) and click it with the Pointer tool.

Splitting a composite path (Modify > Split) applies the Gradient fill to each individual path.

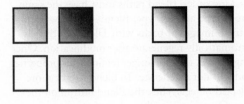

Gradient joined   *Gradient split*

When applying Divide to a clipping path, make sure that it is the top object in the stacking order so that the paste inside's contents are not lost. Hold down Option (Macintosh) or Alt (Windows) when applying Divide to a clipping path to yield a composite path in which each divided area shows a portion of the paste inside's contents.

Divide a   *Subselect and move*
clipping path   *each divided area*
with contents.   *with its contents.*

 Expand Stroke

Use Expand Stroke to create closed paths from open paths.

To expand the stroke of a path:

1 Select a path and choose Expand Stroke.

   Choose Xtras > Path Operations > Expand Stroke, choose Modify > Alter Path > Expand Stroke, or click the Expand Stroke button on the Xtra Operations toolbar.

2 Enter a Width value and click OK.

The Width value sets the width of the resulting closed path, with the appearance that the stroke of the open path has been widened. You can adjust the line cap or the miter limit and click OK. The primary location of these options is the Stroke inspector.

 Inset Path

Following the edge of the original path, Inset Path expands or contracts one or more closed paths by a specified amount.

To create an inset path or paths:

1   Select a closed path and then choose Inset Path.

Choose Xtras > Path Operations > Inset Path, choose Modify > Alter Path > Inset Path, or click the Inset Path button on the Xtra Operations toolbar.

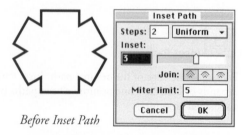

Before Inset Path

2   Set options in the Inset Path dialog box.

After Inset Path

To	Do this
Apply Inset Path to alter the path once	Enter a positive or negative value in the Inset entry field and click OK.
Apply Inset Path to alter the path in steps	In addition to entering an Inset value, enter the number of steps and choose whether you want a uniform, farther, or nearer arrangement of the new paths.

Working with blends

Paths are blended from bottom to top in the stacking order. Blend paths must have the same stroke type and fill type. Blends do not work on bitmap images or paths with Tiled fills. Blends automatically regenerate after modification. Once ungrouped, they no longer retain blend properties and will not regenerate. To blend two or more selected objects, click the Blend button on the Xtra Operations toolbar, choose Modify > Combine > Blend, or choose Xtras > Create > Blend.

Blends between spot colors result in intermediate steps using only tints of those spot colors and will print on just two separation plates. When printing a spot-to-process blend, the spot color is set to overprint the process color. Steps in spot-to-spot and spot-to-process blends are set to process colors if the blend is ungrouped. This also occurs if incompatible colors or fills are chosen, or if the blends are exported to earlier versions of FreeHand or to applications such as Illustrator, which may support spot colors in blends.

To create a blend:

1   Select multiple objects.

2   Click the Blend button on the Xtra Operations toolbar, choose Modify > Combine > Blend, or choose Xtras > Create > Blend.

To blend objects from point to point:

1   Select objects and subselect points within each object.

2   Choose Modify > Combine > Blend.

The selected points determine the transformation pattern of the intermediate blend paths, moving from one path to another. Path direction can also affect blending.

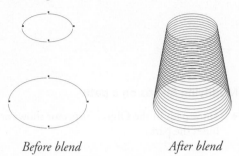

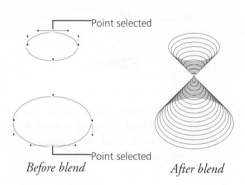

Before blend   *After blend*

Point selected

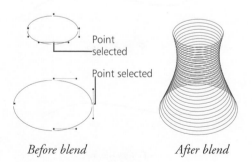

Before blend   *After blend*

Point selected

Point selected

Point selected

Before blend   *After blend*

Modifying blends

◆ Select a blend and enter a value in the Number of steps entry field in the Object inspector to adjust the number of intermediate paths. The greater the value entered, the smoother the blend. The Range % values automatically update.

◆ Designate where the steps begin and end by adjusting the Range % in the Object inspector. The steps appear at even intervals between the original paths. The First entry field affects how closely the steps are placed to the bottom path. The Last entry field affects how closely the steps are placed to the top path.

◆ The number of steps is related to the target printer resolution of the document.

Smoothness of blends depends on the number of steps in the blend and the distance between the steps. For example, a blend 15 inches across with 25 steps would not be as smooth as a blend 2 inches across with 25 steps.

◆ Subselect one of the original paths and make changes.

◆ Change one of the colors by dropping a color chip onto the blend.

To join a blend to a path:

1 Select a path.

2 Hold down Shift and select the blend.

3 Choose Modify > Combine > Join Blend to Path.

Modifying blends on a path

◆ Show path in the Object inspector shows or hides the path.

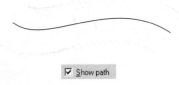

◆ With Rotate on path checked in the Object inspector, the blend is rotated around the path. With it unchecked, the blend is positioned parallel to the path.

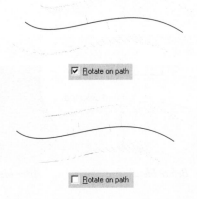

◆ Hold down Option (Macintosh) or Alt (Windows) and click to subselect the path to edit.

The center of the first object in the blend is matched to the first point in the path, and the rest of the blend follows the path. Subselect the path and reverse its direction to make the blend flow in the opposite direction.

Removing a blend from a path

◆ Splitting a blend from a path yields the blend and the path.

◆ Ungrouping a blend from a path yields the path and breaks the blend into the original paths and the steps, which remain in the same position.

Note: Exporting FreeHand 9 documents containing blends along a path to versions of FreeHand earlier than FreeHand 7 causes the blends along a path to be converted to groups.

Blending composite paths and groups

Composite paths can be blended to other composite paths and groups blended to other groups. Groups must contain only simple paths and cannot contain composite paths, images, clipping paths, or other groups.

Use the Type pop-up on the Object inspector to control how differing paths or groups of objects are blended. The Type setting controls how different numbers of paths are blended with one another. The Order setting determines how sub-paths are mapped between objects. Because many factors influence how blended groups and complex paths behave, experiment with the guidelines below to achieve optimal results.

This Type setting	Results in
Normal	Successful blends between most types of composite paths and groups.
Horizontal	Optimal blending between complex paths containing non-overlapping sub-paths. It divides a segmented path into horizontal portions.
Vertical	Optimal blending between complex paths containing non-overlapping sub-paths. It divides a segmented path into vertical portions.

This Order setting	Results in
Positional	Blends organized automatically based upon objects' x and y positions.
Stacking	Blends organized automatically based upon objects' stacking order.

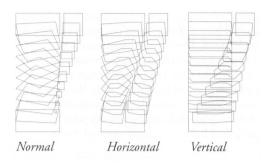

Normal   *Horizontal*   *Vertical*

 Adding drop shadows to objects

Use the Shadow tool in the Xtra Tools toolbar to apply drop shadows to FreeHand vector objects. The Shadow tool does not apply shadows to bitmap images, EPSs, clipping paths, or text. Choose from three different types of shadows: Hard Edge, Soft Edge, and Zoom.

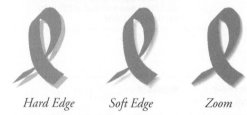

Hard Edge   *Soft Edge*   *Zoom*

To apply a drop shadow:

1   Select one or more objects.

2   Choose Window > Toolbars > Xtra Tools to display the Xtra Tools toolbar, and click the Shadow button.

    Double-click the Shadow tool button to display options.

3   Drag the Shadow tool on the original object or objects to initiate the shadow, move the Keyline preview of the shadow to a desired location, and release the mouse button.

    Moving the Shadow tool moves only the shadow, not the original object. The original object and its shadow comprise a group.

To apply a drop shadow to text, first convert the text to paths. To apply a drop shadow to a clipping path, apply the shadow to an object before using it as a clipping path, or cut the contents of a paste inside to apply the shadow only to the clipping path. Then, select the contents, choose Edit > Cut, subselect the clipping path within its group, and choose Edit > Paste Inside.

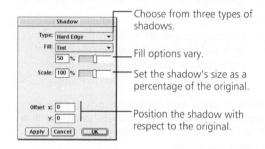

Choose from three types of shadows.

Fill options vary.

Set the shadow's size as a percentage of the original.

Position the shadow with respect to the original.

Setting the drop shadow's fill

Fill options vary depending upon the shadow type. For Hard Edge and Soft Edge shadows, choose from these options in the Fill pop-up:

◆   **Tint**—Define the shadow color as a tint of the original object's color. A value of 0 yields white; a value of 100 yields 100 percent of the original object's color.

◆   **Shade**—Define the shadow color as a percentage of black added to the original object's color.

◆   **Color**—Define the shadow color according to the color chip dropped onto the color well available with this option.

Soft Edge provides these additional options:

◆   **Fade to**—Drop a color onto the Fade to color well to define the shadow's background color. The default is white.

◆   **Soft edge**—Define the degree to which the shadow's edges are softened to the Fade to color. A value of 0 yields a hard edge; a value of 100 softens the shadow throughout.

Designate the color for the Zoom shadow type using two color wells—one for the stroke color and one for the fill color.

The Shadow tool creates incremental colors to achieve the Soft Edge and Zoom effects. Applying soft-edged or zoomed shadows to objects with spot, Hexachrome, or RGB colors yields incremental CMYK process colors.

Embossing objects

Use Emboss to create a three-dimensional effect in which the edges of an object are raised or impressed. Use the Emboss Xtra only on objects that are closed paths with Basic, Gradient, or Pattern fills. Applying the Emboss Xtra creates multiple objects much like blending or smudging.

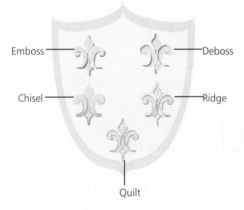

Choose Window > Toolbars > Xtra Operations to display the Xtra Operations toolbar, select one or more objects, and click the Emboss button to display the Emboss dialog box. Choose one of five effects from the buttons across the top: Emboss, Deboss, Chisel, Ridge, or Quilt. Set options, and click Apply to preview the effect, or click OK to apply the effect and close the dialog box.

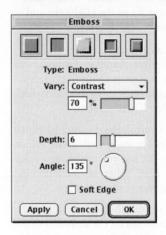

Note: To apply the effect without opening the dialog box, hold down Command (Macintosh) or Control (Windows), and click the Emboss button. Alternatively, choose Xtras > Create > Emboss to display options and apply the effect.

Specifying the relief

◆ **Vary**—The Vary option sets the way in which an object's colors create highlight and shadow. Choose either Contrast or Colors from the pop-up. Contrast uses tints of the path's original colors to create highlight and percentages of black combined with the path's original color to create shadow. Colors uses the colors you specify in the Highlight and Shadow color wells available with this option.

The Emboss Xtra creates incremental colors to achieve each effect. Applying Emboss, Deboss, Chisel, Ridge, or Quilt to objects with spot, Hexachrome, or RGB colors yields incremental CMYK process colors.

◆ **Depth**—Depth controls the distance by which the effect is raised or impressed. Slider values range from 1 to 20, but you can enter a value up to 72 in the field. Values are measured in the document's unit of measurement.

◆ **Angle**—Angle controls the placement of the light source, which affects the direction of the highlight and shadow. Values are measured in degrees.

◆ **Soft Edge**—Check Soft Edge to apply a blended look to the relief. Soft Edge is available only with Emboss and Deboss.

Using the perspective grid

The perspective grid is a non-printing array of lines that converge on one or more vanishing points to create the appearance of three dimensions. Use the Perspective tool to snap objects to the perspective grid. Create and modify vanishing points and grid size to control the three-dimensional appearance of the attached objects. Use the Define Grids dialog box to edit and store custom perspective grids and use them to modify other objects.

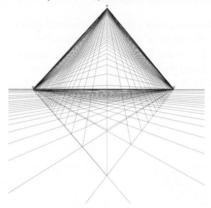

 Perspective tool

Use the Perspective tool to attach objects to the perspective grid. Attach an object to the perspective grid to give it a three-dimensional appearance, which is retained even after the object is released from the perspective grid. Attaching an object to the perspective grid is a two-step process using the Perspective tool and the cursor keys.

To attach an object to the perspective grid:

1 Choose View > Perspective Grid > Show to show the perspective grid.

2 Click the object with the Perspective tool.

3 Drag the object to the desired area of the perspective grid.

4 Tap the appropriate cursor key.

5 Release the mouse button.

Tap this cursor key	To
Left	Attach the object to the left grid.
Right	Attach the object to the right grid.
Up	Attach the object to the floor grid, aligned with the right vanishing point.
Down	Attach the object to the floor grid, aligned with the left vanishing point.

Note: If the perspective grid has only one vanishing point, tap either the left or right cursor key to attach an object to the vertical grid and tap either the up or down cursor key to attach an object to the horizontal grid.

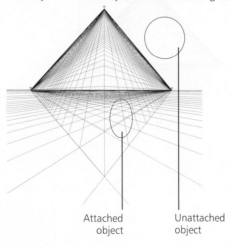

Attached object   Unattached object

To alter an object's perspective appearance, drag the object to a new location on the perspective grid using the Perspective tool. Objects retain their perspective appearance when moved from the grid.

To	Do this
Flip a side grid object horizontally on the grid	1. Select the object with the Perspective tool. 2. Press the spacebar.
Flip a floor grid object vertically on the grid	1. Select the object with the Perspective tool. 2. Press the spacebar.
Move an object while constraining it to the perspective grid lines	Hold Shift while dragging the object. Press Esc to retain the object's perspective appearance when moving it off of the grid.
Reduce an object one pixel in both the x and y directions	1. Select the object with the Perspective tool. 2. Press the 1 key.
Enlarge an object one pixel in both the x and y directions	1. Select the object with the Perspective tool. 2. Press the 2 key.
Reduce an object one pixel in the x direction	1. Select the object with the Perspective tool. 2. Press the 3 key.
Enlarge an object one pixel in the x direction	1. Select the object with the Perspective tool. 2. Press the 4 key.
Reduce an object one pixel in the y direction	1. Select the object with the Perspective tool. 2. Press the 5 key.
Enlarge an object one pixel in the y direction	1. Select the object with the Perspective tool. 2. Press the 6 key.

Objects on the grid update automatically when repositioned using the Perspective tool. Moving objects using the Pointer tool or the cursor keys detaches them from the grid.

Note: When View > Snap to Grid is checked, objects moved using the Pointer tool will snap to the perspective grid but will not automatically obtain a perspective appearance.

Creating and modifying perspective grids

The attributes of the perspective grid determine the look of your three-dimensional objects. By defining the number of vanishing points and their positions, as well as the grid cell size, you can alter the viewer's perspective.

To activate the perspective grid:

◆ Choose View > Perspective Grid > Show.

◆ Click the Perspective tool in the Toolbox.

Double-click to rename a grid.

Select 1, 2, or 3 vanishing points.

Define grid cell size in the document's unit of measurement.

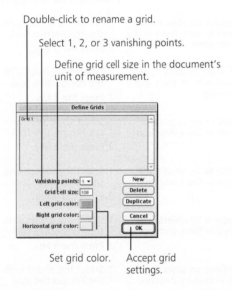

Set grid color.   Accept grid settings.

To create a new grid:

1   Open the Define Grids dialog box by choosing View > Perspective Grid > Define Grids.

2   Click the New button.

The newly created perspective grid appears in the grid list. To change the default grid name, double-click the name and enter a new name. Press Return to accept the new name.

3   Set the number of vanishing points, grid cell size, and grid color.

4   Click OK.

Note: You cannot name a new perspective grid using the same name as an existing grid. To replace a grid in the grid list, first delete the unwanted grid and then create a new one.

Altering grid attributes

Change the number of vanishing points and the grid color using the Define Grids dialog box. Alter the grid angles and orientation by clicking and dragging an active grid area with the Perspective tool. The cursor indicates when the pointer is over an active area.

Left wall   Right wall

Horizon line   Vanishing point

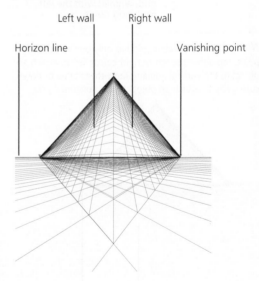

This cursor	Indicates this active area
	Normal cursor; no active area.
	Vanishing point
	Left wall
	Right wall
	Floor
	Horizon line

To	Do this
Hide/show a grid associated with a particular vanishing point	Double-click the vanishing point.
Hide/show the grid floor	Double-click the horizon line.
Add a new grid to the grid list by modifying an existing grid	Hold down the Option key (Macintosh) or the Alt key (Windows) while moving the grid with the Perspective tool. The new perspective grid appears in the Define Grids dialog box with a default name.
Move grid and attached objects	1. Select the objects to be moved. 2. Drag the perspective grid with the Perspective tool while holding the Shift key.
Move grid and clone all attached objects	1. Select the objects to be cloned. 2. Hold down Shift-Option (Macintosh) or Shift-Alt (Windows) and drag the grid.

Removing objects from the grid

When removing objects from the perspective grid, you can choose to retain or discard the perspective transformation from the object.

To remove perspective attributes from a grid object:

1 Select the object with either the Pointer tool or the Perspective tool.

2 Choose View > Perspective Grid > Remove Perspective.

To remove a selected object from the grid and retain perspective attributes, choose View > Perspective Grid > Release With Perspective.

Modifying shape and position

Using transformation tools

The following tools transform points or objects: Move, Rotate, Scale, Skew, and Reflect.

To manually transform a selected object:

1 Select a transformation tool from the Toolbox.

2 Click in the document to establish the center of transformation.

   To set the center of transformation to the center of the object, hold down Control and click with the mouse button (Macintosh only).

3 Drag to transform the object.

   The farther you drag away from the point of transformation, the more control obtained over the transformation.

   Hold down Shift while transforming to constrain to 45° increments.

To numerically transform a selected object:

1 Click the appropriate button in the Transform panel.

2 Enter values in the Center entry fields to set the center of transformation.

3 Adjust settings in the Transform panel and click Apply.

Transforming contents and fills

Each transformation tool offers the option to transform the contents of objects and fills of objects. In addition, the Scale tool offers an option to transform lines. The Contents and Fills settings in the Transform panel affect both manual and numerical transformation.

☑ Contents
☑ Fills
☑ Lines

When you transform groups, stroke widths stay proportional. Check Transform as Unit in the Object inspector to transform stroke widths to show perspective. When these objects are ungrouped, the stroke width reverts to its undistorted state.

Use	To
Move	Precisely move objects a given distance with respect to their current position.
	Positive x values move the selection right and negative x values move the selection left. Positive y values move the selection up and negative y values move the selection down.
	You cannot set a center of transformation for the Move tool.
Rotate	Apply two-dimensional rotations to objects.
	Positive values rotate the selection counterclockwise around its center. Negative values rotate the selection clockwise around its center.
Scale	Enlarge or reduce objects.
	Uncheck Uniform to adjust x and y scaling separately.
	Positive x values enlarge the selection horizontally and negative x values reduce the selection horizontally. Positive y values enlarge the selection vertically and negative y values reduce the selection vertically.
Skew	Obliquely transform objects.
	Positive h values skew the selection to the right and negative h values skew the selection to the left. Positive v values skew the selection up and negative v values skew the selection down.
Reflect	Flip objects.
	A reflect axis of 90° flips the selection horizontally. A reflect axis of 180° flips the selection vertically.

Note: Use the cursor keys to move selected objects in preset increments. Set the increment using Modify > Cursor Distance.

Copying a transformation

To duplicate an object and its transformation, type the number of copies in the Copy field on the Transform panel.

Copies: [0]

Using 3D Rotation

The 3D Rotation Xtra tool applies three-dimensional rotations to two-dimensional objects. See "3D Rotation" in FreeHand Help.

Using transformation handles

Using the Pointer tool, double-click an object or a selection of objects to activate eight transformation handles for the entire selection. Double-click away from the object to deactivate the handles. To prevent activation of the transformation handles, uncheck the General > "Double-click enables transform handles" preference.

Drag the handles to move, rotate, scale, or skew objects without using the Transform tools in the Toolbox or the Transform panel. Moving the Pointer tool over and around the selection changes the cursor to indicate which transformation function is available.

Transformation handles active for selected objects

To activate the transformation handles of a text block, double-click the text block's border. To adjust the kerning or the leading of a text block with transformation handles active, hold down Command (Macintosh) or Control (Windows) and drag the appropriate text block handle. For an explanation of how text block handles work, see "Anatomy of a text block" on page 174.

Cursors indicating transformation functions

To	Do this
Move	Move the cursor over the object within the selection rectangle, and drag the object to a new position. Do not drag the centerpoint.
Rotate	Move the cursor next to one of the handles, and drag to turn the object clockwise or counterclockwise. Hold down Shift when dragging to rotate in 45° increments.
Scale	Move the cursor over one of the handles, and drag to resize the object according to the direction of the cursor. Hold down Shift when dragging to resize proportionally.
Skew	Move the cursor over one of the dotted lines between the transformation handles, and drag to skew the object. Hold down Shift when dragging to constrain the skew horizontally or vertically.
Set the center of rotation	Drag the centerpoint to a new location.

When using transformation handles to move, rotate, scale, or skew an object or objects, holding down Option (Macintosh) or Alt (Windows) copies the entire selection. A plus (+) sign next to the cursor indicates copying.

Working with the centerpoint

Drag the object's centerpoint anywhere in the document to set the center of rotation. To reset a centerpoint, deselect and then reselect the object, or hold down Shift and click the centerpoint.

Centerpoint

To move an object without moving its centerpoint, hold down Command (Macintosh) or Control (Windows), and drag the object to a new location. To add an object to a selection without moving the centerpoint, hold down Command-Shift (Macintosh) or Control-Shift (Windows), and click the additional object.

When using Command-C and Command-V (Macintosh) or Control-C and Control-V (Windows) to copy and paste an object, the centerpoint of the object does not move.

Activating transformation handles in a specified selection

To transform an object within a group or a paste inside, hold down Option (Macintosh) or Alt (Windows), select the object, and release the modifier key. Double-click the selected object to activate the transformation handles, and then move, rotate, scale, or skew it. Pressing Tilde (~) activates transformation handles for the entire group or paste inside without moving the centerpoint.

Press Tilde (~) to activate handles for an entire group.

To transform points within a selected path, select the points, double-click a point to activate transformation handles for the entire selection, and then move, rotate, or scale the points. Pressing Tilde (~) activates transformation handles for the entire path without moving the centerpoint.

Transform panel settings

When moving, rotating, or scaling an object, its move distance, rotation angle, or scale percentage appears in the Transform panel, respectively. Each subpanel of the Transform panel has x and y coordinate fields that indicate the location of an object's center after each transformation.

Check Contents, Fills, or Lines to specify what object attributes are affected by the transformation. Contents refers to the objects pasted inside a clipping path. Fills refers to the objects within a Tiled fill. Lines refers to the strokes of objects.

Creating patterns with reflections of a path

Use the Mirror Xtra tool to create simple or complex patterns by creating one or more reflections of an existing path. To choose the Mirror Xtra tool, select a path, then click the Mirror tool button on the Xtra Tools toolbar.

Click and drag the mirror cursor to specify the halfway point between the selected path and its reflection or the centerpoint of a group of reflections. Keylines show the position of each reflection upon release.

To	Do this
Rotate the keylines around the cursor	Hold down Option (Macintosh) or Alt (Windows).
Constrain rotation to 45° increments	Hold down Option-Shift (Macintosh) or Alt-Shift (Windows).
Toggle between reflect and rotate when setting Multiple mirrors	Press the up or down cursor keys.
Increase or decrease the number of axes when setting Multiple mirrors	Press the right or left cursor keys.

Note: An entire path, text container, or image must be selected when you use the Mirror tool. If only some points on a path are selected, FreeHand selects the entire path to mirror.

Double-click the Mirror Xtra tool to display the Mirror dialog box.

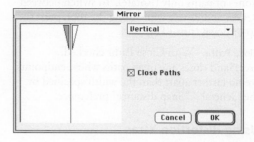

Choose	To create
Vertical	A copy of the selected path flipped along its vertical edge (default).
Horizontal	A copy of the selected path flipped along its horizontal edge.
Horizontal and Vertical	A 2x2 matrix of reflections centered on the cursor location.
Multiple	A radial array of either clones and their reflections or clones only, centered on the cursor location.

Choosing the Multiple option displays additional options.

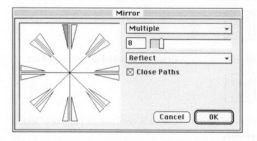

Reflection factor—Type a number 1 through 100 or use the slider to enter 1 through 50. If Reflect is set, the path and its reflection are multiplied. If Rotate is set, only the path is multiplied. To increase the reflection factor while using the tool, press the right cursor key. To decrease the reflection factor, press the left cursor key.

Effect type—Choose between multiple clones of paths and their reflections (Reflect) or multiple clones of paths only (Rotate). To switch between Reflect and Rotate while using the tool, press the up or down cursor key.

Close Paths—With Close Paths checked, FreeHand closes any open paths whose endpoints are no farther apart than the width specified by the General > "Snap distance" preference.

Using distortion Xtras

The following tools distort objects: Add Points, Roughen, Bend, and Fisheye Lens.

Choose Window > Toolbars > Xtra Operations and click the Add Points button. Choose Window > Toolbars > Xtra Tools toolbar and click the Roughen, Bend, or Fisheye Lens button on the Xtra Tools toolbar.

Use	To
Add Points	Add points halfway between every pair of points on a path.
Roughen	Create a jagged effect.
Bend	Create a bloated or spiked effect.
Fisheye Lens	Create a concave or convex effect.

See FreeHand Help for a more detailed explanation about each of these distortion tools.

Note: Another way to distort objects is to use the Modify > Envelope command.

Envelope

An envelope is a hidden wrapper or enclosure that contains one or more objects. Distort and reshape vector objects using the Envelope feature. Choose Window > Toolbars > Envelope to display the Envelope toolbar.

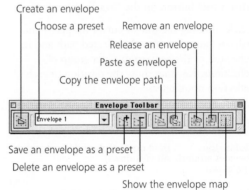

Changes made to an envelope affect the objects contained within the envelope. As with any FreeHand path, use the Pointer tool or any path-changing tool or operation to modify an envelope. For example, dragging a corner point of an envelope outwards causes the objects enclosed to stretch in that direction.

To apply the Envelope effect:

1 Select the object or group to which the envelope will be applied.

2 Choose Modify > Envelope > Create or click the Create button on the Envelope toolbar.

3 Modify the envelope as you would any FreeHand path and note the effect on the contents of the envelope.

To remove the envelope from the FreeHand object while retaining all changes to the object, choose Modify > Envelope > Release or click the Release button on the Envelope toolbar.

Saving envelopes

Save envelope settings for later use by storing envelopes as presets. Envelope presets are retained in the Envelope toolbar.

To save an Envelope effect as a preset:

1 Select an enveloped object.

2 Choose Modify > Envelope > Save As Preset or click the Save As Preset button in the Envelope toolbar.

3 Type a name for the preset in the Name field of the New Envelope dialog box and click OK.

Envelope settings are stored in the file named Envelope (Macintosh) or Envelope.set (Windows) located in the FreeHand 9\English\ Settings\Envelope folder.

Note: Deleting the Envelope settings file removes all of your custom envelope presets.

To	Do this
Apply an envelope	Choose Modify > Envelope > Create, or click the Create button on the Envelope toolbar.
Modify an envelope	Modify the envelope's path as you would modify any FreeHand path.

To	Do this
Undo individual modifications to an envelope	Choose Edit > Undo.
Remove an envelope and all its modifications to the FreeHand objects	Choose Modify > Envelope > Remove, or click the Remove button on the Envelope toolbar.
Remove an envelope and retain the modifications made to the FreeHand objects	Choose Modify > Envelope > Release, or click the Release button on the Envelope toolbar.
Save an envelope as a preset	1. Select an enveloped object. 2. Choose Modify > Envelope > Save As Preset or click the Save As Preset button on the Envelope toolbar. 3. Type a name for the preset in the Name field of the New Envelope dialog box and click OK.
Delete an envelope preset	1. Select the envelope preset that you want to delete. 2. Click the Delete preset button.
Copy a path and use it as an envelope on another object	1. Select the path and choose Edit > Copy. 2. Select an object and choose Modify > Envelope > Paste as Envelope or click the Paste as Envelope button on the Envelope toolbar.
Convert an envelope to a path	1. Select the enveloped object. 2. Choose Modify > Envelope > Copy As Path or click the Copy As Path button on the Envelope toolbar.
View the envelope map	Choose Modify > Envelope > Show Map or click the Show Map button on the Envelope toolbar.

Using Envelopes with Xtras

Because Xtras affect objects in various ways, Envelopes do not work with all Xtras. Use Envelope with the following Xtras:

◆ Color Xtras (Darken, Lighten, Saturate, Desaturate, Name all colors)

◆ Mirror tool

Aligning objects or points

The Align panel options either align or distribute objects or points along a horizontal axis, vertical axis, or both axes. The vertical and horizontal pop-up options determine the position of each alignment.

Choose Window > Panels > Align or choose Modify > Align to display the Align panel.

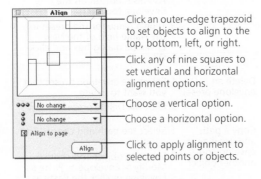

Click an outer-edge trapezoid to set objects to align to the top, bottom, left, or right.

Click any of nine squares to set vertical and horizontal alignment options.

Choose a vertical option.

Choose a horizontal option.

Click to apply alignment to selected points or objects.

Check to orient alignment to page dimensions.

Three rectangles in the preview illustrate the current alignment setting; they do not represent the actual selected points or objects. When a distribute option is set, a fourth rectangle appears. Select objects and double-click a preview area to directly apply the alignment.

When Align to Page is checked, one or more objects are aligned or distributed in relation to the current page dimensions. If only one object is selected, Align to Page must be checked to apply an alignment.

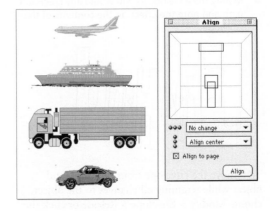

Use	To
Align objects	Align objects based on an object's center or one side of its bounding box.
Distribute objects	Place objects at even distances from one another based on an object's center or one side of its bounding box.

Aligning and distributing points is similar to moving points using automatic curvature; adjacent paths move according to the position of the point rather than the position of its handles. To move points to a position, select at least two points in one or more paths, and choose a setting from the Align panel. To achieve a smooth arc when aligning points, check Automatic in the Object inspector. Align and distribute selected points in a path with other objects.

To use an object's position as a basis for aligning other objects, lock it in position. Select it and the other objects, and then set the alignment. The unlocked objects align to the locked one.

To lock an object, choose Command-L (Macintosh) or Control-L (Windows); to unlock an object, choose Command-Shift-L (Macintosh) or Control-Shift-L (Windows).

Using other methods to distribute objects

To evenly space identical objects across a page, use blending or power-duplicating. Blends quickly create and space objects.

To use a blend to distribute objects:

1 Create an object and copy and paste it.

2 Position the copy where the last object should be and select both the object and its copy.

3 Choose Modify > Combine > Blend.

4 Set the Number of steps in the Object inspector.

To use power duplication to distribute objects:

1 Create the first object and clone it.

2 Transform it with the tools in the Transform panel.

Do not deselect the transformed object before duplicating.

3 Duplicate it and repeat.

Modifying attributes

 Find & Replace Graphics

Use Find & Replace Graphics to search for objects by name or with similar characteristics. The Find & Replace Graphics panel has two tabs: Find & Replace and Select.

Click the Find & Replace tab to find and modify every occurrence of a specific attribute. Click the Select tab to select every object with a given attribute. Designate the range of your search to include the entire document, a page, or only the current selection.

To display the Find & Replace Graphics dialog box, choose Edit > Find & Replace > Graphics, use Command-Option-E (Macintosh) or Control-Alt-E (Windows), or click the Find & Replace Graphics button on the Main toolbar.

Find & Replace

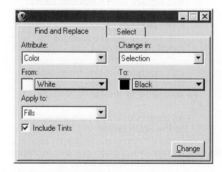

Note: The Find & Replace feature affects hidden objects. The Select feature does not affect hidden objects.

Use	To find
Color	Any color applied to objects and replace with another color.
Stroke width	Strokes within a given range of widths and replace with a new stroke width or modify the width using mathematical equations.
Font	Any font, style, or type size and replace with a font of a given style and size, or modify the size using mathematical equations.
Remove	Invisible objects, overprinting, custom halftones, or contents.
Path shape	Path shapes exactly matching that of the object pasted in the panel and replace with any object, except TIFFs and EPSs.

Applied transformations are considered exact copies. Contents pasted inside a clipping path are not searched. EPSs and TIFFs will not be found. |
| Simplify | Paths with a given number of points and replace with simplified paths according to the Allowable Change value.

Use mathematical equations to specify a range of values. |
| Rotate | All objects and rotate them around their individual centerpoints according to the Rotation angle. |
| Scale | All objects to scale them according to the Scale factor. |
| Blend steps | Blends with a given number of steps and replace with a blend of the given number of steps or resampled at the current printer output resolution.

Use math functions to specify a range of values. |

Select

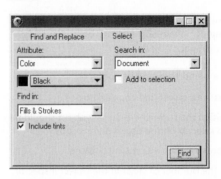

Use	To select objects containing
Color	The specified color.
Style	The specified object or paragraph style.
Same as selection	Matching strokes and fills.
Fill type	A particular fill type or any filled object.
Stroke type	A particular stroke type, any stroked object, arrowhead, or dashed line.
Stroke width	A particular range of stroke width values.
Font	A particular font, style, or range of type size.
Text effect	A particular text effect or any text effect.
Object name	A note matching the object name.

Assign names to objects using Xtras > Other > Set Note. |

Use	To select objects containing
Object type	A given number of points, composite paths, clipping paths, groups, blends, ellipses, rectangles, text, bitmaps, EPSs, envelopes, or instances.
	Check Open paths only to find and select all open paths, so that you may easily fill or remove fills from open paths imported from earlier versions of FreeHand.
Path shape	Path shapes exactly matching the object pasted in the panel.
	Applied transformations are considered exact copies. EPSs and TIFFs will not be found.
Halftone	Halftones.
Overprint	Strokes and fills set to overprint.

Find & Replace Graphics offers options to select and modify object attributes. For all searches, choose a category from the Attribute pop-up and define the search area in the Change in pop-up: Selection, Page, or Document. For numeric entry fields, use equations (+, -, *, /) to specify values.

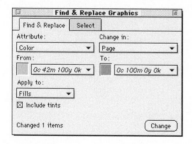

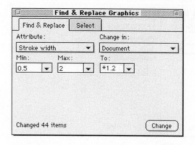

To replace color:

1   Select a From color and a To color from the Color List pop-ups.

Make sure that all the colors in the document are named before finding and replacing.

2   Choose from the Apply to pop-up to confine your search to strokes, fills, or both. Check Include tints to include tints of the From pop-up base color.

3   Click Change to apply the replacement color.

The number of items changed appears at the lower-left corner of the dialog box.

To replace stroke width:

1   Enter minimum and maximum widths to define a search range. Enter a width in the Min entry field and leave the Max entry field blank to search for a specific width.

2   Enter a value in the To entry field to define the replacement width.

3   Click Change to apply the replacement stroke.

Use mathematical equations to search for stroke widths and to define replacement stroke widths. In the example above, all stroke widths between 0.5 and 2 points are increased by 20%.

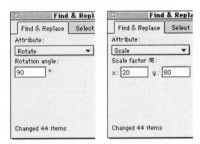

Changed 44 items

Changed 44 items

To replace a font:

1 Select a font type from the From pop-up, choose a style, and enter minimum and maximum point sizes.

2 Enter a replacement font, style, and size.

   You can use mathematical equations to specify font sizes.

3 Click Change to apply the replacement font.

To rotate or scale multiple objects:

1 Choose Rotate and enter a Rotation angle, or choose Scale and enter Scale factor percentages.

   Entering the same percentage in both the x and y entry fields scales objects proportionally.

2 Click Change to apply the rotation angle or the scale factor according to the range of your object search.

   Use Find & Replace Graphics to rotate and scale objects relative to each object's center, which are operations not available when using the transformation tools alone.

To find objects with a magenta fill and a black stroke:

1 Click the Select tab, and search for all objects with a magenta fill. Choose Color from the Attribute pop-up, Document from the Search pop-up, magenta from the Color List pop-up, and Fills from the Find in pop-up.

2 Choose Selection from the Search pop-up, black from the Color List pop-up, and Strokes from the Find in pop-up.

3 Click Find.

Illustrating with stored objects

Use the Graphic Hose tool in the Xtra Tools toolbar to spray frequently used objects on your document page for quick illustration. Each hose consists of up to 10 objects that can reside in a FreeHand document, including groups, blends, text, EPSs, and TIFFs. Choose from a collection of preset hoses, or create your own hoses. Choose Window > Toolbars > Xtra Tools toolbar to display the Xtra Tools toolbar, and click the Graphic Hose button. To spray objects, drag the tool on your document page. The speed and direction that you drag the tool affects how objects are placed.

 Graphic Hose ▶ *Graphic Hose cursor*

Objects comprising a hose

Spraying the hose

Note: Use the left and right cursor keys to increase or decrease the spacing as you spray hose objects. Use the up and down cursor keys to increase or decrease the scale factor as you spray hose objects. See "Specifying an array" on page 142.

Managing hoses

Double-click the Graphic Hose button to display options. The Graphic Hose panel has two buttons: Hose and Options.

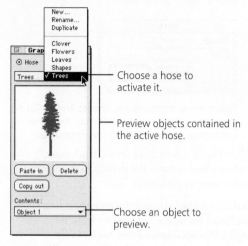

Choose a hose to activate it.

Preview objects contained in the active hose.

Choose an object to preview.

Hose setting

To activate a hose, click the Hose button on the Graphic Hose panel and choose from available hoses listed in the active hose pop-up. The Rename and Duplicate commands in the active hose pop-up only affect the active hose. Choose New when adding a hose to the list. The Contents pop-up lists each object available in the active hose and previews each in the window provided.

To add a new hose:

1 Click the Hose button on the Graphic Hose panel, and choose New from the active hose pop-up.

2 Name your hose in the Hose dialog box, and click Save to add it to the list.

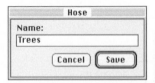

3 Select one or more objects, choose Edit > Cut or Copy, and click Paste in to add it to the list of active hose objects in the Contents pop-up.

When basing a new hose on a default hose, duplicate and rename the default hose to prevent inadvertent modification.

To delete a hose, discard the corresponding FreeHand file of the same name from the English\Xtras\Graphic Hose folder in the FreeHand application folder. If you modify a default hose and cannot retrieve it by using Edit > Undo, you must uninstall and then reinstall FreeHand to regain the default set of hoses.

Managing hose objects

The Contents pop-up lists the objects available in the active hose. To add an object to the active hose, select it, cut or copy it, and click Paste in. The maximum number of objects that can comprise a single hose is 10. Each new object is assigned a name: Object-1, Object-2, and so on. Choose an object name from the Contents pop-up to display it in the preview. Once an object is deleted from the active hose, it is not possible to use Edit > Undo to retrieve it.

Note: Avoid placing too many memory-intensive objects such as lenses, EPS images, and TIFF images in a hose because spraying a great number of these generally results in larger and slower documents.

Specifying an array

On the Graphic Hose panel, click the Options button to specify the way in which hose objects are sprayed in your document. Define how objects are ordered, spaced, scaled, and rotated.

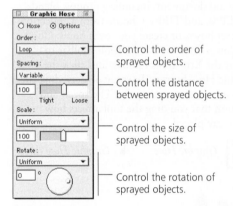

Control the order of sprayed objects.

Control the distance between sprayed objects.

Control the size of sprayed objects.

Control the rotation of sprayed objects.

Options setting

Setting Graphic Hose options

Choose	To
Loop (Order pop-up)	Place objects in the order they appear in the Contents pop-up.
Back and Forth (Order pop-up)	Place objects from first to last and then from last to first in the order they appear in the Contents pop-up.
Random (Order pop-up)	Randomly place objects listed in the Contents pop-up.
Grid (Spacing pop-up)	Space objects in rows and columns defined by a fixed distance.
Variable (Spacing pop-up)	Space objects based on a specified value. Slider values range from 0 to 100, where 0 is Tight and 100 is Loose. Enter a value of up to 100 in the entry field.

Choose	To
Random (Spacing pop-up)	Randomly space objects based on a percentage of randomness ranging from 0 to 200, where 0 indicates no deviation from the value specified in the entry field.
Uniform (Scale pop-up)	Scale objects progressively by a fixed percentage, ranging from 1 to 300.
Random (Scale pop-up)	Randomly scale objects based on a percentage of randomness ranging from 0 to 300, where 0 indicates no deviation from the percentage specified in the entry field.
Uniform (Rotate pop-up)	Rotate objects progressively by a fixed rotation angle.
Incremental (Rotate pop-up)	Rotate objects by progressively increasing or decreasing the rotation angle.
Random (Rotate pop-up)	Randomly rotate objects by applying a rotation angle ranging from 0 to the angle specified in the entry field.

CHAPTER 6
Color, Strokes, and Fills

Using color in FreeHand

The Color Mixer and the Color List are the mainstays of your work environment. Use these panels to create, modify, and organize the colors in your document. Using the Color Mixer, create process colors, adjust hue, lightness, and saturation, and choose colors from the System Color dialog box. Using the Tints panel, create colors that are tints of existing colors.

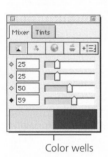

Color chips

Color wells

Create colors using the Color Mixer.

Organize colors using the Color List.

Use the Color List to track the colors in your document. The Color List automatically names colors according to their color component values, such as percentages of CMYK or RGB. When you select an object, its color name appears highlighted in the Color List.

Name your colors for fast, easy, and accurate access. When objects in the document contain unnamed colors—colors that are in a document but not on the Color List—use the Name All Colors Xtra to add them to the Color List. If viewing color names is unnecessary, choose Hide names from the Color List Options pop-up to display only the color chips.

Use the Color List Options pop-up to modify existing colors or add new ones from a variety of custom color-matching libraries.

Color List options include adding, duplicating, and removing colors. Other options convert spot colors into process colors, and vice versa, and convert CMYK colors to RGB colors, and vice versa.

Working efficiently with color

Displaying the Color Mixer

Click this button on the Main toolbar to show or hide the Color Mixer.

- ◆ Choose Window > Panels > Color Mixer.
- ◆ Use Command-Shift-C (Macintosh) or Control-Shift-9 (Windows).
- ◆ Double-click a color chip in the Color List.

Displaying the Color List

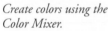

Click this button on the Main toolbar to show or hide the Color List.

- ◆ Choose Window > Panels > Color List.
- ◆ Use Command-9 (Macintosh) or Control-9 (Windows).
- ◆ Double-click a color well in the Color Mixer.

Double-click a color well or color chip almost anywhere in the application to show or hide both the Color Mixer and the Color List.

Viewing colors in the Color Mixer

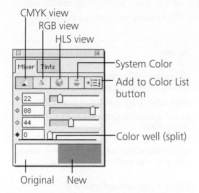

CMYK view
RGB view
HLS view
System Color
Add to Color List button
Color well (split)
Original   New

- **CMYK view**—The Color Mixer displays percentages of the cyan, magenta, yellow, and black color components for the standard, four-color printing process.

- **RGB view**—The Color Mixer displays red, green, and blue color components. RGB values are calculated based on a range of 0 to 255.

- **HLS view**—The Color Mixer displays the hue, lightness, and saturation of an RGB color.

- **System Color**—The Color Mixer displays the Apple Color Picker (Macintosh) or the Windows Color dialog box (Windows).

The color well at the bottom of the Color Mixer is split into two sections. When creating or modifying color, the Color Mixer displays the original color on the left side of the color well and the new color on the right side of the color well. Uncheck the Colors > "Color Mixer/Tints panel uses split color well" preference to view the new color across the entire color well.

Note: The on-screen accuracy of color chips and wells depends on the current settings in the Colors > "Color Management" preference. See Chapter 9, "Color Management," to set on-screen colors to closely approximate colors in your final output.

Drag a color chip onto the Color Mixer color well or hold Option (Macintosh) or Control (Windows) and click the color chip. The Color Mixer displays the color's CMYK or RGB values as appropriate.

- Dragging and dropping a CMYK color changes the Color Mixer to CMYK mode.

- Dragging and dropping an RGB color changes the Color Mixer to RGB mode. When the Color Mixer is in HLS mode, dropping an RGB color onto the color well does not change the mode.

On the Color List, process color names are italicized and spot color names are plain. A triple-dot symbol designates RGB colors. CMYK colors have no symbol. A black hexagon designates Hexachrome colors, as shown on page 151. Colors created in HLS view, Apple Color Picker, and Windows Color dialog box are RGB colors.

Color attributes	Naming convention
CMYK process (italic)	*65c 15m 65y 15k*
CMYK spot (plain)	65c 20m 65y 15k
RGB process (italic; triple dot)	*51r 119g 79b*
RGB spot (plain; triple dot)	51r 125g 79b

Creating colors

To create a CMYK color or an RGB color:

1   Click the CMYK or RGB mode button to display either Color Mixer mode.

2   To adjust color component values, move the sliders or enter values in each entry field. Use the color well to monitor the color as you mix it.

When you switch to RGB mode from CMYK, or vice versa, notice that the sliders and fields change to display the color's relevant component values.

3   Drag a chip from the color well to apply directly to an object's stroke or fill, or add the newly created color to the Color List. See "Applying color directly to objects" on page 149 and "Adding colors to the Color List" on page 150.

Hue, lightness, and saturation

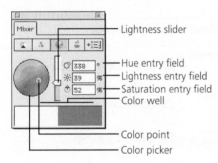

Lightness slider
Hue entry field
Lightness entry field
Saturation entry field
Color well

Color point
Color picker

Click the HLS button to display the HLS color picker. FreeHand displays the hue, lightness, and saturation values of any color appearing in the Color List. The HLS panel produces RGB colors.

◆   **Hue**—Hue is the color itself, such as green, orange, or pink. Switch to CMYK view or RGB view to see the color component values that correspond to the hue that is numerically identified in the Hue entry field and indicated by the color point.

◆   **Lightness**—Lightness indicates how close the hue is to black (0%) or white (100%).

◆   **Saturation**—Saturation refers to the vividness or dullness of the hue. Increasing saturation adds color; decreasing saturation adds gray.

To modify	Do this
Hue	Choose a different color point from the HLS color picker,
	click and drag the color point, or
	enter a new degree value in the Hue entry field.
Lightness	Move the slider or enter a percentage value in the Lightness entry field.
Saturation	Enter a percentage value of saturation in the Saturation entry field.

Displaying the Tints panel

The Tints panel displays options for creating tints. Use the Color Mixer toolbar button to display the Tints panel, unless the Tints panel has been removed from the Color Mixer. Choose Window > Panels > Tints, or use Command-Shift-Z (Macintosh) or Control-Shift-3 (Windows) to display the Tints panel.

Creating tints

Tints are colors derived from percentages of a base color. Choose a base color from the Color List or drag a color onto either base color well.

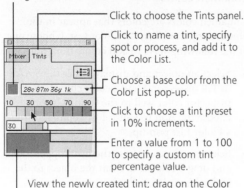

Drag a base color onto the color well.

— Click to choose the Tints panel.

— Click to name a tint, specify spot or process, and add it to the Color List.

— Choose a base color from the Color List pop-up.

— Click to choose a tint preset in 10% increments.

— Enter a value from 1 to 100 to specify a custom tint percentage value.

View the newly created tint; drag on the Color List, a color well, or a graphic element.

View the base color or drag onto a base color.

To create a tint:

1 Display the Tints panel.

2 Drag a color chip onto either of the Tints panel's base color wells, or choose a base color from the Color List pop-up.

3 Click on a preset tint from the tint bar, create a custom tint by moving the slider, or enter a percentage from 1 to 100 in the entry field.

4 Drag a chip from the color well to apply directly to an object's stroke or fill, or add the newly created tint to the Color List. See "Applying color directly to objects" on page 149 and "Adding colors to the Color List" on page 150.

If not on the Color List already, the base color is added to the Color List along with the newly created tint. The tint's name comprises the tint percentage and the original name.

65c 15m 65y 15k ——— Base color
50% 65c 15m 65y 15k — Tint

Applying color directly to objects

Drop a color chip onto the stroke or fill of an object.

Hold down Shift as you drag to force a color to apply to only the fill of an object. Use this method to change any other fill type to Basic.

Hold down Command (Macintosh) or Control-Shift (Windows) as you drag to force a color to apply only to the stroke of an object.

Change any selected object's fill by selecting another fill option in the Fill inspector. The most efficient way to change any fill to a graduated fill or a radial fill is to use modifier keys as you drag a color onto an object.

To force a color to apply as a graduated Gradient fill, hold down Control as you drag a color chip onto an object. Where you drop the color sets the angle of the Gradient fill.

To force a color to apply as a radial Gradient fill, hold down Option (Macintosh) or Alt (Windows) as you drag a color chip onto an object. Where you drop the color sets the fill's center.

For detailed information about applying color to text, see Chapter 7, "Text."

Adding colors to the Color List

Add to the Color List those colors you intend to use in your FreeHand illustration. Create colors in the Color Mixer or choose them from color-matching system libraries.

Adding colors from the Color Mixer or Tints panel

Choose one of the following ways to add colors created in the Color Mixer or tints created in the Tints panel:

Add to Color List button

◆ Click the Add to Color List button on the Color Mixer or Tints panel. Name the color and specify Spot or Process in the Add to Color List dialog box. Hold down Command (Macintosh) or Control (Windows) while clicking the Add to Color List button to bypass the dialog box and reuse the last choice of Process or Spot.

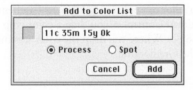

◆ Drag the newly created color from the color well of the Color Mixer or Tints panel and drop it either onto an empty space at the bottom of the Color List or onto the color drop box. Do not drop a color onto an existing color name.

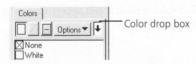

◆ Create a color and choose New from the Color List Options pop-up.

◆ In Windows, right-click any color well on the Color Mixer or Tints panel to choose the Add to Color List command.

Adding Colors from an object with unnamed colors

Unnamed colors are colors that appear in the illustration but not on the Color List. Choose one of the following ways to add colors from objects:

◆ Select an object and display either the Stroke or Fill inspector. Drag a color chip from an inspector color well to the Color List or choose the Add to Color List command from a Color List pop-up.

◆ Select an object, choose the Eyedropper tool, and drag a color chip from the object to the Color List color well.

◆ Choose Xtras > Colors > Name All Colors to add to the Color List all unnamed colors in a document.

See "Naming unnamed colors" on page 152.

Adding Colors from copied or imported objects

The Color List displays colors from some imported file formats automatically, such as FreeHand, Adobe Illustrator, and CorelDRAW. Named colors applied to copied or imported objects, such as EPS files, remain in the Color List even if you delete the objects.

Note: FreeHand adds named spot or process colors from an editable EPS to the Color List upon import. Check the Import > "Convert editable EPS when imported" preference to import EPS files as editable.

Adding colors from a pre-defined library

Listed in the Color List Options pop-up, the predefined color libraries that come with FreeHand are part of commercially available color-matching systems and contain both spot and process colors. Color-matching systems provide printed and on-screen color chips for designers and contain instructions for printers so they print the colors you specify. Consult with your commercial printer to know which color libraries they support and recommend. See "Color libraries" on page 155.

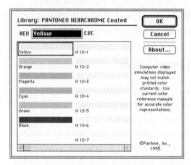

Choose colors from color library dialog boxes, such as this one for the Pantone Hexachrome Coated color library.

Custom colors display the name of the custom color library with a library-specific color reference. Pantone® Hexachrome colors comprise two of the custom color libraries in FreeHand. In the Color List, these colors appear with hexagon-shaped icons to the right of the color names.

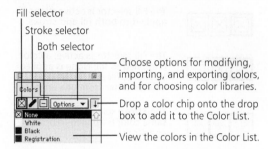

Organizing colors in the Color List

As you drag newly created colors from the Color Mixer and drop them onto the Color List, FreeHand names them. Newly added colors appear at the bottom of the Color List, but you can rearrange them.

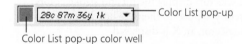

The Color List default colors are None, White, Black, and Registration. These colors cannot be deleted or renamed. Black is a spot black that prints on the process black plate. Registration-colored objects, such as crop marks or trim marks, print solid on all color separations.

Color List pop-ups appear throughout the application to easily apply colors to selected objects or name unnamed colors. These pop-ups show the named colors in the document, replicating the Color List. Each color name has a color chip next to it.

Using the Color List selectors

Use the Color List selectors to view and assign fill and stroke colors. Selecting an object displays the colors in the selectors.

To apply fill and stroke colors to selected objects, drag colors onto selectors, or activate a selector and click on a color name in the Color List.

Newly created objects automatically assume the current fill and stroke color scheme shown in the selectors if the Object > "Changing objects changes defaults" preference is checked.

These selectors	Indicate
▨▨▨	The Fill selector is active; None is applied to both fill and stroke.
▨▨▢	The Fill selector is active; a color is applied to fill; None is applied to stroke; fill and stroke color choices differ from one another.
▨▨▨	The Stroke selector is active; the same color is applied to both fill and stroke.
▢▬▢	The Stroke selector is active; two or more objects are selected and at least one object's fill and one object's stroke differ from the fill and stroke of other selected objects.

A thick, black border indicates the active selector. The selectors display the fill and stroke colors currently applied to them. When None is applied to a selector, an X is displayed.

When two or more objects are selected and do not share the same fill color, a dash is displayed in the Fill selector; the same is true of stroke colors and the Stroke selector. When the fill color and stroke color differ—whether one object or several are selected—a dash is displayed in the Both selector.

Rearranging colors

To rearrange colors in the Color List, click a color name and drag it to a new position. Make sure that you drag the color name and not the color chip; otherwise, you will replace an existing color rather than relocate the one you are moving.

Assigning custom color names

To rename a color in the Color List:

1 Double-click the color name to highlight it and type the new name.

Clicking the color name applies that color to all selected objects. If that is not your intent, deselect all objects before editing a color name.

2 Press Return or click anywhere in the application to apply the name.

When you enter a custom color name directly into the Color List that is the same as one already on the panel, a dialog box prompts you to use a different name.

Naming unnamed colors

Use the Add to Color List button to name unnamed colors. For example, if you drag a color directly from the Color Mixer to an object or from a TIFF image using the Eyedropper tool to the Fill inspector color well, FreeHand does not automatically name the color and does not add it to the Color List.

To name and add the color, click the Add to Color List button in the Color Mixer or Tints panel. Accept the default name or enter a name for the color in the Add to Color List dialog box. Define it as either spot or process and click OK.

Duplicates of names already on the Color List are labeled with a dash and a duplicate-counter number at the end of the name as shown below.

65c 15m 65y 15k ——Original name
65c 15m 65y 15k-1 ——Duplicate name

Click Cancel in the Add to Color List dialog box to leave the color unnamed and omit it from the Color List.

When objects contain an unnamed base color and its tints, the Name All Colors Xtra adds each tint and its base color to the Color List. Name All Colors adds a base color for each tint. If the base color is named, Name All Colors adds only the tints to the Color List.

To name unnamed colors throughout a document, choose Xtras > Colors > Name All Colors to place every color used in the document in the Color List. FreeHand names them in the Color List using their corresponding color values.

Click one or more colors and use Remove or Replace to standardize your colors by eliminating the ones you do not need. Alternatively, choose Xtras > Delete > Unused Named Colors to remove all unused colors if the Color List pop-ups become unmanageable.

Sorting colors

To sort the Color List entries by color name, choose Xtras > Colors > Sort Color List by Name. FreeHand sorts the colors first numerically and then alphabetically. The default colors—None, White, Black, and Registration—remain at the top of the Color List.

Hiding color names

When using FreeHand for process printing, color composite printing, or screen output such as Internet or multimedia, the ability to hide names in the Color List becomes very useful, since it is not necessary to visually distinguish between spot and process colors. When working with custom color libraries, you can view a large number of colors at once.

Choose Hide names in the Options pop-up to hide color names and RGB or Hexachrome icons. This option economizes space on the Color List by arranging color chips in a grid according to the current width of the panel. Changing the width of the Color List reflows the color chips into a new row and column arrangement. A solid border around a single color chip indicates the color is active.

Choosing Hide names from the Color List Options pop-up displays only color chips on the Color List.

You cannot rearrange the Color List when Hide names is turned on. Moving a color either replaces an existing color or adds an existing color to the Color List.

Duplicating colors

To duplicate a color, choose a color on the Color List and choose Duplicate from the Options pop-up. The new color is named "Copy of [original color]."

Removing colors

To remove colors, click a color name on the Color List and choose Remove from the Options pop-up. Removing colors from the Color List does not remove them from corresponding FreeHand objects. These colors remain in the objects as unnamed colors. When removing multiple colors, a dialog box prompts you to either remove all colors or only the unused colors.

◆ **Spot colors**—Convert removed spot colors to process colors. Objects containing these spot-to-process converted colors may not print separations as intended.

◆ **Hexachrome colors**—Convert removed Hexachrome colors to RGB values. The Hexachrome icon appears to the side of the name in the Color List.

◆ **Tints**—Removing a color that is a base color for tints also removes from the Color List all tints that were based on the color.

Note: It is not possible to remove or replace imported spot or process colors from a locked or uneditable EPS. To know whether an imported EPS is locked, switch to Keyline mode, Command-K (Macintosh) or Control-K (Windows). If the EPS displays an X-box, then the EPS is locked.

Modifying color

To alter color component values of an existing color:

1 Drag a color chip from the Color List to the color well in the Color Mixer.

2 Adjust the color values in the Color Mixer by entering new values in any of the entry fields or by moving the corresponding sliders.

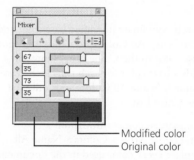

Modified color
Original color

3 Drag a color chip from the Color Mixer's color well and drop it onto the original chip in the Color List.

To prevent color names from automatically changing when altering color values, uncheck the Colors > "Auto-rename colors" preference. The default name of a color is retained when dragging the replacement color chip onto the original color chip.

To replace colors in the Color List:

1 Choose a color name and choose Replace from the Color List Options pop-up.

A dialog box prompts you to choose another color from the Color List or from a color library. With Black, White, None, or Registration chosen, Replace is not available in the pop-up.

2   Choose a color from the Color library pop-up or the Color List pop-up and click OK.

All selected objects with an old color will display the new color.

The Colors > "Auto-rename colors" preference—whether checked or unchecked—does not effect the Replace option from the Color List Options pop-up to replace colors. Also, the preference does not affect colors with custom names.

Converting colors

Designate how a color prints to separations by converting it to either a spot or process color.

◆ **From Process to Spot**—Choose a color name in the Color List. Choose Make spot from the Options pop-up.

◆ **From Spot to Process**—Choose a color name in the Color List. Choose Make process from the Options pop-up.

Converting colors from CMYK to RGB, or vice versa, involves transferring colors from one color space into another.

◆ **From CMYK to RGB**—Choose a color name in the Color List. Choose Make RGB from the Options pop-up. Make RGB changes the CMYK color to the nearest RGB value.

◆ **From RGB or Hexachrome to CMYK**—Choose a color name in the Color List. Choose Make CMYK from the Options pop-up. Make CMYK changes the RGB or Hexachrome color to the nearest CMYK value.

Note: Converted colors may not appear the same as they did before they were converted, especially if a color management preference is active.

Converting colors when exporting

To maintain color consistency when exporting a file in PDF, EPS, and Adobe Illustrator formats, or when dragging and dropping into another application, three conversion options are available from the Convert Colors to pop-up: CMYK, RGB, and CMYK and RGB.

Using FreeHand's Convert Colors to options before exporting is typically more precise than relying on the import conversion features of other applications. For more information, see Chapter 10, "Working with Other Applications."

Color libraries

To add colors from a color-matching system library:

1   Choose a color-matching system library from the Options pop-up on the Color List.

2   Choose colors from the library dialog box and click OK to add them to the Color List.

To import colors from a custom color library:

1   Choose a custom color library from the Color List Options pop-up.

2   Choose the colors to add and click OK.

If a custom color library is stored outside of the Color folder in the FreeHand application folder, choose Import from the Color List Options pop-up to locate and open the library.

Import the colors from a Photoshop color index table into FreeHand so that the color values are the same in either application. Choose Xtras > Colors > Import RGB Color Table, and then choose the Photoshop ACT file that contains the index to import.

To export colors to create a custom color library:

1 Choose Export from the Color List Options pop-up, choose the colors for export, and click OK.

   Export non-Hexachrome colors from the Color List as a custom color library and share them among multiple documents.

2 In the Create Color Library dialog box, type a Library name, and then type a file name. Enter the number of rows and columns and any notes.

3 Click Save as (Macintosh) or Browse (Windows) and specify the FreeHand 9\English\Colors folder as the destination. Click Save.

Converting colors during import and export

Exporting documents to previous versions of FreeHand—When exporting to the FreeHand 5.x format, all colors are converted to CMYK process or spot colors because FreeHand 5.x stores all colors as CMYK. The color names remain unchanged in the original document after export. Colors originally defined as RGB or Hexachrome are stored in CMYK format when opening the document in FreeHand 9.

Importing documents from previous versions of FreeHand—FreeHand 8 and 9 store colors internally as CMYK, RGB, or Hexachrome (CMYKOG). Because FreeHand 5.x stores colors as CMYK, documents converted from this version to FreeHand 9 contain CMYK spot or process colors, even if these colors have RGB color names on the Color List.

Note: For more information on FreeHand's color libraries, see FreeHand Help.

Applying stroke and fill effects to objects

Choosing stroke and fill types

Choose from five stroke types in the Stroke inspector: None, Basic, Custom, Pattern, and PostScript.

Choose from nine fill types in the Fill inspector: None, Basic, Custom, Gradient, Lens, Pattern, PostScript, Textured, and Tiled. An open path, a closed path, or a composite path can have only one fill. Each object within a group can have its own fill.

Compatible output devices

These	Print to
Basic strokes and fills	PostScript and non-PostScript.
Custom strokes and fills	PostScript.
Pattern strokes and fills	PostScript Level 2 or higher. Pattern strokes are designed for use on low- and medium-resolution printers, not for output to film recorders and imagesetters, because the pattern dots appear much smaller on high-resolution output devices.
PostScript strokes	PostScript.
PostScript fills	PostScript. PostScript fills do not print to non-PostScript printers even after exporting FreeHand documents that contain them to file formats such as TIFF or PICT.
Gradient fills	PostScript and non-PostScript.
Lens fills	PostScript and non-PostScript.
Textured fills	PostScript.
Tiled fills	PostScript and non-PostScript.

On-screen and printed appearance

These	Appear
Basic strokes and fills	Solid on screen and in print.
Custom strokes	Solid on screen, but print correctly. In print, color appears on the solid portions of the pattern and transparent areas print correctly—except for the Arrow, Braid, and Neon stroke patterns, which are opaque.
Custom fills	With an opaque pattern of C's on screen but print correctly. In print, color appears only on the solid portions of five of the custom fills. The background of four of the custom fills is opaque—even if there are spaces between repeating patterns.
Pattern strokes and fills	At 72 dpi (dots per inch) on screen and print at a fixed resolution.
PostScript strokes	Solid on screen and print according to the PostScript code. In print, color appears on the solid portions of the pattern and transparent areas print correctly.
PostScript fills	With an opaque pattern of PS's on screen but print according to the PostScript code. In print, color appears on the solid portions of the pattern and transparent areas print correctly.
Gradient fills	Opaque on screen and in print.
Lens fills	As any of a variety of custom effects created by the lens.
Textured fills	With an opaque pattern of C's. In print, color appears only on the solid portions of the pattern, but the background is opaque.
Tiled fills	Transparent. Objects behind them appear through the spaces in the pattern.

Overprinting

Overprinting is one way to avoid trapping problems when printing separations. Check the Overprint option in the Stroke or Fill inspector to print the color of a stroke or fill on top of the colors beneath it.

With the Redraw > "Display overprinting objects" preference checked, overprinting strokes or fills appear as a pattern of white O's on screen but print normally to a PostScript or non-PostScript printer. Check this preference to view strokes and fills on screen. The Overprint setting is available for Basic strokes and fills and Gradient fills.

For a more detailed discussion of overprinting, knocking out, and trapping, see "Overprinting" on page 228 and "Trapping" on page 230.

Basic strokes

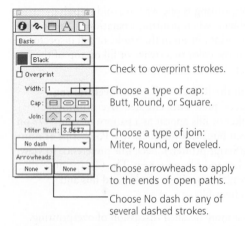

Check to overprint strokes.

Choose a type of cap:
Butt, Round, or Square.

Choose a type of join:
Miter, Round, or Beveled.

Choose arrowheads to apply
to the ends of open paths.

Choose No dash or any of
several dashed strokes.

Stroke inspector: Basic

*The ampersand object has a black stroke
and a fill of None.*

Following are descriptions of the Basic stroke
options appearing on the Stroke inspector. Width
appears for all stroke types.

Width

Width specifies the thickness of a stroke.
FreeHand offers default line widths in the Width
pop-up on the Stroke inspector and throughout
the application. Preset widths range from a
hairline (0.25 of a point) to 12 points. Width
pop-ups display width settings in points
regardless of the unit of measurement set for the
entire document. Type custom widths in the
Width entry field, and then press Return.

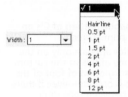

Add or edit the preset width values in the
Object > "Default line weights" preference. Like
that of the Width pop-ups, the unit of
measurement for these width values is always
points.

To apply a Custom stroke width in a different
unit of measurement than that set for the
document, enter a value and a unit override code
into a Width entry field. For example, with the
unit of measurement set to inches, typing "p7" in
the Width entry field converts 7 points to 1.1667
inches. The "#" symbol in the Unit overrides
chart refers to the numerical value.

Unit overrides

Use	For example
#i for inches or decimal inches	7i = 7 inches or 7 decimal inches
p# for points	p7 = 7 points
#p for picas	7p = 7 picas
#m for millimeters	7m = 7 millimeters
#c for centimeters	7c = 7 centimeters
#x for pixels	7x = 7 pixels

Caps

Butt cap

Round cap

Square cap

A butt cap is flush with the end of the path. Round and square caps extend beyond the end of the path by half the stroke width. To change the ends of an open path, select a path and choose another cap option to change.

Joins

Miter join

Round join

Beveled join

Joins define how two path segments meet—miter, round, or beveled. To change the corners in an open or closed path, select a path and choose another join option to change the path's corner or curves.

Miter limit

A miter join automatically becomes a beveled join when the join's miter limit exceeds the value set in the Stroke inspector.

The miter limit is the ratio between the length of the miter join and the stroke width. This measurement sets the maximum length of a miter join. Any length beyond this limit automatically converts the miter join to a beveled join. FreeHand accepts values ranging from 1 to 57.

For example, if you enter 2 as the miter limit for a stroke width of 3 points, the miter join converts to a beveled join when the length of the miter join exceeds 6.

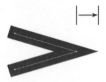

Miter

Beveled join

The arrows indicate the length of the miter join.

Dashed strokes

Dashed strokes are strokes with transparent breaks.

To edit a dashed stroke and create a new one:

1 Hold down Option (Macintosh) or Alt (Windows) while choosing a dash from the dash type pop-up in the Stroke inspector to display the Dash Editor.

2 To set dash sizes, enter values in one or more of the On entry fields. To set the space sizes between dashes, enter values in one or more of the Off entry fields.

Verify the unit of measurement in the Units pop-up at the lower-left corner of the document window.

3 Click OK to add a new dash to the Dash pop-up.

The new dashed stroke appears at the bottom of the Dash pop-up rather than replacing the original dash. FreeHand applies this newly created dashed stroke to any selected paths. If no path is selected, then the dashed stroke applies to the next path created.

The Dash pop-up can display up to 255 dashed strokes. Once you have added new dashed strokes to the Dash pop-up you cannot remove them from the document.

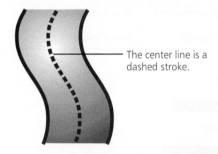

The center line is a dashed stroke.

Arrowhead Editor

Arrowheads extend beyond the end of the path. Create or edit paths using the Arrowhead Editor.

The left pop-up applies an arrowhead to the first point (origin) of the selected path, and the right pop-up applies to the last point. Arrowheads are proportional to the stroke width and extend beyond the end of the path. Arrowheads indicate path direction.

To create an arrowhead from an existing one:

1 Choose Basic from the stroke type pop-up on the Stroke inspector.

2 Hold down Option (Macintosh) or Alt (Windows) and choose an arrowhead to display the Arrowhead Editor.

3 Create or edit the arrowhead.

4 Click New to add a new arrowhead to the Arrowheads pop-up.

Both the left and the right pop-ups can list up to 255 arrowheads. Once you have added new arrowheads to the pop-up you cannot remove them from the document.

To create a new arrowhead:

1 Cut or copy an object from your document.

2 Choose New from the Arrowheads pop-up to display the Arrowhead Editor, and click Paste in.

Custom strokes

A Custom stroke applies a preset repeating PostScript pattern to a path. Modify the width, length of each pattern, spacing between patterns, and color of 22 of the 23 Custom strokes. Neon is the only Custom stroke that is not editable.

◆ **Length**—Set the horizontal distance of a single pattern in a series.

◆ **Spacing**—Set the distance between each occurrence of a repeating pattern.

To edit a Custom stroke, change the width or length of its repeating pattern or the spacing between patterns. Type values in the Width, Length, and Spacing entry fields in the Stroke inspector. Press Return to apply.

A sample of the current Custom stroke is displayed, but modifications to stroke width, length, spacing, or color do not change the sample.

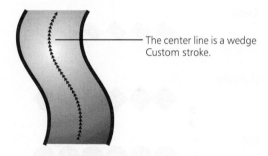

The center line is a wedge Custom stroke.

Note: When transformed, a Custom stroke pattern keeps its original length and spacing. However, the pattern's orientation follows the path's orientation.

Custom stroke catalog

Arrow

Ball

Braid

Cartographer

Checker

Crepe

Diamond

Dot

Heart

Left Diagonal

Neon

Rectangle

Right Diagonal

Roman

Snowflake

Squiggle

Star

Swirl

Teeth

Three Waves

Two Waves

Wedge

ZigZag

Basic fills

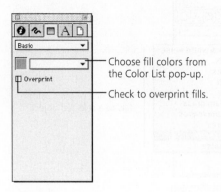

Choose fill colors from the Color List pop-up.

Check to overprint fills.

Fill inspector: Basic

The circle object has a blue Basic fill and a black Basic stroke.

Custom fills

A Custom fill applies a preset, repeating PostScript pattern to a path. Except for "Black and white noise," each Custom fill is editable in the Fill inspector and has its own options.

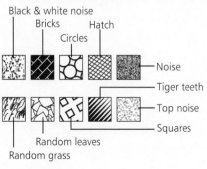

Black & white noise
Bricks
Circles
Hatch
Noise
Tiger teeth
Top noise
Squares
Random leaves
Random grass

Custom fills

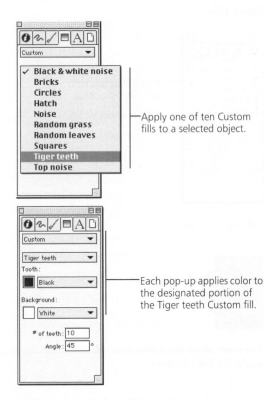

Apply one of ten Custom fills to a selected object.

Each pop-up applies color to the designated portion of the Tiger teeth Custom fill.

Fill inspector: Custom: Tiger teeth

Note: Because a Custom fill prints at one size on all PostScript output devices, it does not scale with its respective object; the fill keeps its original size even though the path itself increases or decreases in size.

Pattern strokes and fills

FreeHand offers 64 editable bitmap patterns for both strokes and fills. Color appears on the solid portions of the patterns.

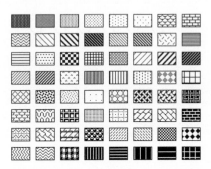

Pattern strokes and fills

Use the Stroke inspector to edit Pattern strokes and the Fill inspector to edit Pattern fills.

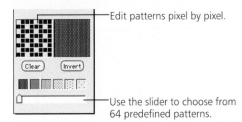

Edit patterns pixel by pixel.

Use the slider to choose from 64 predefined patterns.

Stroke inspector: Pattern

Important: Do not use Pattern strokes and fills when printing to high-resolution output devices, including imagesetters.

Pattern display and preview

An editable display of the pattern appears on the left and a preview of that pattern appears on the right. As you edit the pattern on the left, the overall effect previews on the right.

Clear and Invert

The Clear button removes a pattern from the entry field and displays white until you choose another or create a new pattern. The Invert button inverses pixel color—from black to white or from white to black.

Pattern type

Scroll through the predefined pattern types using the slider at the bottom of the Stroke inspector. The chosen pattern appears in the display and preview.

Note: A Pattern stroke or fill does not transform with its respective object; the stroke or fill pattern keeps its original orientation and size even though the path itself transforms.

PostScript strokes and fills

PostScript applies a stroke or a fill of a unique pattern and shape that you create in the PostScript code entry field. FreeHand sends the PostScript code entered in the Stroke or Fill inspector to the PostScript Interpreter in your printer's Raster Image Processor (RIP). If your code is incorrect, you will receive a PostScript error message when printing.

Enter PostScript code sequences up to 255 characters. Use the spacebar to separate code commands, letting the text wrap on its own. After entering or pasting code, press Return to apply the code to a selected object.

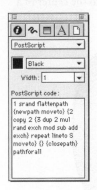

Stroke inspector   *Fill inspector*

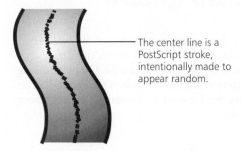

The center line is a PostScript stroke, intentionally made to appear random.

PostScript stroke

PostScript resources

PostScript programming is beyond the scope of this manual. To learn PostScript programming or to find more information about the PostScript description language, consult such books as *Learning PostScript: A Visual Approach*, by Ross Smith (Berkeley, California: Peachpit Press, 1990) and the *PostScript Language Reference Manual*, Second Edition, by Adobe Systems Incorporated (Reading, Massachusetts: Addison-Wesley, 1990).

Gradient fills

Use the top color well to apply color to the start of a graduated fill or to the perimeter of a radial fill. Use the bottom color well to apply color to the end of the graduated fill or to the center of a radial fill.

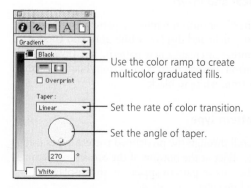

Use the color ramp to create multicolor graduated fills.

Set the rate of color transition.

Set the angle of taper.

Fill inspector: Gradient > graduated

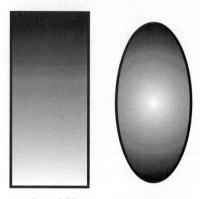

Graduated fill   *Radial fill*

The color transition in graduated fills is always straight. In radial fills it is always circular, regardless of the shape of the fill. Use blends along a path to create fills that follow the contours of an object. See Chapter 5, "Drawing," to learn about blends.

 Graduated fills

Graduated fills consist of smooth color progressions that extend from one edge of an object to its opposite edge at the angle you specify.

Taper

A linear taper progresses in increments of equal width from one color to another. A logarithmic taper progresses from a narrow band of color to increasingly wider increments towards another color.

Linear taper

Logarithmic taper

Angle

Set the graduated fill's angle using the Fill inspector's Angle dial. FreeHand's default angle is 270°. Hold down Shift to constrain the angle to 45° increments. As with all angle dials in FreeHand, 0° is at 3 o'clock, and 90° is at 12 o'clock.

Radial fills

A radial fill consists of a series of concentric color progressions that extend from the farthest edge to the center of an object's bounding box. The centerpoint is set relative to the bounding box.

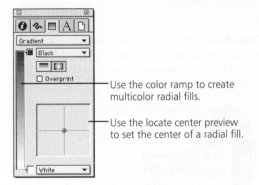

Use the color ramp to create multicolor radial fills.

Use the locate center preview to set the center of a radial fill.

Fill inspector: Gradient > radial

Locate center preview

Drag the knob in the locate center preview to set the centerpoint for radial fills. The knob's default position is the center of the preview. Hold down Shift and click anywhere in the preview to reset the radial fill's center to the center of the fill object's bounding box.

Note: To simultaneously set a radial fill's center position and center color, hold down Option (Macintosh) or Alt (Windows) while dropping the color chip onto the object.

Multicolor fills

To apply a multicolor fill, choose the Gradient option from the Fill inspector. Click either the graduated fill button or the radial fill button. Drop colors onto the color ramp.

Color ramp

The color ramp displays a preview of your fill. Use it to specify colors: a minimum of 2 colors and a maximum of 32.

To	Do this
Add a color to the color ramp	Drag a color chip onto the desired location on the color ramp. A color well for this chip appears.
Reposition a color within the fill	Drag a color chip along the color ramp to a new position.
Place a color in more than one location on the color ramp	Hold down Control (Macintosh) or Alt (Windows) and drag an existing color on the color ramp to copy it to a new location.
Remove a color from the color ramp	Choose a color chip, drag it away from the color ramp to an inactive area, and release the mouse button.
Change a color on the color ramp	Drag a new color onto an existing color chip. To change the colors of the top color well and the bottom color well, choose a new color from the appropriate Color List pop-up.

Note: Changing the fill from multicolor to Basic fills the object with the color displayed in the top color well.

Lens fills

A Lens fill transforms a selected object into any of six special-effect lenses—Transparency, Magnify, Invert, Lighten, Darken, and Monochrome. These effects in turn modify the appearance of images, objects, and text over which the lens is placed.

Spot colors under a lens are converted to process colors for output. Use the Eyedropper tool to capture new colors created by a Lens fill effect.

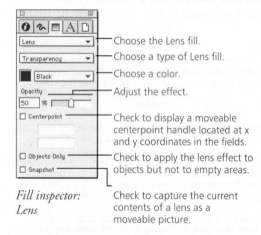

Choose the Lens fill.

Choose a type of Lens fill.

Choose a color.

Adjust the effect.

Check to display a moveable centerpoint handle located at x and y coordinates in the fields.

Check to apply the lens effect to objects but not to empty areas.

Fill inspector:
Lens

Check to capture the current contents of a lens as a moveable picture.

Centerpoint—Check to display a moveable centerpoint handle at the center of a selected lens. Drag the centerpoint anywhere in the document using the Pointer tool. Shift-clicking the centerpoint returns the centerpoint to the center of the lens. Unchecking Centerpoint removes the centerpoint. Deselecting the lens causes the centerpoint to disappear without changing the lens effect.

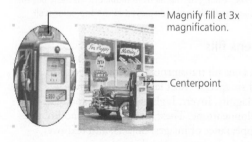

Magnify fill at 3x magnification.

Centerpoint

Objects Only—Check to apply the lens effect to objects, not empty areas, under the lens.

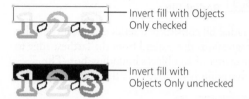

Invert fill with Objects Only checked

Invert fill with Objects Only unchecked

Snapshot—Check to capture the current contents of the lens, allowing the lens to be moved anywhere in the document without changing the lens contents.

With Snapshot checked, the magnify fill retains its contents when moved.

The image remains in the lens without checking Centerpoint.

Note: Choosing a new Lens type automatically unchecks Centerpoint, Objects Only, and Snapshot.

From one Lens fill to another, the options located between the Lens type pop-up and the Centerpoint checkbox on the Fill inspector differ.

Transparency

Enter a number from 0 (completely transparent) to 100 (completely opaque) or use the slider to adjust the opacity of the transparency fill.

Applying a transparency fill to the fairy's wing and gown creates a see-through effect.

Magnify

Enter a number from 1 to 100 or use the slider to adjust the number of times the magnify fill magnifies objects under it.

Centerpoint

The ellipse has a magnify fill set at 3x with a floating centerpoint.

Invert

Colors under the invert fill appear as their complementary CMYK colors (their opposites on a color wheel).

An invert fill applied to an image creates a negative image.

Lighten

Enter a number from 0 (no change) to 100 (completely white), or use the slider to adjust the percentage by which the lighten fill lightens colors under it.

A triangle with no stroke has a lighten fill to simulate a ray of light.

Darken

Enter a number from 0 (no change) to 100 (completely black), or use the slider to adjust the percentage by which the darken fill darkens colors under it.

An object created by tracing the water has darken fill to darken the water.

Monochrome

Choose a color in the monochrome Fill inspector. Colors under the monochrome fill appear as monochrome degrees of that color. Each color under the monochrome fill appears as a tint of the chosen color. The amount of lightness in the original color determines the tint value.

A monochrome fill creates a monochrome effect.

Using Lens fills

A lens does not actually change properties of the objects under it; it creates duplicate objects inside the lens. This is apparent when Centerpoint is checked and the lens is moved from the centerpoint or vice versa.

Remember that using Lens fills, especially on top of each other, can quickly add hundreds of objects to the document, greatly increasing both file size and print time, which may render your file unprintable.

An awareness of the placement of layers, as well as the arrangement of objects within a layer, is key to successful use of Lens fills.

EPS files are not affected by lens-filled objects. An object with a paste inside cannot receive a Lens fill; however, a lens-filled object can be pasted inside another object. Text cannot receive a Lens fill unless the text is converted to paths.

To remove a Lens fill, select the lens-filled object, and then choose None or another type of fill in the Fill inspector, or delete the lens-filled object.

Up to eight lenses can be stacked on top of each other. When a ninth lens is stacked upon eight others, the bottom lens is no longer affected by the lenses above it.

Tiled fills

Tiled fills are patterns based on a repeating object, or tile, that you create. Create a Tiled fill using graphics or text pasted into the Fill inspector. FreeHand will not allow EPSs, bitmap images, or other Tiled fills in a Tiled fill.

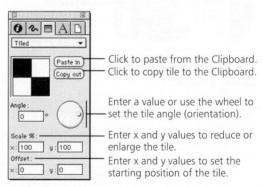

Fill inspector: Tiled

Spacing

The bounding box of each repeating object of a Tiled fill abuts those of its neighbors and determines the space between each object. When the Tiled fill consists of text, the text block determines the size of the tile, unless the text is first converted to paths. The more complex the fill, the slower it prints and redraws on screen.

Scale%

Enter x and y values to set percentages of the original object's height and width. Enter equal values to scale proportionally or different values to create distortion.

Offset

Enter a positive value or a negative value to realign the pattern within the object you are filling by the amount you specify.

◆ Positive x values move the fill to the right.

◆ Negative x values move the fill to the left.

◆ Positive y values move the fill up.

◆ Negative y values move the fill down.

To create and apply a Tiled fill:

1 Create an object to use as the tile and choose Edit > Cut or Copy. If you choose Copy, remember to deselect the original object before proceeding.

2 Select an object. Choose Tiled from the Fill inspector and click Paste in.

Note: To create a Tiled fill with space between its repeating tiles, draw a rectangle with a stroke and fill of None around the tile, and paste them in together.

To realign a Tiled fill within an object:

1 Select the object with a Tiled fill.

2 Display the Transform panel and uncheck the Fills checkbox.

3 Drag the object with the Pointer tool over its Tiled fill, realigning them.

4 Check Fills in the Transform panel and reposition the object as needed.

Textured fills

Textured fills are non-editable PostScript language patterns. Because Textured fills print at one size, they cannot be scaled with an object. Choose a Textured fill from the Fill inspector. The sample displays the currently chosen Textured fill. Note that the sample does not change as you modify the fill color.

Fill inspector: Textured

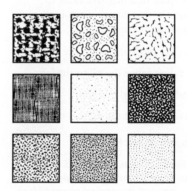

Textured fills

CHAPTER 7

Text

Basic FreeHand text concepts

The Text tool and the Pointer tool are the only tools necessary for working with text, and they appear in the Toolbox.

 Using the Text tool

To	Do this
Create a new text block	Click or click and drag in your document.
Type text	Click in your document and begin typing, or click within an existing text block to place an insertion point and begin typing.
Highlight text	Click to place an insertion point and drag to include the desired characters, words, or paragraphs.
Select a word	Double-click anywhere in the word.
Select a paragraph	Triple-click anywhere in the paragraph.
Select all text within a text block	Choose Edit > Select > All after placing an insertion point to select all text within a text block or linked text blocks. Selecting all text and pressing Delete does not remove the text block, only the characters.
Momentarily switch to the Pointer tool	Hold down Command (Macintosh) or Control (Windows). Release Command or Control to return to the Text tool.
Switch to the Pointer tool	Press 0 (zero) when no text block is selected.

Note: By default, the Text tool reverts to the Pointer tool after you create a text block and move the cursor outside the text block. To change this default, uncheck the Text > "Text tool reverts to pointer" preference.

Using the Pointer tool

To	Do this
Select a text block	Click a text block. Drag to move it, or press Delete to remove it.
Manipulate a text block handle	Double-click a side-middle or bottom-middle handle to turn on or turn off auto-expansion, or click and drag a side handle to adjust kerning, a bottom handle to adjust leading, or a corner handle to adjust the size of a text block.
Link one text block to another	Click and drag from the link box of one text block to the body of another text block.
Finish typing	Click outside the text block.
Switch to the Text tool	Press "." (period), press "A," or double-click a text block. On the Macintosh, use Shift-F9.

Anatomy of a text block

FreeHand text is container-based. There are two kinds of containers, or text blocks: standard and auto-expanding. Text blocks selected with the Pointer tool display eight handles and a link box. Learning how these handles work is crucial to understanding text in FreeHand.

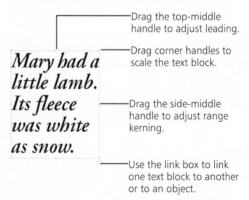

Drag the top-middle handle to adjust leading.

Drag corner handles to scale the text block.

Drag the side-middle handle to adjust range kerning.

Use the link box to link one text block to another or to an object.

Solid middle handles indicate a standard text block. Hollow middle handles indicate an auto-expanding text block. Double-click a handle to switch between solid and hollow.

When switching between standard and auto-expanding, click directly on the appropriate text block handle and not on the border. Double-clicking the border of a text block activates the text block's transformation handles.

A standard text block maintains a fixed size. In contrast, an auto-expanding text block dynamically increases or decreases in size to fit the text it contains.

Use standard text blocks for large amounts of text. In standard text blocks, text automatically wraps from one line to the next. Use auto-expanding text blocks for small amounts of text, like labels and captions.

The highlight color of text block borders are visible on screen in Preview mode—when deselected, only the text is visible. In Keyline mode, both the text block border and the text is visible. If a selected text block does not display its highlight color in Preview mode, check the General > "Smoother editing" > "Highlight selected paths" preference.

See "Applying color to text blocks" on page 188 to assign color to text block borders.

Text blocks selected with the Text tool display only the text rulers and the Text tool cursor. To show or hide the text rulers, choose View > Text Rulers or use Command-/ (Macintosh) or Control-Shift-Alt-T (Windows).

Mary had a
little lamb.
Its fleece
was white
as snow.

Creating text blocks

With the Text > "New text containers auto-expand" preference checked, click the Text tool to create a text block that expands both horizontally and vertically when typing.

To create a standard text block with the Text > "New text containers auto-expand" preference checked, drag the Text tool to the size of the text block. With this preference unchecked, click with the Text tool to create a standard text block, in which text wraps automatically.

On the Macintosh, hold down Control and click with the Text tool to create an auto-expanding text block when this preference is unchecked.

Choose one of the following ways to turn on auto-expansion of existing text blocks:

- Using the Pointer tool, double-click the side-middle handles to turn on or turn off horizontal auto-expansion. Double-click the bottom-middle handle to turn on or turn off vertical auto-expansion.

- Select single or multiple text blocks. Click the horizontal and vertical buttons on the Object inspector to turn on or turn off auto-expansion.

To turn on or turn off auto-expansion for all text blocks within a selection of multiple objects, on the active page, or within a document, use the Find & Replace Graphics panel. Choose Edit > Find & Replace > Graphics, and click the Select panel. Choose Object type from the Attribute pop-up and Text from the Object type pop-up. Specify a search criteria in the Search pop-up and click Find. This selects all text blocks. Click the appropriate buttons on the Object inspector to turn on or turn off auto-expansion.

Auto-expanding text blocks function like standard text blocks, with these exceptions:

- Auto-expanding text blocks can contain only one column.

- The corner handles of an auto-expanding text block do not scale the text block.

- Deselecting an empty auto-expanding text block deletes it.

Manually adjusting spacing and leading

To	Do this
Increase or decrease letter spacing (range kerning)	Drag a side-middle handle.
Increase or decrease word spacing	Hold down Option (Macintosh) or Alt (Windows) and drag a side-middle handle of a single-column text block.
Increase or decrease leading	Drag a top-middle or bottom-middle handle.

To modify range kerning and leading using the Text inspector, the Text menu, or the Text toolbar, see "Adjusting kerning and range kerning" on page 183. For information about word spacing, see "Spacing" on page 198.

Manually scaling standard text blocks

In a standard text block, a dot in the link box indicates text overflow. When this happens, scale the text block, or link the overflow text block to another text block or to an object. An empty link box indicates all the container's text is visible.

To	Do this
Scale a text block	Drag a corner handle with the Pointer tool. Text within the container reflows to fill the new size.
Scale a text block proportionally	Hold down Shift and drag a corner handle. Text within the container reflows to fill the new size.

To	Do this
Scale a text block and text (font size)	Hold down Option (Macintosh) or Alt (Windows) and drag a corner handle.
Scale a text block and text (font size) proportionally	Hold down Shift-Option (Macintosh) or Shift-Alt (Windows) and drag a corner handle.
Reduce the size of a text block to fit the text	Double-click the link box with the Pointer tool.

Only standard text blocks are scalable. Use corner handles when scaling. The top-, bottom-, or side-middle handles change text attributes rather than reflow text. To scale a text block by assigning precise dimensions, select a text block and enter width and height values in the Object inspector.

Linking one text block to another

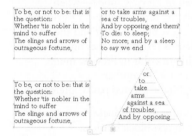

Three text blocks and a path

Link text blocks to flow text from one text block to another or from a text block to an object, such as a path. A linked object acquires text block attributes and retains these attributes even after deleting text from the object. Use the Object inspector and the Text inspector together to format text linked to a path.

To create a link, select the link box of a text block with text overflow and drag the link line to the inside of an empty text block or onto an object. Once objects are linked, text flows into the empty text block or into the object. Link any number of text blocks on a single page or across multiple pages.

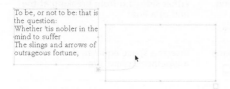

Changes to selected text in a linked text block may affect text in other linked blocks. For example, when enlarging the font size in one text block, text may reflow into the next block.

Breaking links between text blocks

To break a link, click the link box of a text block and drag the link line to an empty area in the document. Text flows back into the last linked text block. Breaking links in the middle of a chain of text blocks leaves empty text blocks after the last linked block.

To break a link and retain text placement:

1 With the Text tool, select the text in the second text block and choose Edit > Cut.

2 Drag a link line from the link box of the first text block to an empty area in the document.

3 Place an insertion point in the second text block with the Text tool and choose Edit > Paste.

   Text remains intact but is no longer linked. The first text block has an empty link box indicating no text overflow and no link.

Cutting or deleting a text block other than the first text block in a linked series does not delete the text itself. When pasting the cut text block, the text is a copy of the original text. After deleting a text block, the existing text reflows across the remaining text blocks.

Deleting empty text blocks or objects

Breaking links may leave empty blocks. With an empty text block selected, press Delete, or choose Edit > Clear, or double-click its link box to delete it. Because deselected text blocks are invisible in Preview mode, choose View > Preview to turn off Preview mode or use Command-K (Macintosh) or Control-K (Windows) to switch to Keyline mode.

To delete all the empty text blocks in a document, choose Xtras > Delete > Empty Text Blocks, or use Find & Replace Graphics to remove all invisible objects. Choose Edit > Find & Replace > Graphics, and click the Find & Replace tab. Choose Remove from the Attribute pop-up, choose Invisible objects from the Remove pop-up, and click Find.

Using the Text Editor

The Text Editor provides another environment for reviewing and editing text. Use it when text is difficult to edit on screen or when editing invisible characters.

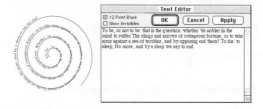

To edit existing text in the Text Editor:

1 Select the text block and choose Text > Editor or use Command-Shift-E (Macintosh) or Control-Shift-E (Windows) to display the Text Editor.

2 Edit the text in the Text Editor.

   Check the 12 Point Black checkbox in the Text Editor to ignore formatting attributes and display text in 12-point black type. This option does not affect the actual text in a document.

3 Click OK, Cancel, or Apply.

- ◆ Click OK to apply changes to the text and close the Text Editor.

- ◆ Click Cancel to close the Text Editor without applying changes.

- ◆ Click Apply to apply changes to the text without leaving the Text Editor.

Here are other ways to display the Text Editor.

- ◆ To create a new text block and open the Text Editor simultaneously, hold down Option (Macintosh) or Alt (Windows) when creating a text block.

- ◆ To simultaneously make the text active and display the Text Editor, hold down Option (Macintosh) or Alt (Windows), and double-click a text block with the Pointer tool.

- ◆ To always edit text in the Text Editor, check the Text > "Always use Text Editor" preference.

- ◆ To display the Text Editor in Windows, right-click a text block, and then choose Editor from the Shortcut menu.

Note: Text in envelopes is editable, but only in the Text Editor. For information about envelopes, see "Envelope" on page 134.

Showing non-printing text symbols

To show non-printing text symbols in the Text Editor, check Show invisibles. These symbols are only visible and editable in the Text Editor, except em dash and en dash, which are visible in all text.

Space	Represents a single space.
Tab →	Represents a tab.
End of paragraph ¶	Represents a hard return at the end of a paragraph.

End of column ⅃	Forces text following the symbol to start at the top of the next column or linked text block.
End of line ↵	Forces text following the symbol to start on the next line.
Non-breaking space ⌣	Inserts a space that prevents text on either side of it from breaking at the end of a line.
Em space ▢	Inserts a space equal to the width of a typeface's point size.
En Space ▯	Inserts a space equal to half an em space.
Thin space		Inserts a space equal to one-fifth of an en space.
Em dash —	Visible in all text. Inserts a dash the width of an em space.
En dash -	Visible in all text. Inserts a dash the width of an en space.
Discretionary hyphen ⌐	Inserts an invisible hyphen indicating where text should break at the end of a line.

Note: Use a discretionary hyphen to hyphenate without checking Hyphenate in the Text Paragraph inspector.

To insert a text symbol in text, whether in the Text Editor or in a text block, place the text cursor in the appropriate place in text, choose Text > Special Characters, and then choose the appropriate symbol. Space, tab, and end-of-paragraph symbols are inserted using the spacebar, Tab key, and Return key, respectively.

Tools to format text

Use the Text inspector, the Text menu, or the Text toolbar to apply precise type specifications to characters, lines of text, paragraphs, and entire text blocks.

Text inspector

Choose Window > Inspectors > Text to display the Text inspector. Apply frequently used type specifications and text formatting from one location.

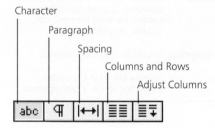

- ◆ Choose the Text Character inspector to set the font, style, size, text alignment, leading, and kerning; shift the baseline; and apply text effects and paragraph styles.

- ◆ Choose the Text Paragraph inspector to set paragraph spacing, indentation, and hyphenation; apply hanging punctuation to paragraphs; and apply rules to paragraphs.

- ◆ Choose the Text Spacing inspector to scale characters horizontally; set word and letter spacing; and keep words and lines of text together to prevent awkward breaks at the ends of lines and columns.

- ◆ Choose the Text Columns and Rows inspector to create columns and rows and to adjust text flow.

- ◆ Choose the Text Adjust Columns inspector to copyfit text precisely.

Text menu

Set the font, point size, style, text alignment, leading, and case; apply text effects; and choose special characters.

Text toolbar

Use the buttons and entry fields to set the font, type size, type style, leading, and text alignment and perform advanced functions. Use Command-Option-T (Macintosh) or Control-Alt-T (Windows) to show or hide the toolbars.

In Windows, the Text toolbar includes buttons for Bold and Italic character styles. Click both Bold and Italic buttons to apply a font's BoldItalic character style, when available. An icon next to the font name indicates whether the font is a TrueType or a device font. Absence of an icon indicates a system font or an unidentifiable font. The Text toolbar contains common text commands.

For more information on the Text toolbar, see "Text toolbar" on page 29.

Selecting text with the right mouse button (Windows)

Many choices available in the Text menu, Text toolbar, and the Text inspectors also appear in the Text shortcut menu. To display text options, right-click one or more text blocks. Right-click a path to choose Flow Inside Path or Attach to Path.

Text shortcut menu

Choosing shortcut commands for text

Choose	To
Edit	Display the Edit menu showing commands applicable to the text block.
Font, Size, Type Style, Effect, Align, or Leading	Specify a font, a font size, a style, a text effect, an alignment, or a leading value.
Editor	Display the Text Editor.
Detach From Path	Separate text from its attached path.
Remove Transforms	Restore a text block to its status before any transformations.
Convert To Paths	Convert text to paths.

Choose	To
Select	Specify a selection domain.
View	Choose a magnification view for the active page.
Arrange	Move the text block by choosing: Bring to Front, Move Forward, Move Backward, or Send to Back.
Lock or Unlock	Lock or unlock the text block's position. Locked text blocks cannot be transformed, cut, copied, or deleted.
Group or Ungroup	Group or ungroup objects.
Properties	Display the Text Character inspector to view text options.

Setting precise type specifications

Applying character and paragraph attributes to text

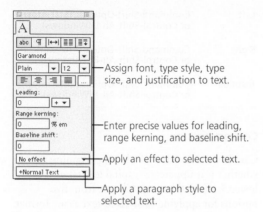

Assign font, type style, type size, and justification to text.

Enter precise values for leading, range kerning, and baseline shift.

Apply an effect to selected text.

Apply a paragraph style to selected text.

Text Character inspector

Use the Text Character inspector to apply attributes to selected characters, a range of text, or an entire text block. To apply text formatting to all text in a series of linked text blocks, place an insertion point, and choose Edit > Select > All. Then assign attributes.

Choose a paragraph style from the pop-up on the Text Character inspector. Save frequently used attributes in paragraph styles, and quickly drag and drop formatting from the Styles panel onto paragraphs. For more information about creating and working with paragraph styles, see "Managing styles" on page 87.

Using font mapping

When a FreeHand document contains fonts not installed on your computer, the Missing Fonts dialog box prompts you to choose a font with which to replace the missing font.

Common text attributes

To specify	Do this
Font	Choose a font from the Text > Font menu, from the pop-up in the Text Character inspector, or the Text toolbar.
Style	Choose a style from the Text > Style menu, or from the pop-up in the Text Character inspector, or the Text toolbar.
Point size	Choose a point size from the Text > Size menu, from the pop-up in the Text Character inspector, or the Text toolbar.
	To specify a point size not in the list, choose Text > Size > Other, enter a value in the Size field, and click OK; or type a value in the point size entry field in the Text Character inspector or the Text toolbar, and press Return.
Paragraph alignment	Choose from the Text > Align menu, click one of the alignment buttons in the Text Character inspector, or the Text toolbar.
Capitalization	Choose a capitalization option from the Text > Convert Case menu.

Clicking a font name in the Font pop-up in the Text Character inspector previews selected text in the chosen font. With no text selected, clicking a font name previews "AaBbCcDd" (Macintosh) or the name of the font (Windows). In Windows, an icon next to the font name indicates whether the font is a TrueType or a device font. Absence of an icon indicates a system font or an unidentifiable font.

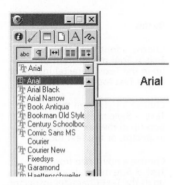

Arial

Text alignment keyboard shortcuts

To align	Use
Center	Command-Shift-Option-M (Macintosh) or Control-Shift-Alt-M (Windows)
Left	Command-Shift-Option-L (Macintosh) or Control-Shift-Alt-L (Windows)
Right	Command-Shift-Option-R (Macintosh) or Control-Shift-Alt-R (Windows)
Justified	Command-Shift-Option-J (Macintosh) or Control-Shift-Alt-J (Windows)

Text style keyboard shortcuts

To apply	Use
Bold	Command-Option-B (Macintosh) or Control-Alt-B (Windows)
Italic	Command-Option-I (Macintosh) or Control-Alt-I (Windows)
Bold Italic	Command-Shift-Option-O (Macintosh) or Control-Shift-Alt-O (Windows)
Plain	Command-Shift-Option-P (Macintosh) or Control-Shift-Alt-P (Windows)

Note: The text style keyboard shortcuts function only when the corresponding font variation is available.

Converting case

Case is the condition of a letter pertaining to whether it is uppercase (capital letters) or lowercase (small letters). Choose from five options for applying to selected text a case format from the Text > Convert Case menu. Letters entered after a case format is applied do not conform to the format.

- **Uppercase**—Converts to uppercase all letters in a selected text block.

- **Lowercase**—Converts to lowercase all letters in a selected text block.

- **Small Caps**—Converts to uppercase all letters in a selected text block, then reduces the point size specified in the Text > Convert Case > Settings dialog box.

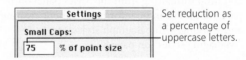

Set reduction as a percentage of uppercase letters.

- **Title**—Converts to uppercase the first letter of each word in a selected text block.

- **Sentence**—Converts to an uppercase letter only the first letter of each sentence in a selected block of text.

Designating exceptions to capitalization options

Checking a Convert Case option under Use Exceptions for protects all words in the list of exceptions when the checked option is applied.

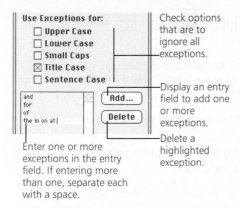

Check options that are to ignore all exceptions.

Display an entry field to add one or more exceptions.

Delete a highlighted exception.

Enter one or more exceptions in the entry field. If entering more than one, separate each with a space.

Note: For custom text shortcuts, see FreeHand Help.

Adjusting leading

Leading in FreeHand is calculated from the baseline of one line of text to the baseline of the next. When assigning leading from the Text menu, choose Solid to set leading equal to the type size of the text and choose Auto to set the leading to 120% of the type size of the text. Choose Text > Leading > Other to display the Leading dialog box. Three options appear in this dialog box, in the Leading pop-up in the Text Character inspector, and in the Text toolbar:

◆ **Extra**—This option increases the standard leading, measured in points. The total leading equals the point size of the type plus the extra leading specified. Choose + from the Leading pop-up in the Text Character inspector or the Text toolbar.

◆ **Fixed**—This option sets the leading to the exact point size specified. Choose = from the Leading pop-up in the Text Character inspector or the Text toolbar.

◆ **Percentage**—This option measures a percentage of the point size of the type. Standard leading is 120%. For example, using 10-point type and entering 120 as the percentage yields a leading of 12 points. Choose % from the Leading pop-up in the Text Character inspector or the Text toolbar.

Adjusting kerning and range kerning

Kerning refers to the space between two letters. Range kerning refers to the letter spacing across a range of characters. To kern precisely, select text and enter values in the entry fields in the Text Character inspector. Each kind of kerning value is a percentage of an em space, which is the space equal to the width of a typeface's point size. Positive values increase spacing; negative values decrease spacing.

To adjust space between two characters:

1 Click between two characters with the Text tool.

2 Enter a percentage value in the Kerning entry field in the Text Character inspector and press Return.

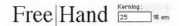

To adjust space between a range of characters (range kerning):

1 Select a range of characters with the Text tool.

2 Do one of the following to apply range kerning:

◆ Enter a percentage value in the Range kerning entry field in the Text Character inspector and press Return.

◆ Hold down Option (Macintosh) or Control-Alt (Windows) and press the right or left cursor key to increase or decrease kerning by one percent of an em.

◆ Hold down Option-Shift (Macintosh) or Control-Alt-Shift (Windows) and press the right or left cursor key to increase or decrease kerning by 10 percent of an em.

Note: For custom text shortcuts, see FreeHand Help.

Shifting the baseline

Use the Baseline shift entry field in the Text Character inspector to shift text upward (superscript) or downward (subscript) in relation to the baseline of the text. Special characters like ® and © usually appear shifted above the rest of the text.

To shift the baseline:

1 Select text with the Text tool.

2 Enter a value in the Baseline shift entry field in the Text Character inspector and press Return.

Enter a positive number to shift the baseline of the text upward or enter a negative number to shift it downward.

Alternatively, use Option (Macintosh) or Control-Alt (Windows) and press the up or down cursor keys to apply a baseline shift.

Note: To create footnotes and superscript special characters like © and ™, select shifted text and reduce the size.

Note: For custom text shortcuts, see FreeHand Help.

Using the text rulers to set tabs and indents

A text block selected with the Text tool displays the text ruler at the top. Text rulers display tab and indent markers above selected text blocks. To show or hide text rulers, choose View > Text Rulers or use Command-/ (Macintosh) or Control-Shift-Alt-T (Windows).

Default tabs left-align at half-inch intervals, regardless of the unit of measurement for the document. To add custom tabs to a document, choose from the five kinds of tabs available on the text ruler: left, right, center, decimal, and wrapping.

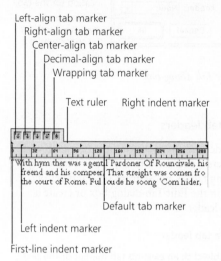

Left-align tab marker
Right-align tab marker
Center-align tab marker
Decimal-align tab marker
Wrapping tab marker

Text ruler   Right indent marker

Default tab marker

Left indent marker

First-line indent marker

When a page is scrolled so that the top of the text block is beyond the top of the document window, the text ruler floats (remains visible) just below the title bar. The text ruler also floats when the text block is rotated 90° and the page is scrolled to the left or the right so that the top of the text block is out of view.

Text ruler floating above text block

Setting tabs

Set a tab for a single paragraph or a range of paragraphs. With paragraphs containing different tab and indent settings selected, only the first paragraph's tab and indent settings appear on the text ruler and the tab area is dimmed. Changes made to these settings affect all selected paragraphs. Drag and drop tab markers to set tabs manually. To move a tab, drag and drop the tab marker to a new location. To remove a tab, drag the tab marker off of the text ruler. Double-click the text ruler to display the Edit Tab dialog box for setting tabs using precise values.

Use	To
Default tabs	Align the left edge of text at half-inch intervals.
Left-align tab	Align the left edge of text to the tab marker.
Right-align tab	Align the right edge of text to the tab marker.
Center-align tab	Align text to the center of the tab marker.
Decimal-align tab	Align text at the decimal point. If the text does not contain a decimal point, the tab right-aligns the text.
Wrapping tab	Flow multiple lines of text between two tab markers.

For the Decimal-align tab example:

1994	9.3%	465
1995	15.5%	775
1996	23.8%	1190

To define a space between two columns created with wrapping tabs, place a wrapping tab on each side of a column, and then place another one at the beginning of the next column.

Mary	Its	And	The
had a	fleece	every-	lamb
little	was	where	was
lamb.	white	that	sure to
	as	Mary	go.
	snow.	went,	

Wrapping tabs

To set tabs by dragging and dropping markers:

1 Place an insertion point or select a range of paragraphs.

2 Drag and drop a tab marker onto the text ruler to specify text alignment.

   All default tabs to the left of the new tab disappear.

3 Place an insertion point and press Tab to align text to the new tab setting.

To set tabs using precise values:

1 Place an insertion point or select a range of paragraphs.

2 Double-click the text ruler to display the Edit Tab dialog box.

   Double-clicking a tab marker displays the Edit Tab dialog box and its specific tab settings.

3 Enter a value in the Position entry field to set the distance from the left edge of the column or text block to the new tab.

4 Choose from the Alignment and Leader pop-ups to define the tab and click OK.

   All default tabs to the left of the new tab disappear.

5 Place an insertion point and press Tab to align text to the new tab setting.

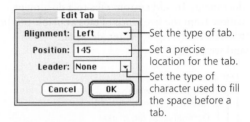

Set the type of tab.

Set a precise location for the tab.

Set the type of character used to fill the space before a tab.

Edit Tab dialog box

Using tab leaders

Tab leaders fill the space occupied by a tab with characters—add them to any type of tab except wrapping tabs. Choose from several types of leaders in the Edit Tab dialog box or create a custom leader.

To add a tab leader:

1 Double-click an existing tab marker or the text ruler to display the Edit Tab dialog box.

2 Choose a tab leader from the Leader pop-up. To enter a custom leader, highlight the entry field, enter a character, and click OK.

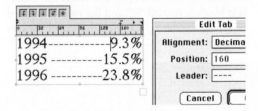

Note: Tabs and tab leaders cannot be used in text on a path.

Setting indents

To set a paragraph indent, place an insertion point or select a range of paragraphs. Drag an indent marker to set the desired margin or indent.

Use	To
First-line indent marker	Set the indent of the first line independently of the rest of the paragraph.
Left indent marker	Set the left paragraph margin.
Right indent marker	Set the right paragraph margin.

To set a hanging indent:

1 Place an insertion point or select a range of paragraphs.

2 Drag the left indent marker to the right to set the paragraph indent, and drag the first-line indent to the left to set a negative first-line indent.

Using the Indents entry fields in the Text Paragraph inspector, enter a positive value in the Left entry field to set the paragraph indent, enter a negative value in the First entry field to set the first-line indent, and press Return. Text lines up to the hanging indent.

Setting margins with the Object inspector

To apply margins to text within a text block or to text flowing inside a path:

1 Select a text block with the Pointer tool.

2 Enter values for left, right, top, and bottom in the Inset entry fields in the Object inspector and press Return.

Entering 0 (zero) as the Inset value positions text against the text block border. Positive values position text inside the text block border, and negative values position text outside the text block border.

Working with text as objects

Text blocks behave like other FreeHand objects—precisely position or scale them by entering values in the Object inspector, duplicate them, group them, send them to different layers, and transform them. In regard to rotating, scaling, skewing, and reflecting, select Text > Remove Transforms to remove all transformations applied to a text block. Transforming a grouped text block transforms the text as well as the text block.

Coloring text and text blocks

Apply color to text blocks as with other objects. All text blocks have two parts—the text and the container. Apply strokes and fills to each part independently.

Applying color to text

To	Do this
Apply a stroke to text characters	Select text with the Text tool and drop a color chip onto the color well in the Basic Stroke inspector or onto the Stroke selector in the Color List.
Apply a fill to text characters	Select text with the Text tool and drop a color chip onto the selected text, the color well in the Fill inspector, the Fill selector in the Color List, or drop a color chip onto the text to apply the color to all characters in the text block.
Remove a color stroke or fill from text characters	Select text with the Text tool and choose None from the Stroke or Fill inspector, or drop the None color chip onto the Stroke or Fill selector in the Color List.

FreeHand

Stroked and filled text

Applying color to text blocks

To	Do this
Apply a stroke to a text block	Select a text block and drop a color chip onto the color well in the Stroke inspector.
	With text selected, check the Display border option in the Object inspector to view the stroked outline.
Apply a fill to a text block	Select a text block and drop a color chip onto an empty area in the text block or onto the color well in the Fill inspector.
Remove color from a text block	Select the text block and choose None from the Stroke or Fill inspector, or drop the None color chip onto the Stroke or Fill selector on the Color List.

The Colors > "Color List shows" preference determines how the Color List selectors behave with selected text blocks. When the preference setting is "Container color," the selectors display the stroke and fill attributes of selected text blocks. Dragging and dropping a color chip onto one of the selectors changes the color of the text block, not the text. When the preference setting is "Text color," the selectors display the stroke and fill attributes of selected text.

Note: With text blocks selected and the Both selector active, selecting colors in the Color List only affects the text fill color. The Both selector is in the indeterminate state. To learn more about the Color List selectors, see "Using the Color List selectors" on page 151.

 Converting text to paths

Convert text to paths to change the shape of individual characters, use text as a clipping path, or apply complicated strokes and fills to the shape of a group of characters. Apply Text > Convert to Paths to text in any PostScript Type 1, PostScript Type 3 font created with Fontographer, or any TrueType font installed on your computer. Text in linked text blocks cannot be converted to paths.

To convert text to paths:

1 Select a text block with the Pointer tool.

2 Choose Text > Convert to Paths, use Command-Shift-P (Macintosh) or Control-Shift-P (Windows), or click the Convert to Paths button on the Text toolbar.

A text block converts to a group, which no longer is editable as text. Choose Modify > Ungroup, use Command-U (Macintosh) or Control-U (Windows), or click the Ungroup button on the Main toolbar to ungroup the converted text to yield individual characters. Each letter in the text becomes an editable path.

◆ Letters with more than one component, such as the letter i, convert to composite paths.

◆ Letters with enclosed areas, such as B and O, convert to composite paths with transparent holes.

◆ All other letters, such as L and Z, convert to a single path.

Select a word or phrase and choose Modify > Join. Once joined, the selected text behaves as a single object. For more information about composite paths, see "Composite paths" on page 113.

FreeHand *Before Joining*

FreeHand *After Joining*

Converting text to paths may degrade the on-screen appearance of text characters because your system's type-handling utility, such as Adobe Type Manager (ATM), no longer maintains the images of the text outlines. Converting text to paths may also reduce the print quality of text, especially at sizes 12 points and less.

Basic text and path formatting

 Attaching text to paths

To place text on a path:

1 Select a text block and a path.

2 Choose Text > Attach to Path, use Command-Shift-Y (Macintosh) or Control-Shift-Y (Windows), or click the Attach to Path button on the Text toolbar.

You can also draw a path, choose Text > Attach to Path, and type directly on the path.

For a closed path, text flows along the top of the path and center-aligns by default. For an open path, only characters up to the first carriage return or tab are displayed. A dot may appear in the link box indicating overflow if the path is shorter than the text.

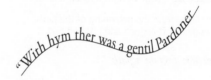

Type specifications of text attached to a path remain intact. Edit text directly on the path or use the Text Editor. To type text directly onto a path, select the path, choose Text > Attach to Path or click the Attach to Path button on the Text toolbar, and begin typing.

To remove text from a path, select the path with the Pointer tool and choose Text > Detach from Path, or click the Detach from Path button on the Text toolbar.

FreeHand automatically adjusts spacing of left-aligned text on a path to avoid overlapping letters due to path curvature. FreeHand does not adjust text on a path in files created in versions earlier than FreeHand 8, unless you detach them from and re-attach them to the path. Conversely, left-aligned text attached to paths in FreeHand 8 or 9 retains the adjustment when opened in previous versions of FreeHand.

If text disappears after choosing Attach to Path, review the Text alignment pop-ups in the Object inspector. Text does not appear on a path with None chosen for both Top and Bottom alignment.

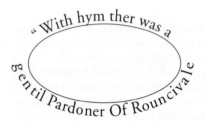

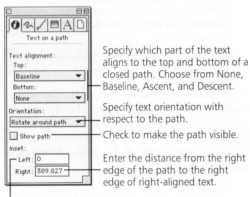

Specify which part of the text aligns to the top and bottom of a closed path. Choose from None, Baseline, Ascent, and Descent.

Specify text orientation with respect to the path.

Check to make the path visible.

Enter the distance from the right edge of the path to the right edge of right-aligned text.

Enter the distance from the beginning of the path to the left edge of left-aligned and justified text.

Object inspector: Text on a path

To place text on the top and bottom of an ellipse:

1   Insert a carriage return at the point where the text should split.

2   Select the text block and an ellipse.

3   Choose Text > Attach to Path.

Applying alignment and orientation to text on a path

Use this orientation	To yield		
Rotate around path	*Text on path* *Baseline*	*Text on path* *Ascent*	*Text on path* *Descent*
Vertical	*Text on path* *Baseline*	*Text on path* *Ascent*	*Text on path* *Descent*
Skew horizontal	*Text on path* *Baseline*	*Text on path* *Ascent*	*Text on path* *Descent*
Skew vertical	*Text on path* *Baseline*	*Text on path* *Ascent*	*Text on path* *Descent*

Text flows in the direction of the path. Path direction is from left to right (clockwise) or from right to left (counterclockwise). To reverse the direction of the text, reverse the direction of the path.

To reverse the direction of text on a path:

1 Hold down Option (Macintosh) or Alt (Windows) and subselect the path.

   When a path is not visible on screen, check Show path in the Object inspector or view the path in Keyline mode.

2 Choose Modify > Alter Path > Reverse Direction.

The path direction and the direction of the text flow reverse.

To move text on a path manually:

1   Place an insertion point in the text or subselect the path with the Pointer tool.

A triangular text handle appears to the left, center, or right of the text, depending on the text alignment. To display text while it moves along the path, hold down Option (Macintosh) or Alt (Windows) while dragging the text handle.

2   Drag the triangular handle to move the text along the path.

The position of the text updates the values in the Left and Right Inset entry fields in the Object inspector.

To move text on a path a precise distance:

1   Place an insertion point in the text or subselect the path with the Pointer tool.

2   Enter a value in the Left or Right Inset entry field in the Object inspector, and press Return.

Flowing text inside a path

FreeHand text can flow inside any open or closed path. To type text directly inside a path, select a path, choose Text > Flow Inside Path, and begin typing.

To flow existing text inside a path and apply an inset:

1   Select both a text block and a closed path with the Pointer tool.

2   Choose Text > Flow Inside Path, use Command-Shift-U (Macintosh) or Control-Shift-U (Windows), or click the button on the Text toolbar.

The path now acts like a text block. Edit the text by double-clicking the path with the Pointer tool, or by placing an insertion point with the Text tool.

3   To apply an inset, display the Object inspector. Enter values in the Inset entry fields.

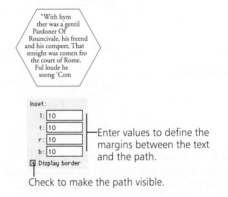

Enter values to define the margins between the text and the path.

Check to make the path visible.

Object inspector: Text in a path

Note: To remove text from a path, choose Text > Detach from Path.

Wrapping text around objects

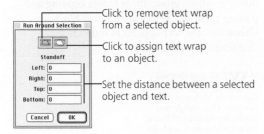

Click to remove text wrap from a selected object.

Click to assign text wrap to an object.

Set the distance between a selected object and text.

Use Run Around Selection to wrap text around a single object, including imported graphics and composite paths. Apply Run Around Selection to objects, not to text blocks. Once assigned, all text automatically wraps around that object.

To display the Run Around Selection dialog box, choose Text > Run Around Selection, use Command-Option-W (Macintosh) or Control-Alt-W (Windows), or click the button on the Text toolbar. Enter values to set the distance between a selected object and text. Values are expressed in the document unit of measurement. Positive numbers begin text flow outside the selected object. Negative numbers keep text within the selected object.

Before applying Run Around Selection, make sure that the object is on top of the text. Select the object. Then, to place the object in front of the text, choose Modify > Arrange > Bring to Front, use Command-F (Macintosh) or Control-F (Windows), or move one layer in front of another. For more about using the Layers panel, see "Simplifying a complex illustration using layers" on page 76.

"With hym ther was a gentil Pardoner Of Rouncivale, his freend and his compeer, That streight was comen fro the court of Rome. Ful loude he soong 'Com hider, love, to me!' This Somonour bar to hym a stif burdoun, Was nevere trompe of half so greet a soun. This pardoner hadde heer as

Before

"With hym ther was a gentil Pardoner Of Rouncivale, his freend and his compeer, That streight was comen fro the court of Rome. Ful loude he soong 'Com hider, love, to me!' This Somonour bar to hym a stif burdoun, Was nevere

After

To wrap text around an object:

1 Select the object and choose Text > Run Around Selection.

   Make sure the object is in front of the text before applying Run Around Selection. Select the object and choose Modify > Arrange > Move Forward or Bring to Front.

2 Click the text wrap button, enter Standoff values, and click OK.

   Text wraps around the graphic's bounding box.

To wrap text around a complex object:

1 Draw a closed path around the object and apply a stroke and fill of None.

   Apply the text wrap to the newly created closed path.

2 With the path selected, choose Text > Run Around Selection.

   Make sure the object is in front of the text before applying Run Around Selection. Select the object and choose Modify > Arrange > Move Forward or Bring to Front.

3 Click the text wrap button, enter Standoff values, and click OK.

Use this technique to create the callout text used by magazines. Create a text block with a border stroke and an inset value. With this text block on top of the main body of text, select the text wrap button in the Run Around Selection dialog box to place the text block inside a column of text or between columns.

Working with inline graphics

An inline graphic is any object pasted into a text block. The inline graphic becomes a text character, responding to text flow and modification like standard text. It has a point size equal to its original height. FreeHand frames the inline graphic with a bounding box, which acts as the border between the graphic and the text.

To place an inline graphic, first cut or copy an object. Place an insertion point in an existing text block and paste the object. To remove an inline graphic, highlight the inline graphic with the Text tool, and cut or delete it. With an inline graphic selected, Graphic element appears in the Effects pop-up in the Text Character inspector.

Inline graphics retain their original graphic attributes when placed in a text block. Operations altering strokes and fills do not affect inline graphics. For example, when applying a color to text, the text displays the new color but the inline graphic remains unchanged.

To use text blocks or text attached to paths as inline graphics, group them before copying and pasting them in the destination text block. Otherwise, the text appears as individual characters when pasted.

"With hym ther was a gentil Pardoner Of Rouncivale, his freend and his compeer, That streight was comen fro the court of Rome. Ful loude he soong 'Com hider, love, to me!' This Somonour bar to hym a stif burdoun, Was nevere trompe of half so greet

Create drop caps using inline graphics.

Positioning inline graphics

After selecting an inline graphic and the surrounding text, use the Text menu, Text inspectors, or Text toolbar to adjust the leading, horizontal scale, range kerning, and baseline shift.

Leading—By default, FreeHand places the bottom of an inline graphic even with the baseline of text and adjusts the leading at the insertion point to accommodate the graphic's height.

Kerning—An inline graphic joins the text character immediately following it. Applying a negative kerning value moves text closer to the graphic. Applying a positive value moves text farther away from the graphic.

Baseline shift—Applying a negative baseline shift moves the inline graphic below the baseline of the surrounding text; applying a positive baseline shift moves it above the baseline of the surrounding text.

Text wrap—Text wraps flush with the graphic's left edge, leaving a slight space at the right edge, in respect to the inline graphic's bounding box.

To modify text wrap, apply Standoff values to the inline graphic. To apply Standoff values with the graphic in the text block, select the inline graphic and choose Edit from the Effects pop-up in the Text Character inspector to display the Run Around Selection dialog box. Enter values.

Graphic along a path—To flow a graphic along a path, paste an object at the insertion point of text on a path.

These graphics flow along a path.

Transforming inline graphics

Applying a Transform function—Move, Rotate, Scale, Skew, or Reflect—to an inline graphic affects the entire text block. Transform the inline graphic before pasting it in the text block for the graphic to retain its assigned attributes. An inline graphic pasted into a transformed text block assumes the text's transformation.

Editing text and text attributes

An inline graphic appears in the Text Editor as a black dot. The black dot acts only as a placeholder when editing text.

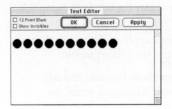

A black dot represents each inline graphic in the Text Editor.

The following are editable attributes of an inline graphic: point size, paragraph spacing, word and letter spacing, baseline shift, alignment, leading, and horizontal scale. Changing the font or type style or applying a text effect does not affect the inline graphic.

When adding an inline graphic to a paragraph, a plus (+) sign appears next to the name of the assigned paragraph style in the Styles panel to indicate an override. Removing this override reduces or enlarges the inline graphic proportionally to match the font size specified in the style. After applying the style, changing the font size of the graphic only approximates its original size.

To edit a paragraph style without altering inline graphics:

1 Deselect all objects. Select a style name on the Styles panel.

2 Choose Edit from the Options pop-up in the Styles panel to display the Edit Style dialog box, change the settings, and click OK.

The new settings apply to the text in the text block, but not to the inline graphic.

To learn more about how to create and edit paragraph styles, see "Managing styles" on page 87.

Applying text effects

To apply a text effect, place an insertion point with the Text tool or select text blocks with the Pointer tool. Choose one of the six available effects from Text > Effect or the Effects pop-up in the Text Character inspector.

To apply an effect using the default settings, choose an effect from the Effects pop-up. To edit the settings, choose Edit from the Effects pop-up to display the Effect dialog box. To display a dialog box and edit settings before applying an effect, choose from the Text > Effect menu commands. The Shadow effect has no settings.

Text effects

Effect	Displays
Highlight	FreeHand
Inline	FreeHand
Shadow	FreeHand
Strikethrough	FreeHand
Underline	FreeHand
Zoom	FreeHand

To speed printing, use the Zoom effect sparingly. It takes longer to print.

Note: The Graphic element effect is used for inline graphics only. For a full description of options available in each Effect dialog box, see FreeHand Help.

If text effects do not display on screen, check the Redraw > "Display text effects" preference. To speed redraw, assign effects after typing text, or work in Keyline mode.

To find and select text with effects:

1   Choose Edit > Find & Replace > Graphics to display the Find & Replace Graphics panel. Display the Select panel and choose Text effect from the Attribute pop-up.

2   From the Effects pop-up, choose an effect to find a specific effect or choose Any effect to locate all effects.

3   Choose Selection, Page, or Document from the Change in pop-up to define the scope of the search.

4   Click Find to select text with the specified effect applied.

This function supports selection of the text effect, but not editing the settings of the applied effect or replacing one effect with another.

Advanced text handling

Spacing and aligning words and characters

Enter values to change the width of characters in proportion to the type size.

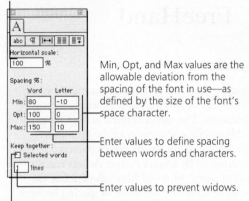

Min, Opt, and Max values are the allowable deviation from the spacing of the font in use—as defined by the size of the font's space character.

Enter values to define spacing between words and characters.

Enter values to prevent widows.

Check to prevent selected works from breaking at the end of a line.

Text Spacing Inspector

Note: A widow is a word or part of a word that occupies the last line of a paragraph. An orphan is the last word or part of a word in a paragraph that occupies the first line of a column.

Scaling text horizontally

Adjust the horizontal scale of selected text to make the text wider or narrower without changing the text's height. Scaling modifies the character shapes but not the character spacing.

To scale characters horizontally:

1   Select text or a text block.

2   Enter a percentage value in the Horizontal scale entry field in the Text Spacing inspector and press Return.

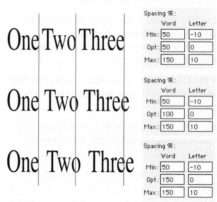

Adjusting Word spacing

Spacing

Spacing % in the Text Spacing inspector is the percentage of spacing between words and characters. The values entered in the Opt entry fields specify a percentage of the optimum spacing values for words and characters determined by a font's design. As text reaches the end of a line, Min and Max values define the range of allowable deviation of spacing between words or characters as measured from the entered Opt values. To apply only Opt values, enter the same value in the Min and Max entry fields.

To adjust the amount of space between words, enter positive values in the Word entry fields. To adjust the amount of space between letters in text, enter positive or negative values in the Letter entry fields.

Adjusting word spacing changes the amount of space between words in a text block without affecting range kerning. Apply character-level spacing attributes by kerning or range kerning.

Note: Entering minimum letter or word values that are less than the optimum values automatically adjusts the spacing for right-justified text down to the minimum. As a result, right-justified text could have tighter spacing than intended.

Keeping words together

Use the Keep together options in the Text Spacing inspector to prevent text from breaking in undesirable ways when it reaches the end of a line, column, or text block.

To keep selected words together, select text and check the Selected words option to prevent text from breaking at the end of a line and creating a widow, a word appearing alone in the last line of a paragraph.

To achieve the same effect, choose Text > Special Characters > Nonbreaking Space to insert an invisible character that prevents words from separating at the end of a line.

Keeping lines together

To keep a specified number of lines together, place an insertion point, enter a number in the Lines entry field in the Text Spacing inspector, and press Return to keep text from breaking at the end of a paragraph or at the end of a text block in a group of linked text blocks.

Enter a value of at least 2 to prevent the first or last line of a paragraph from breaking and leaving a single line at the bottom or at the top of a column.

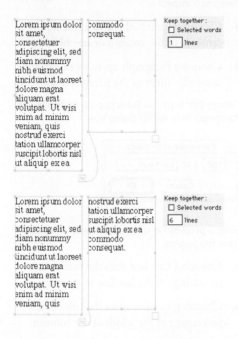

Spacing and aligning paragraphs

Setting paragraph spacing and adding rules

To enhance page layout, use space or page ornaments to create visual breaks between paragraphs.

- Insert paragraph spacing to add space above or below paragraphs.

- Apply indents to create margins between text and the left or right edges of a column or a text block.

- Apply paragraph rules or lines below paragraphs for a stronger visual break.

To add spacing above and below a paragraph:

1 Place an insertion point and display the Text Paragraph inspector.

2 Enter values in the Above and Below entry fields.

The larger the value entered, the greater the amount of space between the paragraph and the one above or below it.

"With hym ther was a gentil Pardoner Of Rouncivale, his freend and his compeer, That streight was comen fro the court of Rome. Ful loude he soong 'Com hider, love, to me!' This Somonour bar to hym a stif burdoun, Was nevere trompe of half so greet a soun. This pardoner hadde heer as yelow as wex, But smothe it

Paragraph spacing:
Above: 0
Below: 0

"With hym ther was a gentil Pardoner Of Rouncivale, his freend and his compeer,

That streight was comen fro the court of Rome. Ful loude he soong 'Com hider, love, to me!'

This Somonour bar to hym a stif burdoun, Was nevere trompe of half so greet a soun. This pardoner hadde heer as yelow as wex, But smothe it

Paragraph spacing:
Above: 10
Below: 10

To create paragraph margins:

1 Place an insertion point.

2 Enter values in the Left and Right entry fields in the Text Paragraph inspector.

Positive numbers place text inside the column or text block, and negative numbers place text outside the column or text block.

"With hym ther was a gentil Pardoner Of Rouncivale, his freend and his compeer, That streight was comen fro the court of Rome. Ful loude he soong 'Com hider, love, to me!' This Somonour bar to hym a stif burdoun, Was nevere trompe of half so greet a soun. This pardoner hadde heer as yelow as wex, But smothe it

"With hym ther was a gentil Pardoner Of Rouncivale, his freend and his compeer, That streight was comen fro the court of Rome. Ful loude he soong 'Com hider, love, to me!' This Somonour bar to hym a stif burdoun, Was nevere trompe of half so greet a soun. This pardoner hadde heer as yelow as wex, But smothe it

Enter a value in the First entry field to set the distance between the first line of text and the left margin of the paragraph. The values in the Indents entry fields reflect the unit of measurement for the document.

To apply and edit paragraph rules:

1 Place an insertion point.

2 Choose from the Rules pop-up in the Text Paragraph inspector.

♦ Choosing Centered places a rule that is centered in the column or text block.

♦ Choosing Paragraph applies a rule of the same alignment as the paragraph above it.

3 Choose Edit from the Rules pop-up to display the Paragraph Rule Width dialog box.

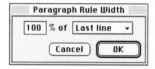

4 Enter a percentage value and choose an option from the pop-up.

♦ Choosing Last line sizes the rule to fit a percentage of the last line in a paragraph.

♦ Choosing Column sizes the rule to fit a percentage of the width of the column.

"With hym ther was a gentil Pardoner Of Rouncivale, his freend and his compeer, That streight was comen fro the court of Rome. Ful loude he soong 'Com hider, love, to me!' This Somonour bar to hym a stif burdoun, Was nevere trompe of half so greet a soun. This pardoner hadde heer as yelow as wex, But smothe it

Paragraph rule 100% of last line

5 Select the text block.

6 Apply a stroke using the Stroke inspector to display the paragraph rules and uncheck Display border in the Object inspector.

A paragraph rule flows with its paragraph, and it is centered vertically in the space below the paragraph.

Setting paragraph alignment

To precisely control how paragraphs align and to fine-tune the length of lines of justified text, use the following: hanging punctuation, ragged width, and flush zone.

◆ Check Hang punctuation to vertically align text to text rather than text to punctuation marks.

◆ Ragged width specifies the minimum distance non-justified text spreads over a column and is expressed as a percentage of the column's width.

◆ Flush zone is a special type of ragged width—it specifies the justification of the last line of a paragraph. As with ragged width, the flush zone value is a percentage of the column's width.

To apply hanging punctuation:

1 Select text or text blocks.

2 Check Hang punctuation in the Text Paragraph inspector to position punctuation marks outside the text block margins.

Text now aligns independently of the following punctuation marks:

' ' " " . , : ; ' '

With hym ther was a gentil
Pardoner Of Rouncivale, his
freend and his compeer,

☒ Hang punctuation

Hyphenation

Click the Hyphenate Edit button in the Text Paragraph inspector to display a dialog box of variables used when hyphenating paragraphs. On the Macintosh, choose the current dictionary from a pop-up listing the installed language dictionaries. In Windows, the pop-up shows only one language at time. With Hyphenate checked, FreeHand applies hyphenation according to the selected dictionary.

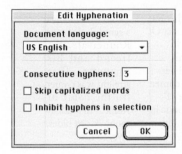

To set the limit for consecutive hyphens within a paragraph, enter a number in the Consecutive hyphens entry field. Check Skip capitalized words to prevent hyphenation of capitalized words. To override hyphenation in selected text, check Inhibit hyphens in selection. To prohibit hyphenation altogether, uncheck Hyphenate.

To set hyphenation points manually, choose Text > Special Characters > Discretionary Hyphen, or use Command-[hyphen] (Macintosh) or Control-Shift-[hyphen] (Windows). With selected paragraphs, check Hyphenate to turn on hyphenation on a per-paragraph basis.

To adjust ragged width:

1 Select text or text blocks.

2 Click the Edit button in the Text Character inspector to display the Edit Alignment dialog box.

—Edit button

3 Enter a percentage value in the Ragged width entry field and click OK.

> "With hym ther was a gentil Pardoner Of Rouncivale, his freend and his computyr, That streight was comen fro the court of Rome. Ful loude he soong 'Com hider, love, to me!'

Ragged width of 0

> "With hym ther was a gentil Pardoner Of Rouncivale, his freend and his computyr, That streight was comen fro the court of Rome. Ful loude he soong 'Com hider, love, to me!'

Ragged width of 95

Entering a value of 95 forces a line of non-justified text to fill 95% of the column's width when the line's original width is less than 95%. The last line of a paragraph and lines that already meet or exceed 95% of the column's width remain unchanged.

Entering a value of 100 creates text that aligns at both the left and right margins of the column or text block.

To adjust flush zone for justified text:

1 Select text or text blocks.

2 Click the Edit button in the Text Character inspector to display the Edit Alignment dialog box.

3 Enter a percentage value in the Flush zone entry field and click OK.

> "With hym ther was a gentil Pardoner Of Rouncivale, his freend and his computyr,
>
> That streight was comen fro the court of Rome. Ful loude he soong 'Com hider, love, to me!'

Flush zone set to 100

> "With hym ther was a gentil Pardoner Of Rouncivale, his freend and his computyr,
>
> That streight was comen fro the court of Rome. Ful loude he soong 'Com hider, love, to me!'

Flush zone set to 50

For example, if justified text has a flush zone value of 50, then the last line of that paragraph justifies to the ragged width distance only if the last line's length meets or exceeds 50% of the column's width.

To force the last line of a paragraph to justify or match the ragged width setting no matter how short it is, set the flush zone value to 0 (zero).

Aligning auto-expanding text blocks

Entering additional text into an auto-expanding text block causes the container to expand while typing. With justified as the alignment, FreeHand uses the width of the longest line in the text block to determine the width of the entire text block. When typing, each line of text fully justifies to fill the width of the longest line of text in the container.

Adjust ragged width and flush zone values of auto-expanding text blocks as for standard text blocks. Width and justification for any line of text in an auto-expanding text block depend upon the width of the longest line of text.

Working with columns and rows

To create columns:

1 Place an insertion point or select a text block.

2 Enter the number of columns in the Columns entry field in the Columns and Rows inspector.

3 Enter precise values in the Height and Spacing entry fields.

4 Press Return to apply column settings.

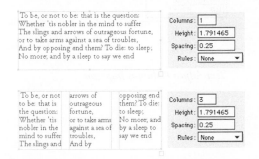

Note: When entering text, choose Text > Special Characters > End of Column to insert a character that automatically moves text to the top of the next column.

To create rows:

1 Place an insertion point or select a text block.

2 Display the Columns and Rows inspector and enter the number of rows in the Rows entry field.

3 Enter precise values in the Width and Spacing entry fields.

4 Press Return to apply row settings.

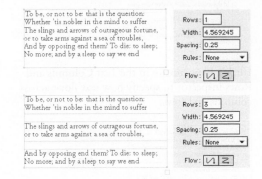

To add rules between columns and rows:

1 Place an insertion point or select a text block.

2 Choose from the Rules pop-up in the Text Columns and Rows inspector.

When choosing Inset, the rules end at the edge of the space set between columns and rows. When specifying a text block inset in the Object inspector, rules end when they reach those margins.

3 To make the rules and the text block border appear, use the Stroke inspector to apply a stroke to the text block.

Uncheck Display border in the Object inspector to hide the border of the text block.

4   Press Return to apply rules settings.

To be, or not to be: that is the question: Whether 'tis nobler in the mind to suffer	The slings and arrows of outrageous fortune, or to take arms	*Full width*
against a sea of troubles, And by opposing end them? To die: to	sleep; No more; and by a sleep to say we end	

To be, or not to be: that is the question: Whether 'tis nobler in the mind to suffer	The slings and arrows of outrageous fortune, or to take arms	*Inset*
against a sea of troubles, And by opposing end them? To die: to	sleep; No more; and by a sleep to say we end	

Click a Flow button in the Text Columns and Rows inspector to specify how text flows across columns and rows.

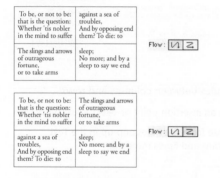

♦ Make text inside an irregular object exactly fit that object.

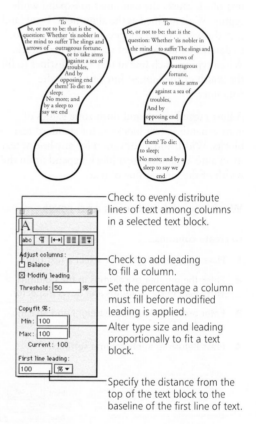

Check to evenly distribute lines of text among columns in a selected text block.

Check to add leading to fill a column.

Set the percentage a column must fill before modified leading is applied.

Alter type size and leading proportionally to fit a text block.

Specify the distance from the top of the text block to the baseline of the first line of text.

Text Adjust Columns inspector

Copyfitting text

Use the Text Adjust Columns inspector to copyfit text to fill columns:

♦ Balance text evenly among columns.

♦ Modify leading to fill columns with text.

♦ Alter text size and leading proportionally to fit the selected text block.

To balance lines of text evenly among columns:

1 Place an insertion point or select a text block.

2 Check Balance in the Text Adjust Columns inspector to distribute lines of text among columns.

An odd number of lines results in one fewer line in the last column.

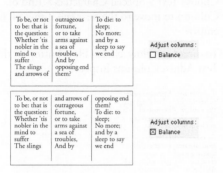

To modify leading so text fills the column from top to bottom:

1 Place an insertion point or select a text block.

2 Check Modify leading in the Text Adjust Columns inspector.

3 Enter a value in the Threshold % entry field to ignore column heights less than a certain percentage.

For example, entering a leading of 50 does not change in columns less than 50% full. This prevents a large amount of leading being applied to only a few lines.

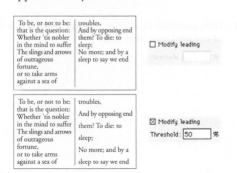

To alter text size and leading with Copyfit %:

1 Place an insertion point or select a text block.

2 Enter minimum and maximum limits for text sizing in the Copyfit % category in the Text Adjust Columns inspector.

Text and leading reduce or enlarge as much as—but no more than—the values set. A value of 100 does not change text.

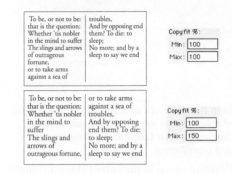

Creating tables and forms

To create a table, choose a method based on the size of the cells in the table.

◆ **Columns and rows**—Use when all cells in the table are uniform height and width.

◆ **Tabs and paragraph rules**—Use when table cells have different heights and widths.

To create a table using columns and rows:

1 Create a text block.

2 Specify coordinates for the text block's width and height in the Dimensions entry fields in the Object inspector, check Display border, and press Return.

3 With the text block selected, specify the number of columns and rows and the space between them in the Text Columns and Rows inspector, and press Return.

Entering values in the entry fields for column height and row width may scale the text block.

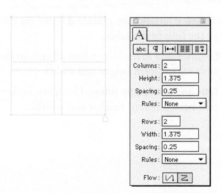

4 Choose Full height from the column Rules pop-up and choose Full width from the row Rules pop-up.

5 To make the rules and the text block border appear, use the Stroke inspector to apply a stroke to the text block.

Uncheck Display border in the Object inspector to hide the border of the text block.

6 With the Text tool, place an insertion point in the first cell in the table and type text.

Choose Text > Special Characters > End of Column to move to the next cell if the cell is empty.

To direct text flow, click a Flow button in the Text Adjust Columns inspector.

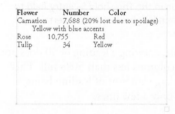

To create a table using tabs and paragraph rules:

1 Drag with the Text tool to create a text block the size of the table.

Flower	Number	Color
Carnation	7,688 (20% lost due to spoilage)	
Yellow with blue accents		
Rose	10,755	Red
Tulip	34	Yellow

2 Drag and drop tabs to set the beginning and end of columns and enter text.

Drag and drop left-aligned tabs to define the left edge of each column. Place an insertion point at the column's beginning and press Tab. Apply wrapping tabs at the left and right edges of columns that contain more than one line of text.

Flower	Number	Color
Carnation	7,688 (20% lost due to spoilage)	Yellow with blue accents
Rose	10,755	Red
Tulip	34	Yellow

3　To change the distance between rows, select text and enter values for Paragraph spacing in the Above and Below entry fields in the Text Paragraph inspector.

Flower	Number	Color
Carnation	7,688 (20% lost due to spoilage)	Yellow with blue accents
Rose	10,755	Red
Tulip	34	Yellow

Paragraph spacing:
Above: 0
Below: 0.125

4　Choose from the Rules pop-ups in the Text Columns and Rows inspector to add lines below rows or columns.

5　To make the rules and the text block border appear, apply a stroke to the text block with the Stroke inspector, and check Display border in the Object inspector.

Flower	Number	Color
Carnation	7,688 (20% lost due to spoilage)	Yellow with blue accents
Rose	10,755	Red
Tulip	34	Yellow

6　To begin a new column, insert a tab on the text ruler to define the edge of the column. To begin a new row, press Return.

Flower	Number	Color
Carnation	7,688 (20% lost due to spoilage)	Yellow with blue accents
Rose	10,755	Red
Tulip	34	Yellow
Periwinkle	1,200	Blue

Note: To create a form, follow the procedures for creating a table, but leave spaces blank.

FreeHand text utilities

Checking spelling

To check spelling in an entire document, deselect all text, choose Text > Spelling to open the Spelling panel, and click Start. To check spelling in selected text, place an insertion point, highlight text, or select text blocks; then open the Spelling panel, and click Start.

The word entry field displays suggested alternatives. Enter a replacement word when the correct word is not in the Suggestion list.

Click Start to begin checking spelling. The button label changes to Ignore. Click to ignore the current occurrence of a suspect word and continue checking.

The suggestion list displays a list of possible replacements for the suspect word.

View the suspect word and, if applicable, the type of error.

View the suspect word within the surrounding text.

Check to scroll the document view to display the found text.

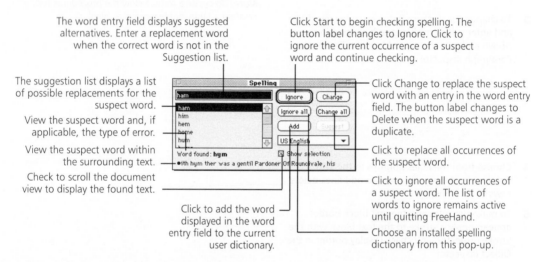

Click Change to replace the suspect word with an entry in the word entry field. The button label changes to Delete when the suspect word is a duplicate.

Click to replace all occurrences of the suspect word.

Click to ignore all occurrences of a suspect word. The list of words to ignore remains active until quitting FreeHand.

Choose an installed spelling dictionary from this pop-up.

Click to add the word displayed in the word entry field to the current user dictionary.

Choose Text > Spelling or use Command-Shift-G (Macintosh) or Control-Alt-S (Windows) to display the Spelling panel. FreeHand's Spelling panel finds and corrects spelling, capitalization, and duplicate word errors.

To add words such as company names or technical terms to the spelling dictionary in use, type the word or name in the Word entry field and click Add. If necessary, enter discretionary hyphens when typing the word.

Choose File > Preferences > Spelling to display the spelling preferences.

♦ Uncheck Find capitalization errors to ignore capitalization during spelling checks.

♦ Uncheck Find duplicate words to ignore duplicate words during spelling checks.

♦ Choose Exactly as typed so that clicking Add on the Spelling panel places selected words in the user dictionary exactly as they are capitalized in the Word entry field.

Inserting special characters

Choose from a variety of non-text characters in the Text > Special Characters menu to force returns and insert spacing in text. See "Showing non-printing text symbols" on page 178.

Note: In the Text Editor, check Show invisibles to display any text symbols inserted among the text.

Using smart quotes

Check the Text > "Smart Quotes" preference to type curly quotation marks with the straight quotation marks key. Choose from the predefined smart quotation marks in the Define quotes pop-up.

Smart Quotes options

Quotes	Usage
" "	American English standard smart quotes are commonly used in Dutch, English, Italian, and Spanish.
„ "	This style is commonly used in Danish, Finnish, and Swedish.
„ "	Low-high quotation marks are commonly used in Czech and German.
„ "	This low-high pair is standard in Hungarian and Polish to mark a quotation within a quotation.
« »	Chevron quotation marks appear as an alternative to smart quotes in French, Greek, Italian, Norwegian, Russian, and Spanish.
» «	Reverse chevron quotation marks are used most often to indicate quotes within a quote in Danish, German, and Hungarian.

The smart single quote for each style is a single character version of the double quote. To enter the single quote version of the selected smart quote, press the apostrophe key. For example, with « » chosen in the Define quotes pop-up, typing ' (apostrophe) results in ‹ ›.

Note: To use more than one style of international smart quotes in a document, change the selection in the Define quotes pop-up before typing a new quote.

Open quotes versus closed quotes

FreeHand opens and closes smart quotes as follows:

- When a quote is preceded by white space or another open quote, pressing the straight quotes or apostrophe key types an open quote.

- When the quote is preceded by a text character, pressing the straight quotes or apostrophe key types a closed quote.

Overriding Smart Quotes

To type a straight apostrophe or quote without changing the preference for the entire document, hold down Control and press the apostrophe or quotation mark key. Use this to include feet and inch marks; for example, 5' 6" in a document with smart quotes.

Note: On some international keyboards, pressing the Control key does not override the Smart Quotes preference.

Finding and replacing text

Choose Edit > Find & Replace > Text or use Command-Shift-F (Macintosh) or Control-Alt-Z (Windows) to display the Find Text panel. The Find Text panel locates and replaces or deletes any character, word, phrase, or special character anywhere in the document. Find and replace a phrase up to 255 characters long. For example, change all occurrences of "Monday afternoon" to "Tuesday morning." Convert a special character such as a white space in imported documents to tabs, or replace all double hyphens with em dashes.

The Find Text panel finds and replaces words according to the selection. With nothing selected, FreeHand searches the entire document.

Note: When Change all completes, a message appears at the lower-left corner of the Find Text panel indicating the number of occurrences changed.

To find and replace text:

1   Select text or text blocks and choose Edit > Find & Replace Text to open the Find Text panel.

2   Enter text in the Find entry field and in the Change to entry field, or choose from the Special character pop-ups for each field.

3   Check the appropriate checkboxes.

4   Click the Find button and click Change to review individual occurrences of text or click Change all to find and replace all occurrences of text in the selection or the document.

To find and delete text, leave the Change to entry field empty. Clicking Change deletes the found text.

To place a special character in the Find or Change to entry fields, choose its name from the Special pop-up list or type its code directly into the entry field.

Note: In the Text Editor, check Show invisibles to display any text symbols inserted among the text. See "Showing non-printing text symbols" on page 178.

Check to find and replace text exactly as entered.

Choose special characters.

Click to find the text in the Find entry field.

Enter text to locate.

Enter replacement text.

Check to find and replace only complete words, not text within words.

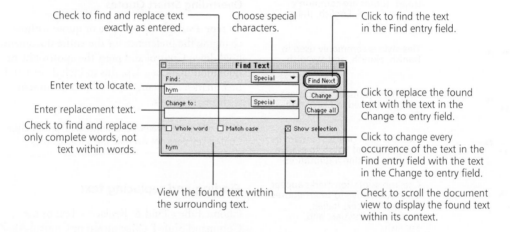

Click to replace the found text with the text in the Change to entry field.

Click to change every occurrence of the text in the Find entry field with the text in the Change to entry field.

View the found text within the surrounding text.

Check to scroll the document view to display the found text within its context.

Special character codes

Choose	Code	To find or replace
Tab	^t	Tab characters
Paragraph	^p	Paragraph marks
End of Column	^d	End of column markers
End of Line	^n	End of line markers
Non-Breaking Space	^S	Non-breaking spaces
Em Space	^M	Em spaces
En Space	^N	En spaces

Choose	Code	To find or replace
Thin Space	^T	Thin spaces
Em Dash	Option-Shift-[hyphen]	Em dashes
En Dash	Option-[hyphen]	En dashes
Discretionary Hyphen	^[hyphen]	Discretionary hyphens
Caret	^^	Caret "^" characters

Choose	Code	To find or replace
Any single character	^@	Any single letter, number, special character, or space. For example, enter "^@bc" to find "abc", "1bc", or "&bc".
Any single letter	^*	Any single letter of the alphabet. For example, enter "c^*t" to find "cat" or "cot".
Any single number	^#	Any single number. For example, enter "12^#" to find any number between 120 and 129.
White space	^w	Any combination of white space other than a single space character, including: tabs, non-breaking spaces, em spaces, en spaces, and thin spaces. For example, enter "^w" to find white space separating columns of numbers in an imported text file. Then replace it with a single tab character (^t).

Finding and replacing fonts

Use Find & Replace Graphics to locate and replace font, style, and point size. Choose Edit > Find & Replace > Graphics, use Command-Option-E (Macintosh) or Control-Alt-E (Windows), or click the Find & Replace Graphics button on the Main toolbar.

To select or replace text:

1 Display the Find & Replace panel and choose Font from the Attribute pop-up.

   To find text with a particular font, style, or point size without replacing those attributes, click the Select tab to display the Select panel and choose Font from the Attribute pop-up.

2 Choose Selection, Page, or Document from the Change in pop-up to define the scope of the search.

   On the Select panel, choosing Selection changes the Add to selection option label to Remove from selection. Use Remove from selection to deselect text blocks containing a particular font from currently selected objects.

3 Choose the fonts and styles to find and replace using the From and To pop-ups.

   To ignore the font and find and replace the style and size only, choose Any font from the From pop-up and No change from the To pop-up.

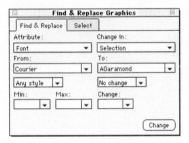

4 Enter values in the Min or Max entry fields to find or select a specific type size or a range of type sizes.

   To find or select a specific point size, use the Min entry field. To find or select a range of sizes, enter values in both the Min and Max entry fields. To ignore size, leave these entry fields blank.

5 Click Change on the Find & Replace panel or Find on the Select panel to replace or select text attributes.

   The number of objects changed or selected appears in the lower-left corner of the panel.

For more information about options available in the Find & Replace Graphics panel, see "Find & Replace Graphics" on page 137.

CHAPTER 8
Printing

Printing in FreeHand

Printing from FreeHand is straightforward even when you require high-resolution, professional quality output. Powerful, prepress capabilities include the following:

◆ **PPD (PostScript printer description) files**—
    Associate the optimized print settings for a specific PostScript printer with a document.

◆ **UserPrep files**—Work around the limitations of particular professional-quality output devices.

◆ **Print preview**—View and adjust how a document will print.

◆ **Print settings**—Customize print setup configurations.

◆ **Output options**—Determine how the final document will export or print to a PostScript output device.

◆ **Printing PostScript files to disk**—Generate PostScript files to give to your service provider.

◆ **Overprinting**—Overprint the background instead of knocking out.

◆ **Document report**—Generate a detailed description of the document.

◆ **Collect for Output**—Gather all the external images and fonts necessary for printing your document and place them in a common location.

◆ **Scaling**—Change horizontal and vertical scaling of your document when printing, leaving the original document unchanged.

◆ **DCS 2.0 support**—Generate pre-separated files for optimized printing performance.

Choosing an output device

Before sending your document to print, determine the type of output device to use based on your project requirements. Ask the following three questions:

◆ What is your final output device?

    If you require high-quality or accurate color reproduction, use a high-resolution PostScript output device available through a service bureau, commercial printer, or other service provider.

◆ What are your budget limitations?

    If you are working with a limited budget, choose output devices available at your workplace.

◆ What is your project schedule?

    An external service provider requires additional coordination.

Print to	To
A 300 to 1200 dpi desktop printer	Print initial black-and-white or color proofs of your illustrations.
An imagesetter	Print high-resolution, camera-ready art or color separations on either paper or film.
Dye sublimation or high-resolution proofing device (such as 3M's Matchprint)	Print high-resolution color proofs.
A film recorder	Create 35mm slides of your illustrations.

Page description languages

An output device uses a page description language to create an image on a medium such as paper. When you print, printer-driver software translates your document into the page description language your output device understands. Three common page description languages are PostScript, Printer Control Language (PCL), and QuickDraw.

PostScript

The PostScript language, created by Adobe Systems to meet the requirements of graphic artists, is the standard for desktop publishing. Because PostScript is resolution- and device-independent, the same PostScript language commands can be printed on different devices at various resolutions. Many FreeHand features use PostScript capabilities, including overprinting, Custom strokes and fills, PostScript strokes and fills, Textured fills, and halftone screens.

PostScript has three versions, Level 1, Level 2, and PostScript 3. Your FreeHand document will print with either Level 2 or PostScript 3, but will print more accurately when both the printer output device and the installed printer-driver software support PostScript Level 2. PostScript Level 2 includes support for more complex graphics than Level 1 as well as faster printing of bitmap graphics, patterns, and halftones.

PCL and QuickDraw

PCL, developed for MS-DOS compatible computers by Hewlett Packard, and QuickDraw, developed for the Macintosh by Apple Computer, are general-purpose page description languages. Despite wide use, PCL and QuickDraw lack support for many features required by professional graphic artists.

Effects available only through the PostScript language, such as PostScript strokes and fills or EPS files, will not print to a non-PostScript output device. A general rule is a non-PostScript output device prints only what you see on your monitor.

Setting up to print (Macintosh)

The printer driver software you select determines the options you see in the Print dialog box. FreeHand supports printing with LaserWriter driver 8.4 or later. Choose File > Print, use Command-P, or click the Print button on the Main toolbar to display the Print dialog box.

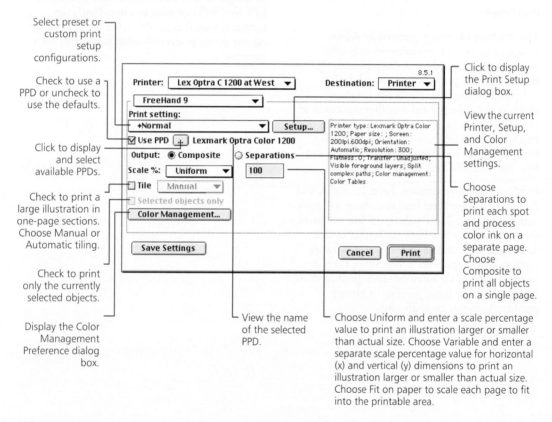

Select preset or custom print setup configurations.

Check to use a PPD or uncheck to use the defaults.

Click to display and select available PPDs.

Check to print a large illustration in one-page sections. Choose Manual or Automatic tiling.

Check to print only the currently selected objects.

Display the Color Management Preference dialog box.

Click to display the Print Setup dialog box.

View the current Printer, Setup, and Color Management settings.

Choose Separations to print each spot and process color ink on a separate page. Choose Composite to print all objects on a single page.

View the name of the selected PPD.

Choose Uniform and enter a scale percentage value to print an illustration larger or smaller than actual size. Choose Variable and enter a separate scale percentage value for horizontal (x) and vertical (y) dimensions to print an illustration larger or smaller than actual size. Choose Fit on paper to scale each page to fit into the printable area.

This dialog box appears when using the PostScript LaserWriter driver version 8.5.1.

To further customize your printing and output settings, display the following dialog boxes from the main Print dialog box:

◆ **Print Setup**—Preview your document before printing and choose paper sizes, ink settings, and other prepress options.

◆ **Color Management Preferences**—Any changes made in this dialog box are reflected in the Colors panel of the Preferences dialog box. Color Management preferences are not saved as part of the Print setting. For more information see Chapter 9, "Color Management."

Printing to a non-PostScript printer

When you select a non-PostScript printer in the Chooser, the options vary depending upon the printer you choose.

Choose File > Print, use Command-P, or click the Print button on the Main toolbar to display the Print dialog box. Choose File > Page Setup to display the Page Setup dialog box and customize your printing options.

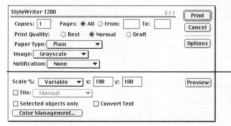

The options above the line are determined by the printer driver. The options below the line are FreeHand specific.

Common non-PostScript printer options

Use	To
Quality	Determine the quality of output.
Pages	Print the entire document or a specific page range.
Copies	Specify the number of printed copies.
Print Back to Front	Determine the order in which to print your document pages.
Print in Grayscale	Print a color document in grayscale.
Scale (FreeHand specific)	Print an illustration larger or smaller than actual size (Uniform); print an illustration with horizontal (x) and vertical (y) dimensions that are larger or smaller than actual size (Variable); scale each page to fit into the printable area (Fit on paper).
Tile (FreeHand specific)	Print a large illustration in one-page sections. Choose from Manual or Automatic tiling.
Selected objects only (FreeHand specific)	Print only the currently selected objects.
Convert Text	Convert text to objects during print time.
Color Management (FreeHand specific)	Display the Color Management Preferences dialog box.
Preview (FreeHand specific)	Display the Print Preview dialog box.

Setting up to print (Windows)

The printer driver software you select determines the options you see in the Print dialog box. Choose File > Print, use Control-P, or click the Print button on the Main toolbar to display the Print dialog box.

Print the entire document, the current page, a specific page range, or only selected objects.

View the current system printer. Choose from available printers. FreeHand saves the choice within the document or template.

Specify the number of printed copies.

Choose Separations to print each spot and process color ink on a separate page. Choose Composite to print all objects on a single page.

Choose preset or custom print setup configurations.

Click to display and choose from available PPDs.

Check to use a PPD or uncheck to use defaults.

View the name of the selected PPD when Use PPD is checked.

Display the Color Management Preference dialog box.

Choose Uniform and enter a scale percentage value to print an illustration larger or smaller than actual size. Choose Variable and enter a separate scale percentage value for horizontal (x) and vertical (y) dimensions to print an illustration larger or smaller than actual size. Choose Fit on paper to scale each page to fit into the printable area.

Click to display the Print Setup dialog box.

Check Print to file to create a PostScript file.

View the current settings chosen in the Print Setup, Output Options, and Color Management dialog boxes.

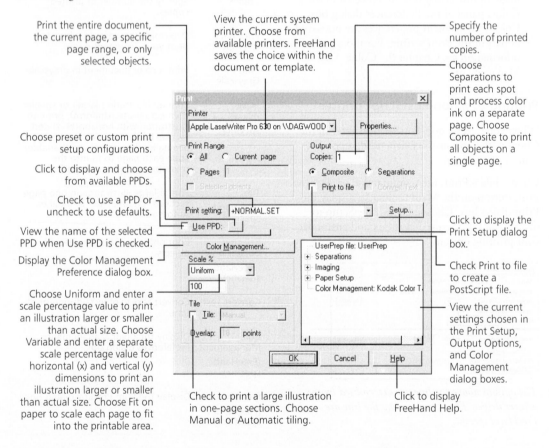

Check to print a large illustration in one-page sections. Choose Manual or Automatic tiling.

Click to display FreeHand Help.

This dialog box appears when printing to a PostScript printer.

To further customize your printing and output settings, display the following dialog boxes from the main Print dialog box:

◆ **Printer Properties**—Options in this system-level dialog box vary depending upon the printer selected. The most common options are changing orientation and paper size.

♦ **Print Setup**—Preview your document before printing and choose paper sizes, ink settings, and other prepress options.

♦ **Color Management Preferences**—Any changes made in this dialog box are reflected in the Colors panel of the Preferences dialog box. Color Management Preferences options are not saved as part of the Print setting. For more information, see Chapter 9, "Color Management."

Printing to a non-PostScript printer

Choose a non-PostScript printer in one of the following locations:

♦ From the available Printer pop-up in the Print dialog box

♦ From the File > Printer Setup dialog box

♦ From the Windows operating system

Note: For more about choosing a printer, please consult your operating system help.

Choose File > Print, use Control-P, or click the Print button on the Main toolbar to display the Print dialog box.

Print the entire document, the current page, a specific page range, or only selected objects.

View the current system printer. Choose from available printers. FreeHand saves the choice within the document or template.

Display printer properties for the current printer.

Specify the number of printed copies.

Convert text to objects during print time.

Display the Color Management Preference dialog box.

Display the Print Preview dialog box.

Choose Uniform and enter a scale percentage value to print an illustration larger or smaller than actual size. Choose Variable and enter a separate scale percentage value for horizontal (x) and vertical (y) dimensions to print an illustration larger or smaller than actual size. Choose Fit on paper to scale each page to fit into the printable area.

Check Print to file to create an output file.

Click to display the FreeHand Help.

Check to print a large illustration in one-page sections. Choose Manual or Automatic tiling.

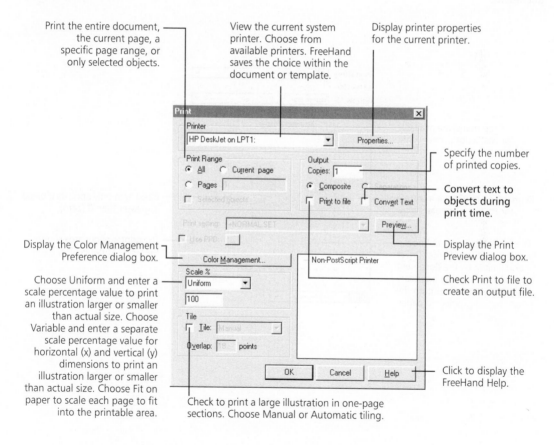

Using print preview

Use print preview to see and adjust how your document will print with the current print settings on the paper you have selected. Choose File > Print or use Command-P (Macintosh) or Control-P (Windows). For PostScript printers, click the Print Setup button to display the Print Setup dialog box.

For non-PostScript printers, click Preview to display the Print Preview dialog box. Check Automatic Orientation to print both portrait (tall) and landscape (wide) pages in the same document.

With Automatic tiling checked in the main Print dialog box, a text banner reading Automatic tiling appears below the preview window. Manual tiling displays your document in the print preview. Print preview shows the zero point and as much as will print above it and to the right.

FreeHand matches print preview to your output choices. For example, if you choose Fit on paper in the Scale pop-up in the main Print dialog box, print preview scales the selected page and displays it on screen at the correct size.

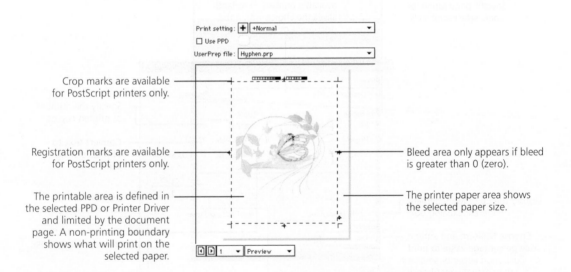

Crop marks are available for PostScript printers only.

Registration marks are available for PostScript printers only.

The printable area is defined in the selected PPD or Printer Driver and limited by the document page. A non-printing boundary shows what will print on the selected paper.

Bleed area only appears if bleed is greater than 0 (zero).

The printer paper area shows the selected paper size.

Changes you make in the Separations, Imaging, and Paper Setup tabbed panels in the Print Setup dialog box will update the preview. For example, switching from emulsion up to emulsion down causes the image in the print preview area to flip horizontally, indicating that the emulsion is now on the bottom. The negative image does not preview.

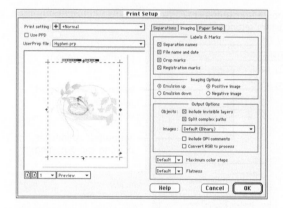

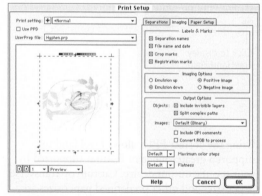

Checking the Emulsion down option changes the image in the preview area.

Repositioning your document

Moving the document in the print preview area affects where the image prints on the paper only during a given print session. The saved document is not affected.

When you point to the print preview area, the cursor becomes a grabber hand. Use it to reposition objects on the paper for printing.

The Reset arrow is displayed when you point to the gray area of the print preview pasteboard. Click with the Reset arrow to restore the original location.

Changing viewing modes

You have three choices for viewing your document in the print preview area:

- ◆ **X-Box**—Displays the page with an X and the bleed. Choose X-Box to speed the opening of the Print Setup dialog box.

- ◆ **Keyline**—Displays the objects on the page in Keyline view.

- ◆ **Preview**—Displays the objects on your page as they will print.

Setting up PostScript prepress options

Click Setup in the main Print dialog box to display the Print Setup dialog box. Choose from preset configurations or create custom print settings and save them.

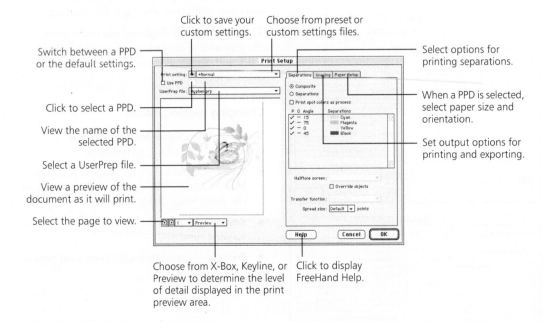

Click to save your custom settings.

Choose from preset or custom settings files.

Switch between a PPD or the default settings.

Select options for printing separations.

Click to select a PPD.

When a PPD is selected, select paper size and orientation.

View the name of the selected PPD.

Set output options for printing and exporting.

Select a UserPrep file.

View a preview of the document as it will print.

Select the page to view.

Choose from X-Box, Keyline, or Preview to determine the level of detail displayed in the print preview area.

Click to display FreeHand Help.

Choosing a PPD

PostScript Printer Description files (PPDs) contain optimized print settings for specific PostScript printers. Remedy unexpected printing behavior by choosing the correct PPD for your output device. Printing results are best when you use PPD information.

Using the correct PPD allows FreeHand to support a greater range of features supported by your specific output device. Custom or Transverse paper sizes and other predefined paper sizes are accessible. The PPD files contain optimized screen information for related printers: screen ruling settings and screen angles customized for each process ink and for spot color inks. These optimized screens produce the best possible results when printing color separations on PostScript imagesetters. Specific values in PPDs vary.

To use a PPD, check Use PPD in either the main Print dialog box or the Print Setup dialog box. Click the edit button to choose from available PPDs. The name of the selected PPD appears to the right of the edit button. With Use PPD unchecked, FreeHand uses the selected printer defaults, which limit your choice of paper sizes.

Choosing a PPD associates that PPD with your document until you uncheck Use PPD or select a different PPD file. FreeHand will use the PPD information when you print.

On the Macintosh, when you use LaserWriter 8.4 or later, leaving Use PPD unchecked uses the default information from the PPD selected in the Chooser.

Working with UserPrep files

Included with FreeHand are several UserPrep files designed to help customize FreeHand for high-end printing to specific output devices.

Choose from the list of installed files containing PostScript code in the UserPrep file pop-up in the Print Setup dialog box to modify printing to PostScript printers. Choose None to print without a UserPrep file. You do not need a UserPrep file when printing to most desktop printers.

On the Macintosh, these files are located in the UserPrep folder in the FreeHand application folder. In Windows, UserPrep files (PRP) reside in the FreeHand 9\Userprep folder.

For complete information on available UserPrep files and how and when to use them, see the UserPrep ReadMe in the application folder. The ReadMe includes a summary of each UserPrep file.

Setting up printing configurations

Choose a print setting file from the pop-up or click the plus (+) button to save your custom settings. Save your file in the FreeHand 9\English\Settings\PrintSet folder to have them appear in the Print setting pop-up.

If you have modified a print setting file by making changes in the Print Setup dialog box, a plus (+) symbol precedes the file name in the Print setting pop-up. To restore the unmodified print setting, choose that setting from the pop-up. If the unmodified print setting does not restore, the PPD has moved or is unavailable. Each print setting is a separate file stored in the PrintSet folder. To remove a print setting file, delete it.

Changes to settings in the main Print dialog box and in the Separations (ink) section of the Separations panel are not saved as part of your print setting files.

Choose from the prepress options available on the three panels in the Print Setup dialog box:

◆ **Separations**—Select options for printing separations.

◆ **Imaging**—Set output options for printing and exporting files.

◆ **Paper Setup**—Select paper size and orientation.

The Separations panel

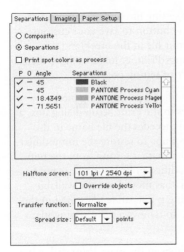

Use	To
Composite or Separations	Determine whether each ink will print on one page or separate pages. Use Composite to print all on one. Use Separations to print each spot and process color ink on a separate page.
Print spot colors as process	Convert all spot colors to their closest CMYK equivalent at print time. This does not affect the document.
The P column in the Separations ink list	Indicate a separation will print for that ink. When a check mark appears in this column, the ink will print. A dash indicates that the ink will not print.
The O column in the Separations ink list	Indicate an ink will overprint. A check mark indicates overprinting and a dash indicates knocking out. Object-level overrides are not reflected. A diamond indicates that an overprinting threshold has been set for a specific ink. Click to change the status.
The Angle column in the Separations ink list	Display the screen angle for an ink. Click to change the angle.

Use	To
Halftone screen	Display optimized screen ruling (lpi) and resolution (dpi) settings from the selected PPD file. Some devices support custom values for screen ruling and resolution. Choose Other to enter custom settings.
Override objects	Override object-level halftone settings for the current print session.
Transfer function	List available transfer functions. Use these functions to modify halftone dot values. The options are based on the information in the selected PPD.
Spread size	Enlarge the boundaries of all Basic strokes and fills to compensate for slight misregistration.

Screen ruling

Screen ruling, measured in lines per inch (lpi), is the number of lines or rows of halftone dots printed per inch on the page. A high screen ruling prints the dots close together, creating sharp, distinct colors and images. A low screen ruling prints the dots farther apart, creating a coarser effect.

Because different types of paper absorb inks differently, the characteristics of your paper and the press, in conjunction with design choices, determine the screen ruling you should use.

Guidelines for specifying screen rulings

Screen ruling (lpi)	Type of printing
65 to 85	Newspapers or point of purchase displays on absorbent, uncoated stock
90 to 133	Business publications, freestanding inserts, or newspaper coupons on coated stock
133 to 150	Menus, travel publications, or yearbooks on medium- to high-quality coated stocks
Above 150	Coffee table books, museum-quality prints, fine art reproductions, automobile promotional brochures, or annual reports on high-quality coated stock running on highly accurate presses

Screen rulings for grayscale images

As you increase the screen ruling for a given printer resolution, the maximum available number of grays decreases. The maximum number of grays you can produce in an image is 256. The maximum number of grays that can be used in Gradient fills or blends depends on the capability of your final output device and the maximum steps value.

At resolution (dpi)	Use screen ruling (lpi)	To print this many grays
300	53 to 60	26 to 33
600	71 to 85	51 to 72
1200 or 1270	65 to 128	89 to 256
2400 or 2540	90 to 150	256
3386 or 3600	150 to 300	128 to 256

Object-level halftones

To apply object-level screen angles and rulings, select an object, choose Window > Panels > Halftones, enter a screen angle and a screen frequency, and press Return. The values you enter in the Halftones panel override ink-level settings for that object. It is important to remember that a screen frequency less than 20 lpi can cause PostScript errors.

In addition to setting object-level screen angle and frequency, you can apply special halftone dot shapes. The options are Default, Round dot, Line, and Ellipse. Although you can adjust object-level screen angles and rulings for full-color images, each separation of the image prints with the angle and ruling specified. This can cause moiré patterns when printed on a commercial press.

If your output does not match the specified halftone, check driver settings such as PostScript Level 1, Enhanced Grayscale, or other printer-specific settings, which may interfere with FreeHand object-level halftones.

For example, when printing on an imagesetter that uses a proprietary screening solution, such as Agfa's Balanced Screening Technology, values you enter may be overridden by ink-level settings or may cause PostScript errors.

To restore the default settings for halftone angle and frequency, backspace to clear the entry fields and press Return.

Note: If you are having printing problems, use Find & Replace Graphics to search for object-level halftones or check Override Objects in the Separations panel of the Print Setup dialog box.

The Imaging panel

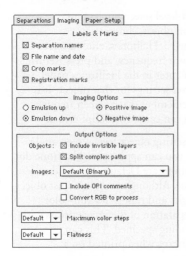

The Paper Setup panel

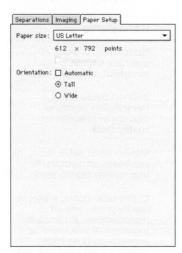

Use	To
Labels & Marks	Add separation names, file name and date, crop marks, and registration marks to output according to the options checked. Choose a paper size large enough to accommodate these marks, which print outside the border of the document page.
Emulsion up and Emulsion down	Control whether the emulsion is on the top or the bottom when looking at the right-reading side of your film.
Positive image and Negative image	Control whether the document prints as a positive or negative image on film.
Output Options, Maximum color steps, and Flatness	Adjust output options. This section appears duplicated in the Output Options dialog box displayed when you choose File > Output Options. For complete details about these prepress options, see "Choosing output options" on page 234.

Use	To
Paper size	List available paper sizes for the selected PPD. This pop-up is unavailable when no PPD is selected. The height and width of the paper chosen display below the pop-up.
Transverse	Rotate your entire document (including crop marks, halftone screen angles, etc.) by 90° on the imagesetter paper or film at print time. Transverse is available when printing to an imagesetter that supports custom page sizes.
Orientation	Control whether the document prints on the selected paper size in portrait (tall) or landscape (wide) orientation. Check Automatic when you have pages in your document with different page sizes and orientations.

Choosing the right paper size

The Paper size list displays paper sizes defined in the selected PPD file. If the selected printer type supports custom paper sizes, Custom in the paper size pop-up and the Transverse checkbox are available. Most imagesetters define regular paper sizes and Transverse paper sizes, which are paper sizes rotated 90°. When a document prints parallel to the paper path, a substantial amount of imagesetter film or paper normally is wasted on the sides of the image. Transverse pages print perpendicular to the paper path. More transverse pages fit on a given length of paper or film, wasting less media on the sides of the image.

Note: Make sure your page fits completely on the imagesetter media when transversed.

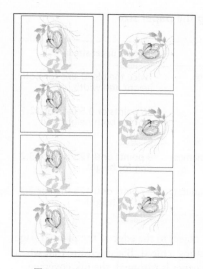

Transverse   Transverse
checked   unchecked

Letter

Custom

Custom transverse

Tall orientation

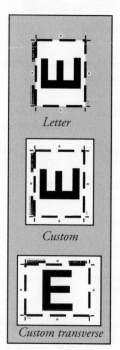

Letter

Custom

Custom transverse

Wide orientation

In general, print on a paper size that matches your largest page size. However, when printing separations, you may want to print bleeds, the file name, the separation name, and crop marks—which means you must use a paper size that is larger than your page size.

Calculating the paper size

To print	Increase paper size by
Bleed objects	Twice the bleed size for both height and width.
Crop marks	36 points or 0.5 inch or 12.7 mm for both height and width.
Separation names	9 points or 0.125 inch or 3.2 mm for height.
File name and date	9 points or 0.125 inch or 3.2 mm for height.

Printing an object to the edge of the printed page requires creating a bleed. Bleeds ensure that when the printed paper is trimmed, the ink coverage extends to the edge of the paper.

Overprinting

When one colored object overlaps another, unless overprinting is turned on, the top object will cut out the overlapped portion when printing separations. This knockout may cause a small white border between overlapping objects when printed, which is the result of misregistration. To easily identify overprinting objects on screen, check the Redraw > "Display overprinting objects" preference. O's will appear on screen for overprinting objects. Use Find & Replace Graphics to locate objects set to overprint, and to turn off overprinting for those objects.

If you want your EPS to overprint in another application, check Overprint when exporting an object with a spot color as an EPS. Otherwise the EPS will knock out the background upon placement in the new application.

Trapping is another way to compensate for misregistration. Talk to your service provider before getting started for advice on whether to overprint or trap, and which settings to use. See "Trapping" on page 230.

In general, use overprinting when you want to print a spot color directly on top of an underlying object or background color. You can also use overprinting to inexpensively add a third spot color to a two-color document. For example, overprinting a red spot color on a yellow background gives you orange in that area, without affecting the red and yellow used elsewhere. Overprinting works best when you overprint a dark color on top of a light-colored object or background.

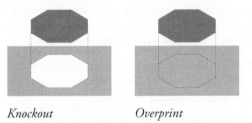

Knockout   *Overprint*

FreeHand supports overprinting the following object types:

Object	Overprinting default status	Check the Overprint checkbox in the
Text in text blocks	Black ink set to overprint	Fill inspector
Fills in text blocks	Off	Fill inspector
Basic stroke	Off	Stroke inspector
Basic or Gradient fill	Off	Fill inspector
Bitmap images	Off	Fill inspector

You cannot set an imported EPS to overprint inside FreeHand. Objects in the original EPS file control whether an EPS overprints.

Overprinting images

Set bitmap images to overprint by selecting them and checking the Overprint checkbox in the Fill inspector. A color image will appear on the process plates containing its specific color values and will overprint all spot plates. A grayscale or transparent grayscale image to which a spot color or CMYK value has been assigned will also overprint.

Overprinting works best for spot colors. Overprinting using process colors may give unexpected results. While FreeHand will allow you to overprint a grayscale image to which a process color has been applied, it is not recommended.

What you see on your monitor screen can differ greatly from the final results that emerge from your printer. See Chapter 9, "Color Management."

In the following examples, the image on the left shows a process TIFF overprinted on a process background. The image on the right shows a spot TIFF overprinted on a process background.

On the computer monitor, the two overprinted TIFFs look identical.

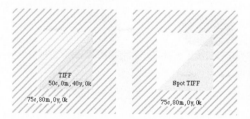

When printed, the results are very different.

Overprinting Gradient fills

Just like any other object, overprinting Gradient fills may overcome trapping problems by allowing a filled object to overprint on the correct color plates. Do not overprint indiscriminately—unless you are familiar with overprinting, it can result in a third color in the overprinted area that is not what you expected.

Check the Overprint checkbox in the Fill inspector to set any Basic or Gradient fill to overprint. The results of overprinting vary greatly depending upon the colors used in the fill and the background. You will get the best results overprinting an object with a Gradient fill on a spot color background. The filled object will overprint on the spot plate, eliminating trapping problems.

If you overprint an object with a Gradient fill on a process background, the results will vary based on the CMYK values in the background and the CMYK values used in the Gradient fill.

For more detailed information about Gradient fills, see Chapter 6, "Color, Strokes, and Fills."

Overprinting inks

To set overprinting document-wide for specific spot or process colors, set the desired inks to overprint in the Separations panel in the Print Setup dialog box by clicking in the Overprint column. Set inks to overprint for a single print session or save the overprint status as part of your document. Inks with a check mark in the O column will overprint. Inks with a dash will knock out. Inks with a diamond have an assigned ink overprint threshold.

We recommend setting inks to overprint on a document level only if you have a thorough understanding of working with separations and overprinting.

Set an overprint threshold to specify a limit for shades of an ink to be overprinted. For example, set an overprint threshold of 90% for the black ink when you want all objects that contain 90% or more of black to overprint. Objects containing less than 90% black will knock out. To set the overprint threshold, click in the O column in the Separations panel to display the Overprint Ink dialog box. Enter a value in the percentage entry field. Grayscale images containing inks with an overprint threshold will always knock out.

Trapping

When the inks used for adjacent objects print out of register, unsightly gaps or color shifts appear between the objects. Trapping compensates for misregistration by expanding a lighter object to slightly overlap a darker one.

Traditionally, trapping is a prepress task handled by a commercial printer. FreeHand's drawing tools can be used by designers and production artists to create traps. However, you may want to leave this task to prepress professionals.

Spread size is a printing option that can be used as a substitute for trapping all objects with Basic strokes and fills. As a general rule, use either manual trapping or spread size.

When considering how to trap your documents, begin by talking to your commercial printer about what needs to be trapped, who is responsible for trapping, and how traps will be created.

However trapping is accomplished, your printer should determine the trap width, which is the amount of overlap for each trap. Differences in paper characteristics, sheet size, screen rulings, and press conditions require different trap widths. The following guidelines illustrate commonly used trap widths for printing on an offset sheet-fed or web press. If you resize a document, traps you specify may be the wrong size.

Trap size guidelines

Screen ruling	Trapping values*	
lines per inch	inches	points
65	0.0077 to 0.0308	0.55 to 2.20
100	0.0050 to 0.0200	0.36 to 1.44
133	0.0038 to 0.0152	0.27 to 1.08
150	0.0033 to 0.0132	0.24 to 0.96
200	0.0025 to 0.0100	0.18 to 0.72

Note: *The lower value assumes excellent press registration when the press is off by no more than half the distance between a row of halftone dots. The higher value assumes less exact press registration when the press is off by a full row of halftone dots.

Chokes and spreads

When two colors meet, the darker color defines the visual edge and determines the direction of the trap. You can minimize the visual impact of traps by creating a choke to trap a dark foreground object to a light background or by creating a spread to trap a light foreground object to a dark background.

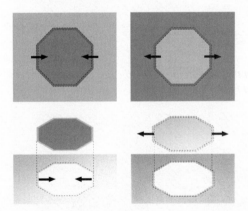

To create a choke:

1 Select the dark foreground object.

2 Apply a Basic stroke with a width equal to twice the size of the trap and use the light background color as the stroke color.

3 Check Overprint in the Stroke inspector and uncheck it in the Fill inspector.

To create a spread:

1 Select the light foreground object.

2 Apply a Basic stroke with a width equal to twice the size of the trap and use the light foreground fill color as the stroke color.

3 Check Overprint in the Stroke inspector and uncheck it in the Fill inspector.

To trap a foreground object to a dark background object:

1 Select the foreground object and choose Edit > Clone.

2 Apply a Basic stroke with a width equal to twice the size of the trap and use the foreground object's fill color as the stroke color. Check Overprint in the Stroke inspector for the stroke.

3 Choose Edit > Cut.

4 Select the dark background object and choose Edit > Paste Inside.

To trap a foreground object to a light background object:

1 Select the foreground object and choose Edit > Clone.

2 Apply a Basic stroke with a width equal to twice the size of the trap and use the light background color as the stroke color. Check Overprint in the Stroke inspector for the stroke.

3 Choose Edit > Cut.

4 Select the background object and choose Edit > Paste Inside.

For information on using the Trap Xtra to create traps, see FreeHand Help.

Printing sections of a document

Most desktop printers only print standard paper sizes such as A4, US Letter, and US Legal. If your illustration is larger than the largest paper size your printer can accommodate, use one of these techniques to print your document:

♦ Select Fit on paper or scale a page down in the main Print dialog box to fit on the printable area of the selected paper size.

♦ Use the Manual or Automatic tile options in the main Print dialog box to print portions of a page at full scale.

♦ Print only some of the objects in your document by printing only visible layers.

Scaling for print

Choose from three scaling options for printing—Uniform, Variable, or Fit on paper. The document retains the Scale selection, but the settings do not affect the scale of the original document. Print preview shows the effect of the current Scale settings.

Uniform—Uniformly scale a document's dimensions for print. Selecting Uniform displays an entry field in the Print dialog box. Enter a percentage from 10% to 1000%, accurate to four decimal places.

Scale %: [Uniform ▼] [100]

Variable—Independently scale horizontal (x) and vertical (y) dimensions of a document. Selecting Variable displays entry fields for x and y dimensions in the Print dialog box. Enter percentages from 10% to 1000%, accurate to four decimal places.

Scale %: [Variable ▼] x: [100] y: [100]

Fit on paper—Reduce or enlarge artwork, crop marks, and bleeds for print to fit the selected printer paper size.

Scale %: [Fit on paper ▼]

Using tiling

To use Manual tiling to print a portion of an illustration:

1 For each page you want to print, drag the ruler's zero point to the lower-left corner of the portion of the page you want to print.

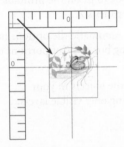

2 Choose File > Print to display the Print dialog box and enter the desired page number in the page range entry field.

3 Check the Tile checkbox to turn on tiling, choose Manual from the pop-up, and choose a paper size on which the page fits.

In the print preview window, use the grabber hand to adjust the position of the tile.

To use Manual tiling to print multiple pages of a document on a single page:

Use this technique to print all pages of a document containing small custom pages such as business cards on a single sheet of paper or strip of imagesetter film.

1 With the rulers displayed, select the upper-right page in your document to make it the active page.

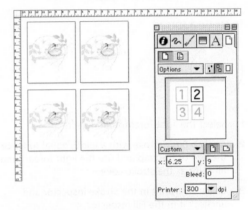

2 Drag the ruler's zero point to the lower-left corner of the lower-left page in the document.

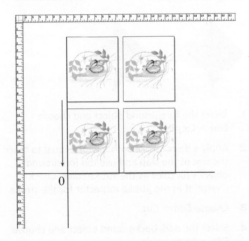

3 Choose File > Print to display the Print dialog box and enter the page number of the upper- right page in the page range entry field.

4 Check the Tile checkbox to turn on tiling, choose Manual from the pop-up, and choose a paper size in the Paper Setup panel large enough to contain all the pages.

Check Print Preview to make sure that all of the pages you want to print display in the printable area for the upper-right page. Use the grabber hand to adjust the position of the tile.

To use Automatic tiling:

1 Choose File > Print, use Command-P (Macintosh) or Control-P (Windows), or click the Print button on the Main toolbar to display the main Print dialog box.

2 Check the Tile checkbox to turn on tiling and choose Automatic from the pop-up.

The overlap value determines how much of the illustration will be duplicated on adjacent tiles.

Printing only some objects in a document

You have several choices when you want to print only some of the objects in your document during a specific print session:

◆ Check Selected objects only in the Print dialog box to print the currently selected objects.

◆ In the Imaging panel in the Print Setup dialog box, uncheck the Include invisible layers option and uncheck layers on the Layers panel to make them invisible and prevent them from printing.

◆ Move layers you do not want to print below the separator line on the Layers panel.

◆ In Windows, right-click a selected object and choose Print Object from the shortcut menu.

Printing PostScript files to disk

To create a PostScript file, choose File > Print and choose File as the destination (Macintosh) or choose File > Print and check Print to file (Windows).

When preparing a PostScript file for a prepress service provider, ask them which settings are best for their system before you begin.

If the PostScript file will be printed directly to an output device, make sure the selected PPD matches the output device and make sure Use PPD is checked. For prepress applications, choose File > Export to use an EPS format.

When fonts in your document are not installed on the final output device (Macintosh)

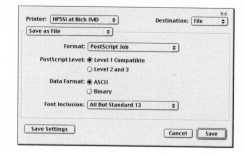

On the Macintosh, the LaserWriter 8.4 and later drivers support including PostScript or TrueType fonts in a PostScript file. To avoid PostScript errors, use this option when fonts in your FreeHand document are not installed on the final output device.

From the Font inclusion pop-up in the Create File dialog box, you have the options None, All, and All But Standard 13 to specify which fonts to include in the PostScript file. Choosing None will not include any fonts in your document, resulting in a smaller file that downloads faster. However, font substitution may occur unless all of the fonts used are resident in the printer. Choosing All eliminates font substitution, but results in the slowest download time. Choosing All But Standard 13 downloads all fonts except the standard fonts included in virtually all printers and imagesetters. Font substitution will only occur if the printer uses a non-standard version of these fonts, or if one of them is missing entirely.

Choosing output options

Output options affect a document when you print to a PostScript output device or export from FreeHand to EPS by choosing File > Export.

Choose File > Output Options to display the Output Options dialog box. The same options for output appear duplicated for convenience in the Imaging panel in the Print Setup dialog box.

- ◆ **Include invisible layers**—Check to print and export objects on all foreground layers.

- ◆ **Split complex paths**—Check to split paths into smaller sections as they are printed and exported, reducing the likelihood of memory-related PostScript errors. Paths split based on the printer resolution.

  To avoid printing problems, uncheck this option if a document contains an EPS pasted inside a complex path.

- ◆ **Images**—Choose from this pop-up to determine how bitmap image data is sent to the printer or included in an exported file.

Use	To
None	Include OPI comments rather than image data. This is frequently used with Include OPI comments.
ASCII	Encode image data as ASCII characters. This option is readable by either platform, but creates a larger file and prints slower than other options.
Binary	Encode images as binary data for use on the Macintosh. Files with binary encoded data are smaller and print faster on the Macintosh, but cause PostScript errors when printed from Windows.
Binary (Cross Platform)	Encode images as binary data for either Macintosh or Windows.

- **Include OPI comments**——Check to include OPI comments with the document when printing or exporting.

- **Convert RGB to process**—Check to convert RGB images to process colors upon output when creating an EPS or a composite. Check Convert RGB to process if you plan to print a bitmap image file to a printer that does not color separate RGB images.

- **Maximum color steps**—Use to limit the number of colors in graduated and radial fills when you have trouble converting an EPS file to a color electronic prepress system such as Crosfield, Linotype-Hell, or Scitex. The available choices are Default, 126, and 256. If an EPS file generates more than the maximum number of colors in the prepress system's line-work format, enter a number smaller than 256 until the file converts successfully. Adjust values with caution—reducing the number of colors may also reduce the smoothness of color transitions.

- **Flatness**—Enter values above zero to speed printing of curved path segments and reduce memory-related PostScript errors. The flatness value controls how smoothly curves print. Values between zero and three are barely discernible to the eye. Values above ten may result in visibly flattened curves, especially at low resolutions.

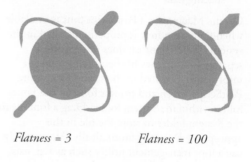

Flatness = 3   *Flatness = 100*

How fonts affect printing

Choosing the type of font is the first step in making sure the type on your pages displays and prints correctly. For production work, it is critical to use either PostScript or TrueType fonts exclusively. If you are working with a prepress service provider or service bureau, ask for a recommendation on font formats before beginning.

Use a type manager to improve on-screen text display and font management. Adobe Type Manager (ATM) is the only type-management utility that supports all of the text effects available in FreeHand. ATM requires PostScript (Type 1) fonts, but does not require output to a PostScript printer.

Working with PostScript fonts

PostScript fonts are the best choice if your final output device is a PostScript printer or imagesetter, or if you want to export your document as an EPS file. All text effects and transformations are available for PostScript fonts.

PostScript fonts have three components:

- The screen or bitmap font for a specific point size (Macintosh)

- The printer or outline font

- Font metrics—the information used to compose the font—including kerning and spacing data.

On the Macintosh, a PostScript font is available when the screen font is properly installed in the system. The Macintosh does not require a separate font metrics file because font metric information is stored in the screen font. Store PostScript screen and printer fonts in the Fonts folder within the System folder. Drag a font file to the System folder to store the file in the appropriate location automatically. Alternatively, use a font management utility such as Extensis Suitcase or Alsoft Master Juggler.

In Windows, a PostScript font is available if the font is installed using a font management utility such as ATM (Windows 95, 98, or NT) or using Start > Settings > Control Panel > Fonts (Windows NT).

Working with TrueType fonts

TrueType fonts are best if your final output device is a desktop printer, especially a non-PostScript printer. TrueType fonts retain quality when scaled, but text effects and transformations may not display or print to a PostScript printer as effectively as a PostScript font with ATM.

Bitmap fonts such as PCL (Windows) are often included with non-PostScript printers. PCL fonts generally provide a limited, non-scalable set of sizes, cannot be transformed, and do not support special text effects.

Avoid using TrueType fonts when you plan to print to a PostScript printer. If there are duplicate fonts in both TrueType and Type 1 format, conflicts are likely, and you may get unexpected results. Because identically named PostScript and TrueType fonts usually contain subtle design and metric differences, a font name conflict can result in unexpected output, such as a different line length.

Unlike PostScript fonts, all the information needed to print or display any point size is included in a single TrueType font file.

On the Macintosh, TrueType fonts are located in the Fonts folder within the System folder.

In Windows, TrueType fonts are installed through the program in the Fonts Control Panel and normally reside in the Windows folder.

Handling missing fonts

When you open or import a graphic or text file containing fonts that are not installed in your system, the Missing Fonts dialog box appears.

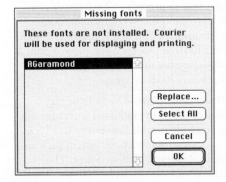

The Missing Fonts dialog box lists all fonts used in the document but not available in your system. Click Replace to choose a replacement font from among the installed fonts in your system. Choose a style from the Text style pop-up. Any missing fonts you do not replace will display and print in the default replacement font: Courier (Macintosh) or Arial (Windows). The font remains intact in your document.

The Missing Fonts dialog box will not appear if you use ATM's font substitution feature. Instead, a temporary font substitution occurs automatically upon open or import. When you import an EPS, the Missing Fonts dialog box alerts you to missing fonts, but will not replace them.

Using Document Report

Use Document Report to compile documentation for your own prepress review, or as a guide to fill out documentation required by your service bureau. Choose from among the options available to generate a detailed description of your document in a report format. Service providers can print out the report before running your job to determine the file's exact contents and avoid costly mistakes.

Choose File > Report to display the Document Report dialog box, which has nine categories:

- **Document**—Includes document-level options, such as the file name, location, and size.

- **Pages**—Includes options describing the dimensions and orientation of each page.

- **Objects**—Includes object-level options, such as assigned names and notes, halftone settings, and status of imported images.

- **Fonts**—Includes specifications for each font in the document.

- **Text blocks**—Includes options for reporting the font, color, location of the bounding box, line and paragraph count, and first line of text for each text block.

- **Layers**—Includes options describing each layer's status and position.

- **Styles**—Includes a description of each object style and paragraph style assigned.

- **Colors**—Includes options for color name, value, and separation status for each color. With Color Management turned on, your settings in the Color Management preferences appear in the report.

- **Output options**—Describes the output options chosen in the Output Options dialog box.

For a complete listing of the options available in each category of the Document Report, see FreeHand Help.

To use Document Report to generate a printed or on-screen report:

1   Choose File > Report to display the Document Report dialog box.

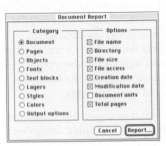

2   Click each category to display the available options.

3   Customize your report by checking and unchecking options in each category to meet your needs, or the needs of your service provider.

Hold down Option (Macintosh) or Control (Windows) and click any of the Options checkboxes to turn all displayed options on or off in a selected category.

4   Click Report to display your report on screen.

The Document Report Viewer appears, including your detailed report by category.

Collecting components for output

The Collect for Output command gathers components needed to print the current document and copies those components to a common location. Use Collect for Output when preparing a document to send to a service bureau. Collect for Output saves a copy of the following components:

◆   The original FreeHand document

◆   Each linked graphic

◆   A FreeHand document report

◆   All fonts in the document except fonts embedded in EPS files

◆   The print set file chosen in the Print Setup dialog box at the time of collection

◆   The PPD chosen in the Print Setup dialog box at the time of collection

To use Collect for Output:

1   Choose File > Collect for Output.

If you have not saved the FreeHand document, a dialog box will prompt you to do so. Canceling this dialog box stops the Collect for Output process.

2   In the Document Report dialog box, choose items you want in the document report, and click Report (Macintosh) or OK (Windows).

For more information on Document Report, see "Choosing output options" on page 234.

3   In the Save dialog box, type the name of the report file, choose a destination for the collected materials, and click OK.

All collected materials, including the newly generated document report, are copied to the location you choose.

Note: License agreements vary from font to font. Before distributing any font, make certain that the font's license agreement gives you the right to do so.

CHAPTER 9
Color Management
···

Managing colors in FreeHand

Color management is the process of maintaining color consistency throughout a workflow, from your monitor to the final product. As you design color illustrations in FreeHand, naturally you want the colors of your final product to match the colors you see on your monitor.

However, monitors display colors using additive RGB color, while printing presses recreate colors using subtractive CMYK color. Because the RGB gamut, or range of colors, is much larger than the CMYK gamut, some colors projected on a monitor can only be approximated in print.

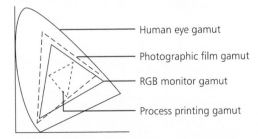

- Human eye gamut
- Photographic film gamut
- RGB monitor gamut
- Process printing gamut

For more information about colors, see "Color, Strokes, and Fills" on page 145.

Illustrations typically pass through one or more electronic devices or software applications on the way to final output. Printing a FreeHand document to a local printer, for example, involves FreeHand, your computer's monitor and operating system, and the printer. Color interpretation from one device or application to another can vary. Even colors in artwork created strictly for the Internet can vary from monitor to monitor.

Furthermore, some elements of a FreeHand illustration may come from another electronic device or another software application. One device or application's interpretation of colors may differ from that of another device or application. Even between devices or applications of the same type—or even the same brand—color interpretation may vary due to age, wear, current settings, and other factors.

This chapter describes each option for managing colors in FreeHand. To use color management, choose a Colors > "Color Management" preference option. Clicking Color Management in the Print dialog box also displays the color management options. If you do not want to use color management, choose None from the pop-up.

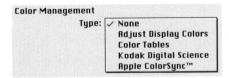

Choose from five color management options.

Note: The Apple ColorSync option is available only on Macintosh.

Adjust Display Colors—Adjust color values visually to match colors from a color swatch book or printed samples, or use specific numeric values.

Color Tables—Use FreeHand's RGB-to-CMYK and CMYK-to-RGB color conversion tables to manage colors without Kodak Digital Science (KDS) or Apple ColorSync (Macintosh only) extensions installed on your computer. The conversion tables use selected data from KDS or Apple ColorSync extensions and interpolate color values during conversion.

Kodak Digital Science—Use the Kodak Digital Science (KDS) engine to actively manage monitor profiles, separation-printer profiles, composite printer profiles, and rendering intent information to include FreeHand in your color management strategy.

Apple ColorSync—If your Macintosh computer has the Apple ColorSync color management engine, the Apple ColorSync profiles exist as an alternative to KDS.

Note: Apple ColorSync is available only on Macintosh.

Choose	When
Adjust Display Colors	Precise color matching is unnecessary but you want to calibrate monitor colors to approximate colors from a swatch book or printed samples.
Color Tables	You want to use limited color management based on KDS or Apple ColorSync data, when, for example, the KDS extensions are not installed.
Kodak Digital Science (KDS)	FreeHand is part of a strategy to manage color throughout your workflow, and you need full color management.
Apple ColorSync	Your Macintosh computer has the Apple ColorSync color management engine installed, FreeHand is part of a strategy to manage color throughout your workflow, and you need full color management.
None	Final output is RGB, web-safe colors, or color management is unnecessary.

Turning color management off for spot colors

When using the Color Tables, KDS, or Apple ColorSync color management option, unchecking Color manage spot colors disables color management for the screen display of spot colors, thereby reducing the processing time for complex illustrations that contain spot colors. Use the appropriate swatch book (for example, Pantone) to reference spot colors.

Using Adjust Display Colors

Use Adjust Display Colors to calibrate monitor colors visually to match sample output colors or numerically to match specific color values. For example, compare colors from a swatch book to monitor colors.

To match monitor colors with a printer's output, print sample colors on the printer and compare the printed output with monitor colors. This color management option is simpler than KDS or Apple ColorSync, but may be less accurate.

Note: FreeHand 9's Adjust Display Colors option is the same as the Adjust Display Colors option in FreeHand 4, 5, and 5.5, and 8.

To calibrate your monitor using Adjust Display Colors:

1 Choose a set of test colors to which you want to calibrate your monitor.

   Use a color swatch book or print sample colors from the target printer.

2 Choose Adjust Display Colors in the Colors > "Color Management Type" preference.

   The Calibrate button appears under the pop-up.

3 Click Calibrate to open the Display Color Setup dialog box.

Color management

Type: [Adjust Display Colors   ▼]

[Calibrate...]

Click to open the Display Color Setup dialog box.

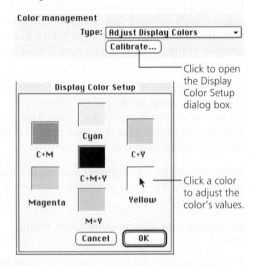

Click a color to adjust the color's values.

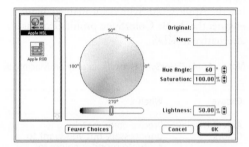

Apple Color Picker

4 Click any color in the dialog box to display an Apple Color Picker or Windows Color dialog box.

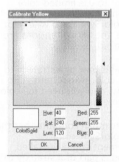

Windows Color dialog box

5 Hold color samples from the output device or color swatch book next to the color on the screen to compare and adjust the on-screen color to match the sample.

Using profiles and color conversion

Generally, a thorough color management strategy has seven steps:

1   Specify colors you want to use.

2   Calibrate your monitor.

3   Measure colors you want to use.

4   Build or specify profiles for each device in the workflow.

5   Convert RGB colors to CMYK colors.

6   Print proofs to the output device.

7   Print the final output.

A color management system such as Kodak Digital Science or Apple ColorSync ties these steps together for effective color management.

Using a color management system requires an understanding of color management that exceeds the scope of this chapter. If your task requires color management and the concept is new to you, we recommend researching the topic before using the Kodak Digital Science or Apple ColorSync option.

Building or specifying profiles

A profile describes a device's behavior regarding colors. It is created by measuring the output range of a particular color device under controlled conditions.

When a document requires extremely accurate color reproduction, sophisticated measuring instruments, such as spectrophotometers or colorimeters, and special software are used to create custom profiles for the actual devices used to produce the document. These profiles precisely map the color gamut and other characteristics of each device.

While custom profiles are the ideal approach, building them requires a thorough knowledge of color management and color management tools.

The Kodak Digital Science and Apple ColorSync color systems help you manage color in FreeHand using standard profiles approved by the International Color Consortium (ICC). Manufacturers furnish model-specific, ICC-compatible profiles that appear on FreeHand's Color Management pop-ups when the "Kodak Digital Science" or "Apple ColorSync" preference is chosen. Available custom profiles also appear.

FreeHand reads all ICC version 2-compatible profiles. Additional manufacturer profiles are available on the Internet at www.colorsync.com. Also check device manufacturers' web sites for profiles.

Simply stated, to calibrate is to adjust the device colors to match the device profile. Whether the profiles are custom or vendor-supplied, each device in the workflow must be calibrated to its profile for effective color management. However, custom profiles are more accurate than vendor-supplied profiles. Consult the device's documentation for each device to learn how to calibrate it.

Note: The Color Tables option is described on page 247.

Using Kodak Digital Science or Apple ColorSync

Use Kodak Digital Science (KDS) or Apple ColorSync (Macintosh) to integrate FreeHand with your overall color management strategy. Choose from a variety of ICC-compatible manufacturer profiles, as well as any available custom profiles.

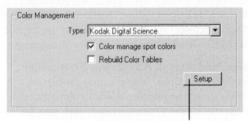

Click to display both Basic and Advanced preferences, including monitor, printer, and intent choices.

Note: System-level color-related features, such as Gamma Control, may conflict with FreeHand's color management systems.

The Kodak Digital Science option is unavailable when the KDS extensions are not in your computer's System folder (Macintosh). To restore the extensions, drag and drop a copy of the Kodak extensions from the FreeHand CD-ROM onto your closed System folder (Macintosh).

If KDS is still unavailable:

◆ Macintosh users can search for extension conflicts with other color management extensions.

◆ Windows users can run the RegKodak.exe utility in the FreeHand 9\Support folder on the FreeHand installation CD-ROM.

If either of these remedies is unsuccessful, uninstall and re-install FreeHand.

Both KDS and Apple ColorSync have the same setup options. The KDS engine is installed when FreeHand is installed. If your Macintosh computer has the Apple ColorSync engine installed, FreeHand recognizes it. If not, the Apple ColorSync option is unavailable in FreeHand.

Rebuilding Color Tables

Because FreeHand uses both the KDS and Apple ColorSync (Macintosh only) color management engines, you can specify whether the Color Tables are to be rebuilt upon changing the color management preference.

◆ Check Rebuild Color Tables for FreeHand to automatically rebuild Color Tables each time a new color management option is chosen.

◆ Uncheck Rebuild Color Tables for FreeHand to retain the same Color Tables when switching from one color management option to another.

Unchecking this option allows experimentation with color management settings without disturbing the Color Tables. FreeHand only rebuilds the Color Tables when the Preferences dialog box is closed with KDS or Apple ColorSync set and the Rebuild Color Tables option checked. FreeHand uses the Color Tables only when CMS Type is set to Color Tables and not when using KDS or Apple ColorSync.

Selecting profiles and intents

Choosing the KDS or Apple ColorSync options displays a Setup button. Click Setup to open the Color Management Setup dialog box, and then choose basic and advanced setup options.

Setting the monitor profile

Choose an ICC-compatible monitor profile from the Monitor pop-up. This option refers to the monitor you use to create illustrations.

Setting the monitor to simulate final output

In the Monitor simulates pop-up, choose from three options: None, Composite printer, and Separations printer. Base your choice on the final output device so that your monitor displays within the color gamut of that device.

For example, an artist designing graphics for on-screen display may opt for the brighter RGB colors by choosing None from the Color management Type pop-up, choosing Adjust Display Colors, or choosing None in the Monitor simulates pop-up.

Note: The web safe color library is recommended for artwork designed exclusively for on-screen display. See Chapter 6, "Color, Strokes, and Fills," for more information.

Choosing None in the Monitor simulates pop-up affects neither the monitor display nor the printer profiles. As you view your document on screen, the monitor displays colors according to the monitor profile. The CMYK colors are displayed as RGB according to the printer profile.

The monitor displays RGB colors based on the monitor profile. However, if the Monitor simulates setting is either Composite printer or Separations printer, then FreeHand uses the appropriate printer profile to adjust the RGB colors.

Setting printer profiles

When printing a document for separations output, choose the appropriate profile from the Separations printer pop-up. The Separations printer options show ICC-compatible CMYK and Hexachrome printer profiles.

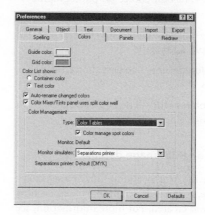

When printing a document for composite output, click the Setup button. Check the Composite simulates separations option, then choose the appropriate profile from the Composite printer pop-up. The Composite printer settings show ICC-compatible CMYK and RGB printer profiles. Choose the correct profile for your composite printer.

Leaving either the Composite printer pop-up or the Separations printer pop-up set to Default (CMYK) provides reasonable results for most printers. On the Macintosh, these defaults are built into FreeHand. In Windows, the defaults are stored with the default monitor profile. However, for best results, use custom profiles.

Setting the rendering intent

The KDS and Apple ColorSync options offer a choice of rendering intents for RGB and CMYK gamuts. Choose one of four options from the Intent pop-up:

Perceptual—The best choice for photographic images.

Saturation—The best choice for colorful artwork such as graphs and charts.

Relative Colorimetric—The best choice for illustrations.

Absolute Colorimetric—The best choice for matching logo colors.

Choosing an RGB image default

To improve the display and output of a selected RGB image, assign a device profile based on how the image was created. For more information, see "Color management of RGB images" on page 247.

Using the Composite simulates separations option

With Composite simulates separations checked, choose Separations printer in the Monitor simulates pop-up so the monitor displays colors that match the output of the separations printer. The Composite simulates separations option bases composite printing on the separations printer profile; it prints simulated separation proofs on a composite printer.

If you are proofing a four-color separation job on a composite printer, you will generally want to check the Composite simulates separations option. With this setting, proofs printed on the composite printer will more accurately match the final printed product.

Note: When printing as a composite using a device that performs in-RIP separations, as some Scitex systems do, uncheck Composite simulates separations.

Printing separations using a Hexachrome printer profile

In addition to Default (CMYK), a generic Hexachrome profile is available for six-color (CMYKOG) output when a more suitable profile is not available. Choose a Hexachrome profile to separate to six-color output. When the printer profile is a Hexachrome printer profile, the monitor displays Hexachrome colors as if the Monitor simulates setting is None, and it displays CMYK colors as if the printer profile is Default (CMYK). Colors print as follows:

◆ **Hexachrome colors**—Hexachrome color library process colors remain unchanged and print using the defined Hexachrome values.

◆ **RGB color**—RGB process colors and RGB TIFFs separate into Hexachrome.

◆ **CMYK colors**—CMYK process colors and CMYK TIFFs remain unchanged when printing as Hexachrome. CMYK colors do not appear on the orange plate or the green plate.

◆ **Spot colors**—Any color defined as a spot color (CMYK or RGB) prints on its own spot plate unless Print spot colors as process is checked in the Separations tabbed panel of the Print Setup dialog box, in which case the colors separate to CMYK values.

Naming color profiles for cross-platform use

To use color profiles between Macintosh and Windows, add a period and the three-letter extension ICM to the profile name. Avoid special characters such as a slash (/) and parentheses. When sharing files between Macintosh and Windows operating systems, name the profiles with no more than 27 characters followed by a period and the ICM extension. (For example, my_printer.icm.) This naming convention is important when assigning RGB images with device profiles.

Store profiles either in FreeHand's ICM folder or in the System\ColorSync Profiles folder (Macintosh) or Windows\System\Color folder (Windows 95/98).

Using Color Tables

Use Color Tables for limited color management without Kodak Digital Science or Apple ColorSync extensions installed on your computer. This option manages only CMYK display and RGB conversion. TIFFs cannot be individually profiled while using Color Tables.

The conversion tables interpolate color values during conversion. When FreeHand is installed, two files named CMYKtoRGBtable and RGBtoCMYKtable are placed in the System folder (Macintosh) or two files named RGB2CMYK and CMYK2RGB are placed in the FreeHand 9 folder (Windows). These files initially contain default data for the Color Tables option to use. When the Rebuild Color Tables option is checked and either KDS or Apple ColorSync is chosen, the Color Tables are rebuilt using the chosen profiles.

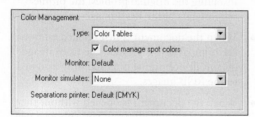

When Color Tables is chosen, the Monitor and Separations printer option choices are displayed without a pop-up. These Kodak Digital Science Advanced Color Options are not available when Color Tables is chosen. However, the options None and Separations printer are available in the Monitor simulates pop-up.

The Color Tables option is available whether the KDS or Apple ColorSync extensions are installed, but the color tables cannot be rebuilt if the extensions are installed.

To change Monitor or Separations printer options when using Color Tables:

1 Choose the Color > Color Management > "Kodak Digital Science" or "Apple ColorSync" preference.

2 Click the Setup button.

3 Change any monitor or separations printer option in the Color Management Setup dialog box and click OK.

4 Check the Rebuild Color Tables option.

5 Click OK in the Preferences dialog box.

6 Choose the Color > Color Management > "Color Tables" preference.

The newly chosen options are displayed in the Color Management area of the Color preferences dialog box.

Color management of RGB images

To improve the display and output of a selected RGB image, use the Object inspector to assign a device profile based on how the image was created. For example, if you scanned an image, assign the appropriate scanner profile using the RGB image default pop-up in the Advanced Color Management dialog box. To open this dialog box, choose the Colors > "Kodak Digital Science" or Colors > " Apple ColorSync" preference, then click Setup. The RGB image default pop-up displays both monitor and input device profiles.

The profile determines the colors that the image displays and prints within that profile's color gamut. The default setting of None displays and prints RGB images according to the Monitor profile.

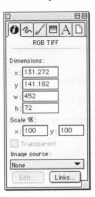

When you select an RGB image, the Object inspector shows the type of RGB image, as well as its source.

Use the Image source pop-up in the Object inspector to individually assign images with device profiles without changing the default profile in the Color preferences. The Image source pop-up is not affected by the Object > "Changing options changes defaults" preference. It is available only with the Kodak Digital Science or Apple ColorSync Color Management option.

The Image source pop-up is useful when importing several images from different sources. For example, one image may have been adjusted to the monitor in Photoshop and another image to a scanner.

Tracking device profiles of relocated RGB images

Before moving a document with profiled images to another computer, install the necessary profiles on the new computer. When the profiles are not available, the following dialog box appears when opening the document:

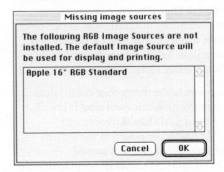

The Missing image sources dialog box lists the missing device profiles needed to support your RGB images.

◆ When the document is reopened after installing the original profiles, the profile assignments of the RGB images remain intact.

◆ When the document is first opened without the original device profiles, the RGB image default device profile is temporarily assigned to the RGB images.

◆ When the document is opened without the original device profiles and you choose a new device profile to replace the temporary default, the new device profile is assigned to the RGB images.

Color conversion of RGB images when exporting an EPS file

◆ With the Convert RGB to Process option unchecked in the Output Options dialog box, FreeHand exports RGB image colors as RGB colors. These EPS files are intended for composite printing and will not reliably separate to CMYK.

◆ With the Convert RGB to Process option checked, RGB colors export as CMYK colors according to the separations printer profile. If there are Hexachrome colors in the document when exporting, a warning states that Hexachrome colors will export as CMYK process colors.

Note: With a Hexachrome profile chosen as the separations printer profile, RGB colors separate into Hexachrome when printing, but not when exporting.

Color conversion of RGB images for printing

◆ With the Convert RGB to Process option unchecked in the Output Options dialog box, FreeHand prints RGB image colors as RGB colors. When this option is unchecked, documents will not reliably separate to CMYK.

◆ When printing separations, the RGB image colors convert to CMYK or CMYKOG colors.

CHAPTER 10
Working with Other Applications

· ·

File types

Vector graphics

Vector graphics describe shapes mathematically, retaining smooth edges and fills at high magnifications. Lines and shapes drawn in FreeHand are vector graphics.

Bitmap images

Bitmap images describe shapes using an array of pixels. Macromedia Fireworks and Adobe Photoshop are examples of applications that create bitmap images.

Bitmap images often appear more photorealistic than vector graphics. However, bitmap images become pixelated and rough-edged when magnified. Bitmap image files are often larger in file size than vector graphics, especially at greater dimensions or higher resolutions.

FreeHand can import and transform bitmap images, but cannot edit them.

Bringing files into FreeHand

Use one of the following actions to import graphics or text:

◆ Import

◆ Paste

◆ Drag and drop

The import method you choose affects how you manage and store your illustrations and imported objects.

Import

To import a file:

1 Choose File > Import, or use Command-R (Macintosh) or Control-R (Windows).

2 Select a file and click Open.

If the file selected for import contains a preview, it displays when the file is selected.

To set format-specific import options for HPGL and DXF (Windows), choose the file type and click Setup to open an additional dialog box. See FreeHand Help for further details about import options.

3 Position the import cursor where you want to place the upper-left corner of the graphic or text block.

4 Click the mouse button to place the graphic at its actual size.

Resize an imported object by dragging its corner handles. Hold down Shift as you drag to constrain the proportions of the image as you resize it.

To resize a bitmap image in specific increments based upon the printer resolution, hold down Option (Macintosh) or Alt (Windows) as you drag to resize the image.

Imported vector graphics are converted to FreeHand format and are stored in the current FreeHand document. The EPS file format is an exception. By default, an EPS graphic is linked to the FreeHand document, not embedded.

A preview of a linked graphic is placed into your document. Storing a preview (linking) rather than the entire imported file (embedding) makes your document smaller.

By default, bitmap images are linked to the FreeHand document, not embedded. To force bitmap files to embed upon import, check the Import > "Embed images and EPS upon import" preference. To embed images that have already been imported, use the Links dialog box.

FreeHand correctly imports clipping paths for both EPS and TIFF images.

Choosing a format

Most applications save or export files in several formats. Choose a graphic or text file format based on one of the following:

- The file formats supported by the exporting application
- The file formats imported by FreeHand
- Your final output device and production requirements
- Specific attributes you want to import

To import from	Do this
Fireworks	Save as PNG, or export as TIFF, GIF, JPEG, or BMP.
Acrobat	Open directly in FreeHand.
Illustrator	Open directly in FreeHand.
Photoshop	Open directly in FreeHand.
PageMaker	Export text as RTF. Export a single page by printing to file as EPS.
CorelDRAW	Open versions 7 and 8 directly in FreeHand.
QuarkXPress	Export text as RTF. Export a single page as EPS.
Word processors (Word, WordPerfect)	Save text as RTF.
3D modeling applications	Save as AutoCAD DXF or bitmap.

Note: To import from Adobe Photoshop 3 or 4, check Photoshop's 2.5 Format Compatibility preference before saving in Photoshop.

Note: EPS files exported from PageMaker or QuarkXPress are not editable in FreeHand.

Importing multipage documents

Choose File > Open, not File > Import, to import a multipage document into FreeHand 9 and retain the original document's page layout. Import by opening documents in these formats:

- Acrobat PDF
- FreeHand 5, 5.5, 7, or 8
- CorelDRAW 7 or 8
- Adobe Illustrator 7

Importing these formats using the Open command retains the multipage format. Importing these formats using the Import command consolidates the contents of all pages onto the FreeHand pasteboard.

Copy and paste

Pasting is another way to import and embed a graphic. It is most efficient for transferring objects from one FreeHand document to another. Pasting is also a good way to transfer graphics or text from an application that cannot export in a file format supported by FreeHand's other import methods.

Graphics copied from a source application and pasted into the active FreeHand document appear in the center of the screen.

Different applications support varying formats, so an application may copy more than one format to the Clipboard. The format that provides the most information about the object is placed. FreeHand pastes a vector graphic, or a bitmap, if a vector graphic is not available.

Choosing the format

Use Paste Special to specify the format in which an object from another application pastes into FreeHand.

For example, use Paste Special to paste text from Microsoft Word as unformatted text. To do so, choose Edit > Paste Special, choose unformatted text (TXT), and click OK.

Drag and drop

Drag and drop objects into FreeHand from applications that support Apple's Drag Manager (Macintosh) or OLE Drag and Drop (Windows). Some of these applications include Netscape Navigator (Macintosh), Fireworks, Photoshop, and Illustrator. Drag and drop objects from one FreeHand document to another.

To drag and drop graphics:

1 Select a graphic in an application and drag it over an open FreeHand document.

2 Position the cursor where you want to drop the selection and release the mouse button.

Results of importing

Vector graphics import as editable paths. Bitmap graphics import in their original format.

FreeHand can import the following file formats:

Vector

- ◆ Adobe Illustrator 1.1 through 7 (AI)
- ◆ AutoCAD (DXF)
- ◆ CorelDRAW 7 and 8 (CDR)
- ◆ FreeHand 5 through 8 (FH5, FH7, FH8)
- ◆ HPGL Graphics (PLT) in Windows only
- ◆ Micrografx Designer 3.x (DRW) in Windows only

Bitmap

- ◆ Adobe Photoshop 3.0 through 5.0 (PSD)
- ◆ GIF
- ◆ JPEG
- ◆ Macintosh Picture (PICT and PICT2)
- ◆ Portable Network Graphic (PNG)
- ◆ Targa (TGA)
- ◆ Tagged Image File Format (TIFF)
- ◆ Windows Bitmap (BMP)

Note: Photoshop PSD files imported into FreeHand can still be edited in Photoshop, either by launching Photoshop and editing, or by opening the original source file in Photoshop.

Other

◆ Computer Graphics Metafile (CGM) in Windows only

◆ Windows Metafile (WMF) in Windows only

◆ Windows Enhanced Metafile (EMF) in Windows only

◆ DCS2 EPS

◆ Encapsulated Postscript (EPS)

◆ Acrobat Portable Document Format (PDF)

◆ ASCII text (TXT)

◆ Rich Text Format (RTF)

Note: CGM, DRW, EMF, PLT, and WMF can be imported into FreeHand only in Windows.

Importing and exporting DCS EPS files

Use DCS EPS (Desktop Color Separation Encapsulated PostScript) files to increase the speed of printing high-resolution EPS files. Each DCS 1.0 EPS is split into five files: one low-resolution composite preview file and one file for each of the four process colors. The DCS 2.0 format is a single file containing all of the data within the five DCS 1.0 files. FreeHand can import DCS 1.0 and DCS 2.0 files and export DCS 2.0 files.

To use a DCS 1.0 EPS, import the low-resolution file from the DCS separations. When FreeHand creates process color separations, it automatically gathers information from the four other component files of the DCS EPS and outputs them to the appropriate plates.

To use a DCS 2.0 EPS, import the single DCS file. FreeHand automatically uses the low-resolution data for display and the high-resolution data for output to the appropriate plates.

To export a FreeHand object or illustration as a DCS EPS, choose File > Export > DCS2 EPS. FreeHand exports a single DCS 2.0 EPS file containing a color preview.

Import a DCS as a linked image—do not embed it. For more information about linking and embedding, see "Linking and embedding" on page 262.

Colors

Colors in imported vector or editable EPS files are not always added to the Color List automatically. To add colors to the Color List when importing an editable EPS created in Adobe Illustrator, check the Import > "Convert editable EPS when imported" preference.

Other ways to add colors to the Color List from imported graphics include:

◆ Choosing File > Open instead of importing.

◆ Choosing Xtras > Colors > Name All Colors. This adds colors from imported vector graphics by their CMYK process color or RGB color name.

◆ Using the Eyedropper tool to add colors from any imported bitmap image. (The Eyedropper tool does not work on a bitmap preview of an EPS.)

Sending information to other applications

FreeHand transfers graphics and text to other applications through these methods:

◆ Export

◆ OLE 2.0 (Windows)

◆ Copy and paste

◆ Drag and drop

◆ Publish as HTML

Export

Exporting converts an illustration into one of several standard file formats that are compatible with many applications on the Macintosh and in Windows. When choosing an export method, consider the FreeHand export formats in the following table.

FreeHand export formats

Macintosh	Windows
Adobe Illustrator 1.1 through 7	Adobe Illustrator 1.1 through 7
ASCII Text	ASCII Text
Windows Bitmap (BMP)	Windows Bitmap (BMP)
Desktop Color Separations 2.0 (DCS2 EPS)	Desktop Color Separations 2.0 (DCS2 EPS)
Flash Player Movie 3 & 4 (SWF)	Flash Player Movie 3 & 4 (SWF)
FreeHand 5.0 through 8	FreeHand 5.0 through 8
GIF	GIF
JPEG	JPEG
Generic EPS	Encapsulated PostScript
Macintosh EPS	

Macintosh	Windows
MS-DOS EPS	EPS with TIFF Preview
Acrobat PDF	Acrobat PDF
Photoshop 3 EPS	Photoshop 3 EPS
Photoshop 4/5 EPS	Photoshop 4/5 EPS
Photoshop 5 PSD	Photoshop 5 PSD
PICT	
PICT (paths)	
PICT2 (paths)	
Portable Network Graphic (PNG)	Portable Network Graphic (PNG)
QuarkXPress EPS	QuarkXPress EPS
RTF Text	RTF Text
TIFF	TIFF
Targa (TGA)	Targa (TGA)
	Windows Metafile (WMF)
	Windows Enhanced Metafile (EMF)

When exporting an EPS or PDF file to another application, optimize color consistency by converting the colors to CMYK, RGB, or both. The Export EPS and PDF Export dialog boxes have this option.

To choose a color conversion option before dragging and dropping or copying and pasting colors from FreeHand to another application, use the Export > "Convert colors to" preference.

URLs in a FreeHand document export correctly to SWF, PDF, and HTML formats. For more information on how to assign URLs to FreeHand objects, see FreeHand Help.

To export:

1 Choose File > Export, or use Command-Shift-R (Macintosh) or Control-Shift-R (Windows) to display the Export Document dialog box.

2 Choose the file format from the Format pop-up.

3 Type a file name and select the destination.

Check Selected objects only to export only selected objects, not the entire FreeHand document.

4 Click Export.

Choose File > Export Again to update the most recent exported document. Export and Export Again are similar to Save As and Save, in that both Export and Save As require a new document name, while both Export Again and Save update an already-named document.

If you choose Export Again, the Export dialog box appears if the document you are updating is not a version of the most recently exported document. When Selected objects only is checked, Export Again continues to export selected objects only.

Automatic export and launch

To open an exported file in another application upon export, check the Open in external application option in the Export Document dialog box. With this feature turned on, FreeHand immediately launches the external application. For example, you may want to open exported Flash animations using Flash or a web browser. Each export type can be linked to a specific external application, and these settings are retained for future exporting.

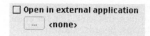

Choosing an export format based on output device

To output to	Use
Low-resolution PostScript printer	Any compatible file format. An EPS or TIFF image prints most consistently, however.
Non-PostScript printer	Any compatible file format except EPS and DCS. Avoid effects that require a PostScript printer, such as Textured or Custom strokes and fills.
High-resolution printer or imagesetter	EPS and DCS EPS for vector graphics, or CMYK TIFF for color bitmaps. Because pattern fills and strokes are device-dependent effects, avoid using them because they probably will not produce the desired results.
Slide recorder	An EPS format if your slide recorder supports PostScript, or use a bitmap image format without PostScript effects.
Plotter, vinyl cutter, or sign-making machine	A graphic saved in a compatible vector graphics format.
World Wide Web	Flash Player format (SWF) to display FreeHand illustrations as a Flash vector graphic or animation or A compressible bitmap format such as GIF, JPEG, or PNG created at screen resolution or HTML using Publish as HTML.
Multimedia	A bitmap format such as PICT, BMP, TIFF, GIF, or JPEG at screen resolution.

Choosing an export file format

To	Export as
Preserve prepress-ready color	Any CMYK EPS format.
Print to a non-PostScript printer	TIFF. JPEG. Enhanced Metafile (Windows).
Open in FreeHand 7.x	FreeHand 7.x document.
Open in FreeHand 8.x	FreeHand 8.x document.
Preview EPS on a Macintosh	QuarkXPress EPS. Macintosh EPS (Macintosh). EPS with TIFF preview (Windows).
Preview EPS in Windows	QuarkXPress EPS. EPS with TIFF preview (Windows).
Export editable text with formatting	RTF text.
Export editable text without formatting	ASCII text.
Edit in Fireworks	FreeHand 8.x document.
Edit in Photoshop	Photoshop 5 document (PSD), EPS, or TIFF.
Edit in Illustrator	Adobe Illustrator.
Create a cross-platform EPS file for use in QuarkXPress	QuarkXPress EPS.
Use an EPS file on a non-Macintosh or non-Windows system	Generic EPS.
Create a bitmap image of the document	TIFF, JPEG, GIF, PNG, BMP, or Targa.

To	Export as
Create graphics for reduced-color and pre-built custom palettes	GIF
Create a color-separated EPS for use through OPI or other client-server software	DCS 2.0 EPS

Exporting an EPS

Exporting an EPS file is the best way to preserve prepress-ready color. When saving as an EPS, consider the following items:

- **Multiple pages**—When you choose an EPS format, each page exports to a separate EPS file. Specify the page range to export.

- **Editable EPS**—Editable EPS is a special EPS format that can be opened and edited in FreeHand, then saved as an EPS without having to export. To save documents in this format, choose Editable EPS as the format in the File > Save As dialog box. This option is only available for one-page documents. Editable EPS always saves with a preview (Macintosh).

- **Fonts (Windows)**—If the PostScript Type 1 or TrueType fonts used are not installed in the final PostScript output device, include fonts in the EPS file. Click the Setup button in the Export Document dialog box and check Include fonts in EPS.

- **DCS 2.0 EPS**—When exporting an EPS for use through OPI or other client-server software, consider exporting the EPS as a DCS 2.0 EPS. The single DCS 2.0 EPS file contains a low-resolution color preview as well as color-separation data.

- **Output Options**—Output options affect export to EPS as well as printing. Choose File > Output Options to include invisible layers or choose from data formats including Binary (Macintosh) and Binary (Cross Platform). See "Choosing output options" on page 234.

To maintain color consistency among applications when exporting an EPS, use the Convert Colors to option in the Export Document dialog box to convert colors to CMYK, RGB, or both upon export.

Choose	To
CMYK	Produce standard CMYK output.
RGB	Rasterize (convert) in Fireworks or Photoshop 4 or later.
CMYK and RGB	Transfer documents to an application with a PostScript RIP, such as Illustrator 7, or Photoshop 4 or 5.

Note: The RGB option and the CMYK and RGB option are not recommended for separations output.

Importing and exporting text

Use the same methods to import and export text as those used to import and export graphics. FreeHand supports two text formats: RTF (Rich Text Format) and ASCII (plain text). RTF text files retain text formatting of the original document while ASCII text files do not.

To import text files:

1 Choose File > Import to display the Import Document dialog box.

2 Select a file and click Open.

3 Click or click and drag in the document to place the imported text.

   Click to place the text file at its original size. Click and drag to set the position and the size of the text block. Once imported, edit as any other text.

Note: FreeHand English does not support double-byte vertical text, which is typical in some Asian languages. When importing such text, FreeHand English simulates vertical alignment by rotating the text block; however, the character orientation defaults to vertical.

To export text files:

1 Choose File > Export to display the Export Document dialog box. Name the text file and choose a location for it.

2 Choose RTF text or ASCII text from the Format (Macintosh) or Save as type (Windows) pop-up, and click Export.

   Only text (no graphics) exports from the FreeHand document. Linked text blocks export in the order that they are linked. Unlinked text blocks export in their stacking order from back to front, first page to last page.

You can drag and drop text to import it and export it from FreeHand. The destination application must support dragging and dropping text. To import or export small amounts of text, use Copy and Paste.

Rich Text Format (RTF)

FreeHand preserves these attributes when importing or exporting an RTF file:

◆ Font

◆ Size

◆ Style—Plain, Bold, Italic, and BoldItalic

◆ Effect—Shadow, Strikethrough, and Underline (import and export); Outline, Subscript, and Superscript (import only)

◆ Color

◆ Margins

◆ Tabs—left, right, center, and decimal

◆ Tab leaders—line, dotted line, and dashed line (the default presets)

◆ Indents

◆ Alignment—left, right, center, and justified

◆ Baseline shift

◆ Letter spacing

◆ Linked text

◆ Horizontally scaled text

Restrictions include the following: Custom tab leaders default to dashed tab leaders. Custom Strikethrough effects default to the effect's default setting. The Underline effect supports single, dotted, dashed, dot-dash, and dot-dot-dash underlines. All other custom Underline effects default to single underline.

Replacing missing fonts upon import

When importing an RTF file containing fonts and text styles not installed on your computer, the Missing Fonts dialog box prompts the selection of installed fonts and text styles to replace the missing ones. For more information about options available in the Missing Fonts dialog box, see "Handling font substitution" on page 268.

Exporting text with inline graphics

Adhere to these guidelines to successfully export text containing inline graphics from FreeHand for use with other applications:

◆ FreeHand exports text with inline graphics to FreeHand versions 5.5 and later.

◆ FreeHand exports inline graphics to other applications as EPS export format (except Photoshop 3 EPS format), or in any bitmap format (BMP, GIF, JPEG, PNG, Targa, and TIFF).

   When exporting a file containing text with inline graphics to a file format that does not support them, bullets replace the inline graphics in the exported file.

◆ To save a file in Adobe Illustrator, Photoshop 3 EPS, or FreeHand 5.0 export formats, convert the text with inline graphics to paths before exporting.

Object Linking and Embedding (Windows)

OLE is a Windows standard for sharing information between applications. One application acts as an OLE client, or "container," maintaining the other application's objects, while the other application acts as a server, providing objects as well as editing its own objects.

FreeHand supports OLE 2.0 only as an OLE server application. Choose Insert Object from any Windows application supporting OLE 2.0. Selecting FreeHand 9 launches FreeHand and creates a new file. After updating and exiting, double-click FreeHand to launch the application and open the file.

Copy and paste

Graphics and text can also be exported by copying them to the Clipboard. They can then be pasted into other applications that can read the exported format.

When you copy an object and switch to another application, FreeHand automatically converts data on the Clipboard to the file types specified in the File > Preferences > Export dialog box.

To choose the format that FreeHand copies to the Clipboard for that copy only, use Edit > Copy Special.

To maintain color consistency among applications when copying an EPS, choose the appropriate format to convert colors to CMYK, RGB, or both in the Preferences dialog box.

Choose	When
CMYK	Using CMYK colors exclusively, or when pasting to an application that does not support RGB PostScript, such as Photoshop 3.
RGB	Using RGB colors exclusively, or when pasting to an application that supports RGB EPS, such as Photoshop 4 or 5.
CMYK and RGB	Using both types of colors, or when pasting to an application that supports both color models in a single document, such as Illustrator 8. This setting forces the target application to convert the colors.
Photoshop 4/5	Copying with the specific intention of pasting into Photoshop 4 or 5.

Note: The RGB option and the CMYK and RGB option are not recommended for separations output.

When copying and pasting into Photoshop, check the Export > "Clipboard output formats: Adobe Illustrator™" preference (Macintosh).

Drag and drop

Move objects from FreeHand to other applications that support Apple's Drag Manager (Macintosh) or OLE Drag and Drop (Windows). Some of these applications include Netscape Navigator (Macintosh), Fireworks, Photoshop, and Illustrator. Drag and drop objects from one FreeHand document to another.

The color conversion preference options described in the previous section, "Copy and paste," apply to drag and drop export as well.

To drag and drop graphics:

1   Select a graphic in FreeHand and drag it over an open document in another application.

2   Position the cursor where you want to drop the selection and release the mouse button.

Rasterize in FreeHand

When FreeHand graphics require conversion to bitmap images, rasterize them directly in FreeHand. The rasterized objects become an embedded TIFF file residing in the FreeHand document.

If a graphic is too large to rasterize directly in FreeHand, an error message appears. For more complex graphics, use the FreeHand export option. Macintosh users may opt to increase the memory allocation for FreeHand.

To rasterize one or more objects in FreeHand:

1   Select one or more objects.

2   Choose Modify > Rasterize, or use Option-Command-Shift-Z (Macintosh) or Alt-Control-Shift-Z (Windows).

The Rasterize dialog box appears.

3   Type or choose a resolution, choose an anti-aliasing setting, and click OK.

The original vector objects are deleted and are replaced with a bitmap image.

Linking and embedding

Creating a link to a graphic displays a preview. When printing or exporting, FreeHand uses the high-resolution source graphic, not the preview. Every time a document containing a link is opened, FreeHand checks the link. If the source graphic cannot be found, the graphic is not displayed or printed.

Creating an embedded graphic copies the source graphic and stores it in the FreeHand document. The same graphic now exists both externally as the source graphic and internally as an embedded graphic. FreeHand no longer requires the external graphic for display or printing.

To always embed graphics, check the Import > "Embed images and EPS upon import" preference.

Note: DCS EPS files should not be embedded in a FreeHand document.

Linking conserves disk storage space since it creates a reference to a graphic rather than making a second copy of the graphic. Linking may require less RAM because a low-resolution preview of the graphic is displayed. Updating changed graphics is easier when graphics are linked because the graphic updates automatically when the document opens.

A disadvantage of linking is the possibility of breaking links to your graphics by moving or renaming them. Graphics with broken links do not display or print until the link is re-established.

Note: Storing linked images on a network server can slow FreeHand performance.

When graphics are embedded, you do not have to have the original graphic files in order to print or view the illustration. The embedded graphic is part of the document. Embedding is useful when you want to transport the illustration without having to worry about breaking links, although the illustration file is larger with the graphics embedded instead of linked.

A disadvantage of embedding is that it increases the amount of RAM necessary to display the document.

Managing links

When linking or embedding a graphic, FreeHand records the graphic's file name and disk location. When you open, export, or print the illustration containing a link, FreeHand looks for the linked graphic by its file name. If the source graphic is not in its original folder, FreeHand looks for it in the same folder as the FreeHand document.

When moving a document to another computer or to a storage device for transport, save imported graphics in the same folder as the document or embed all the external graphics in the document.

Use the Collect for Output command to gather all components, including linked graphic files, needed when preparing a document to send to a service bureau. See "Collecting components for output" on page 238.

Links dialog box

Choose Edit > Links to display the Links dialog box, or select a linked or embedded graphic and click the Links button in the Object inspector.

Broken links

A link to an imported graphic breaks when any of the following occurs:

♦ The graphic is moved out of the folder or disk from which it was originally imported, and it is not in the same folder as the illustration in which it was placed.

♦ The file name of the graphic changes.

♦ The file's path changes, including a server name change.

View the file name.   View the image type.

View the file size.

View the page number of the document on which the upper-left corner of the image appears.

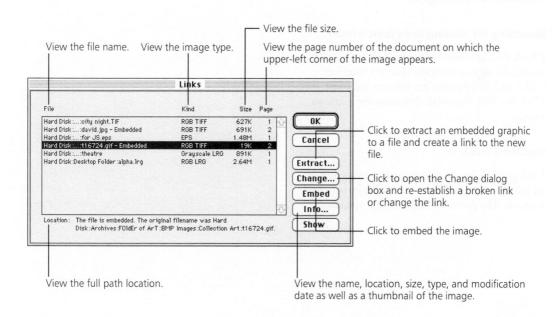

Click to extract an embedded graphic to a file and create a link to the new file.

Click to open the Change dialog box and re-establish a broken link or change the link.

Click to embed the image.

View the full path location.

View the name, location, size, type, and modification date as well as a thumbnail of the image.

Re-establishing a broken link

When opening a document with a broken link, the Locate File dialog box asks you for the new location of the graphic. To search for all missing links, select the first missing file's name and check Search the current folder for missing links. To search for only the first missing link, leave the option unchecked.

After locating the graphics, save the links to the graphics' new location by saving the document. Choosing an updated or different graphic updates the preview. Clicking Cancel in the Locate File dialog box prevents the link from re-establishing itself. FreeHand displays an X-box and the graphic does not print or export. FreeHand asks for the location of the graphic each time the document is opened until you re-establish the link or delete the graphic from the document.

The Links dialog box lists files with broken links in italic with "????" listed under Size. To re-establish the link, choose the unlinked file from the list and click the Change button. Navigate to the renamed or moved file to link it to your FreeHand document again.

Searching for missing links (Macintosh)

Check the Document > "Search for missing links" preference to automatically search a specified folder and its subfolder for missing links first. Click the Edit button to designate the folder to search.

Updating a link

Update a link by saving a more recent version of an imported graphic using the same file name and location. The preview automatically updates.

Working with bitmap images in FreeHand

FreeHand supports TIFF, GIF, JPEG, PNG, Targa, BMP, and Photoshop (PSD) bitmap formats.

In most cases, all bitmap formats behave in FreeHand exactly as TIFF images behave. Use the Links dialog box to embed, extract, or change links to these files.

FreeHand can apply Photoshop plug-ins to bitmap files. However, once a bitmap image has been modified with a plug-in, it is converted to a TIFF and is embedded in the FreeHand document. After applying a plug-in to a bitmap image, choose Edit > Links to extract the embedded image to an external TIFF file.

Grayscale bitmaps can be set to Transparent and the ramp can be edited.

To colorize a grayscale bitmap, apply a fill color.

Exporting FreeHand objects as bitmaps

To set default export options for bitmap images, choose the Export > "Bitmap export" preference. Alternatively, choose File > Export, choose a bitmap file type, and click Options (Macintosh) or Setup (Windows) to display the Bitmap Export Defaults dialog box.

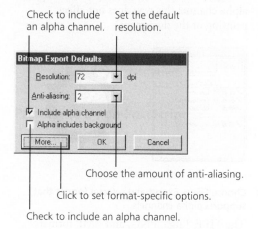

Check to include an alpha channel.

Set the default resolution.

Choose the amount of anti-aliasing.

Click to set format-specific options.

Check to include an alpha channel.

For detailed descriptions of format-specific options, see FreeHand Help.

RAM

Higher resolution and higher anti-aliasing settings in the Bitmap Export Defaults dialog box may require larger amounts of RAM when rasterizing vector images.

If insufficient RAM is available, a dialog box appears informing you that FreeHand does not have enough RAM to complete the operation. If this dialog box appears, use lower resolution or anti-aliasing settings and re-export.

On the Macintosh, allocate more memory to the FreeHand application by quitting FreeHand, selecting the FreeHand application file, choosing File > Get Info in the Finder, and changing the Preferred Size under Memory Requirements. In Windows, close other open applications to increase the amount of memory available to FreeHand.

Working with alpha channels

By using alpha channels, FreeHand can export bitmap images with complex masking and transparency for use in image editing applications. An alpha channel is a layer of a graphic that defines which areas of the graphic are transparent and which areas of the graphic are opaque.

Use alpha channels to quickly define an outline or edge of an object. This is useful when creating a graphic for a web page, or in multimedia or video production when you want to see a background graphic through areas of the image you are creating. FreeHand does not support alpha channels upon import.

FreeHand can export an alpha channel in these formats:

- ◆ TIFF
- ◆ Targa
- ◆ PNG
- ◆ BMP

Creating an alpha channel

When exporting a bitmap format that supports alpha channels, check Include alpha channel in the Bitmap Export Defaults dialog box to automatically create an alpha channel on export. The formats must be exported as 32-bit to support alpha channels. Click the More button in the Bitmap Export Defaults dialog box to choose 32-bit with Alpha.

The alpha channel is a mask or outline of all the objects on your page. When opening the image in an application that supports alpha channels, the edges of objects in the image can be easily defined.

Original graphic   *Alpha channel that FreeHand exports*

Transparency

Use a background layer to define custom areas of transparency on graphics exported as bitmap images with alpha channels.

Note: The Lens fill's Transparency option is a simple way to apply a transparency effect. See "Lens fills" on page 167.

To define a custom transparency:

1 Create a graphic.

2 On a background layer, draw the desired mask.

Use only black, white, or grays for masking. White areas in the background layer appear opaque in the resulting bitmap, while black areas appear transparent. Grays or Gradient fills appear transparent with lighter grays appearing more opaque and darker grays appearing more transparent. Because a background layer does not print, defining an alpha channel this way does not affect printing of the document.

3 Choose File > Export and select a format that supports alpha channels.

The TIFF, Targa, PNG, and BMP formats support alpha channels. For GIF files, which don't support alpha channels, see Step 4 for creating a transparency.

4 Click Options (Macintosh) or Setup (Windows). In the Bitmap Export Defaults dialog box, set the resolution and anti-aliasing. Check Include alpha channel and Alpha includes background.

Note: To create a transparent color in a GIF image, specify an index color and check Include alpha channel.

5 Click the More button, select the 32-bit format, and click OK.

Resizing bitmap images

Resize an imported bitmap image by dragging its corner handles. Hold down Shift as you drag to constrain the proportions of the image as you resize it.

To resize the image in specific increments based upon the printer resolution, hold down Option (Macintosh) or Alt (Windows) as you drag to resize the image.

Scanning (Macintosh)

Using a scanner and the corresponding Photoshop acquisition plug-in, FreeHand can receive data directly from scanners. Consult the documentation for the scanner you are using for specific instructions on settings and options. When you use an acquisition plug-in to scan data into FreeHand, the resulting image is an embedded TIFF image.

See "Working with PNG, GIF, JPEG, and PSD images" on page 267.

Launch and edit

Select an external application that launches from within FreeHand for editing imported bitmap images.

To set the external editor:

1   Choose a format from the Object > "External Editors for: Object" preference.

2   Click the [...] button, choose an editor from the Choose External Editor dialog box, and click Open (Macintosh) or OK (Windows).

To use an external editor:

1   Select an image.

2   Choose Edit > External Editor or hold down Option (Macintosh) or Alt (Windows) and double-click the image.

With the Object > "Warn before launch and edit" preference checked, a dialog box is displayed to confirm that the launch and edit command is intentional. Click OK to launch the application.

If enough RAM is available, the application chosen as the external editor launches with the selected image opened. An Editing in Progress dialog box appears in FreeHand when the external application opens.

3   After editing and saving your image in the external editor, click Done in the Editing in Progress dialog box.

Any changes made to the image automatically update the placed image.

Working with PNG, GIF, JPEG, and PSD images

PNG, GIF, JPEG, and PSD files are bitmap images. In most cases, PNGs, GIFs, JPEGs, and PSDs behave in FreeHand exactly as TIFF images behave. Use the Links dialog box to embed, extract, or change links to these files.

FreeHand can apply Photoshop plug-ins to these files. However, once an image has been modified with a plug-in, it is converted to a TIFF and is embedded in the FreeHand document. After applying a plug-in to an image, choose Edit > Links to extract the embedded image to an external TIFF file.

Note: Because PNG is an extensible format, extra data may be appended to any of these files by other applications, such as Macromedia Fireworks. Since that data is specific to the application in which the file was created, FreeHand will ignore, but not delete, any such data.

When opening a Fireworks source PNG file in FreeHand, the extra data is not imported; only the bitmap data is imported.

Handling font substitution

Replacing missing fonts

The Missing Fonts dialog box appears when FreeHand opens or imports a graphic containing fonts that are not installed in the system. From this dialog box, replace a missing font with a font installed in your system. When fonts are replaced, the text of the replaced font loses all the manual kerning data that was applied. Although most fonts exist for both Macintosh and Windows, fonts may need to be respecified when you transfer the illustration.

Choose	To
Replace	Replace missing fonts originally contained in the document but not currently installed.
	The Replace Font dialog box opens, letting you select a replacement font and style.
Select all	Select all of the missing fonts in the Missing Fonts dialog box and replace them all with one font.
Cancel	Cancel the opening of the document.
OK	Allow the document to be opened without replacing fonts. The missing fonts are temporarily displayed and printed in system default fonts.

Automatic font substitution

The Missing Fonts dialog box does not appear if you use Adobe Type Manager's (ATM) font substitution feature. Instead, a temporary substitution occurs when the illustration is opened.

Using ATM's font substitution feature

ATM automatically applies each missing font's metrics and weight to a multiple master font, and marks the font name with a diamond in the font menu. Line breaks and word spacing are preserved, but the subtleties of the letter forms may be lost.

If you are concerned about typography, open the ATM control panel and uncheck Enable Font Substitution (Macintosh only).

Xtras

Using the PDF Import and Export Xtras

FreeHand can open PDF documents that contain Acrobat notes (sometimes called annotations) and hotspots linked to URLs on the web and export FreeHand documents to PDF that contain notes, envelopes, symbols, embedded fonts, gradients, and links to URLs.

Managing conversion upon import

By default, Acrobat notes are imported to a separate layer called the Notes layer. If the path cannot be discerned, URLs are imported to a separate URLs layer. If you don't want to import notes or URLs, deselect them on the File > Preferences > Import panel.

FreeHand imports its own linear and radial PostScript 3 gradient fills. PostScript 3 gradient mesh fills are imported as 10% black fills. Hotspot annotations are imported as rectangles on the URLs layer.

Managing text conversion upon import

The PDF Import Xtra does not provide automatic font substitution. When fonts specified in the PDF file are not present on your computer, the Missing Fonts dialog box appears and provides the option to select replacement fonts. As is always the case when substituting fonts, the appearance of the converted document may differ from the original.

The PDF Import Xtra supports all font formats allowed by PDF. These include PostScript Type 1 and TrueType fonts.

Some PDF documents contain a large number of individual text blocks. This is a normal occurrence resulting from the manner in which the PDF creation tool structured the original PDF document. After opening a PDF in FreeHand, consolidate the text blocks using FreeHand's text manipulation methods.

When exporting a FreeHand document to PDF format, check Editable text format on the PDF Export dialog box so the text retains its original formatting when imported back into FreeHand. If Editable text format is unchecked, text imports in several blocks.

Managing graphic conversion upon import

PDF supports RGB, grayscale, and monochrome bitmap images. RGB colors are not converted to CMYK upon import. Modify these images just like any placed or imported bitmap image. EPS objects in a PDF document open as editable objects.

Depending on the structure of the original PDF document, an entire page may appear as a single object with the graphic objects pasted inside. Select the objects and choose Edit > Cut Contents to release them.

Exporting PDFs

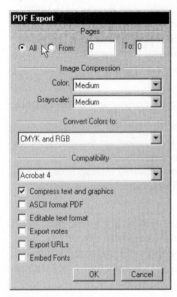

PDF Export Options

Use	To
Pages	Specify pages for export.
Image Compression	Compress the bitmap image using JPEG compression.
Convert Colors to	Determine the color conversion: CMYK only, RGB only, or both.
Compatibility	Determine PDF type for export: Acrobat version.
	Determine whether to include notes and URLs to other objects and pages within the same document.
	Determine whether to imbed fonts.

To export a PDF file:

1   Choose File > Export to display the Export Document dialog box, and choose PDF from the Format (Macintosh) or Save as type (Windows) pop-up to display the Export Document dialog box.

2   Click Options (Macintosh) or Setup (Windows) to display the PDF Export dialog box. Set options and click OK.

Specify the number of pages, image compression, color conversion, and compatibility.

3   Name the file, and click Export in the Export Document dialog box.

Notes, URLs, and fonts

To export notes, links to URLs, or embedded fonts, choose what you want to export on the Export Options dialog box.

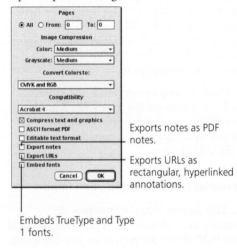

Exports notes as PDF notes.

Exports URLs as rectangular, hyperlinked annotations.

Embeds TrueType and Type 1 fonts.

Image compression

The compression level of your bitmap images affects the PDF file's size and quality of printing. Higher compression levels yield smaller file sizes but result in printed bitmap images of a lower quality. Little or no compression yields larger documents that print with higher quality.

When designing a PDF document for print, choose little or no compression. When designing a PDF document for on-screen display, choose higher levels of compression.

Color conversion

Choose a setting in the Convert Colors to pop-up to export a PDF document with a color gamut suited for on-screen or print media.

Choose	To
RGB	Force document colors to convert to RGB for on-screen viewing. For example, use a bitmap editing application to edit images in a FreeHand PDF file for output to the Internet.
CMYK	Force document colors to convert to CMYK for printing color separations. For example, import a FreeHand PDF file into QuarkXPress for four-color output.
CMYK and RGB	Maintain the integrity of both RGB and CMYK colors for on-screen output or for import into other applications. For example, import a FreeHand PDF file into Adobe Illustrator.

Acrobat compatibility

The Acrobat-compatible format determines which options are available.

♦ Acrobat 3 and 4 support compressed text and graphics, the ASCII text format, notes, URLs, and the Editable text format.

♦ Acrobat 2 supports ASCII format and Editable text format.

♦ Acrobat 1 imposes the ASCII format. Other options are not available.

With ASCII format checked, documents are exported as 7-bit. With ASCII unchecked, documents are exported as 8-bit. Check this option if problems occur when sharing PDF files on older networks and e-mail systems.

In general, leave Editable text format unchecked for read-only output, whether on screen or in print. Check this option only when you plan to edit the document in FreeHand or Adobe Illustrator after exporting it to PDF. Checking this option yields a larger PDF document.

For export limitations, see FreeHand Help.

Exporting Flash animations

The Flash Export Xtra exports a FreeHand document as an animated movie in the Flash Player movie (SWF) format. Import the SWF file into Macromedia Flash, view it with the Flash Standalone Player, or view it in a web browser (Netscape Navigator or Microsoft Internet Explorer). Download the Flash Player for free from www.macromedia.com.

To export a FreeHand file to the Flash SWF format, choose File > Export. In the Export Document dialog box, choose Flash SWF from the Format pop-up (Macintosh) or the Save as type pop-up (Windows). Click Options to display settings for path compression, image compression, text, number of pages to export, method of animation (layers, pages, or both), frame rate, full-screen playback, and protection from importing by other users.

Path compression

This option affects graphic quality by controlling the precision used to convert FreeHand paths to Flash paths. More precision specifies more points on a path; less precision specifies fewer points on a path. Options range from None (highest quality, no compression, most points) to Maximum (lowest quality, greatest compression, fewest points).

Trace dashed strokes

Each dash segment converts to a separate object, which increases export time and file size.

Image compression

Bitmap images convert to JPEG format upon export. This option controls the image quality and the compression of color JPEG files. Options range from None (highest quality, lowest compression) to Maximum (lowest quality, highest compression).

Text

◆ Choose Maintain blocks to keep all the text together in a FreeHand text block for editing in Flash 3 or later.

◆ Choose Convert to Paths to convert text to vector paths, so the text is no longer editable as text. Text attached to a path or text flowing inside a path is automatically converted to paths and therefore is not editable in Flash.

◆ Choose None to omit all text from the exported file.

Pages

This option specifies all pages or a range of pages. Each frame is the same size as the first page exported.

Animation

Choose any combination of the Animation options to export layer-based frames, page-based frames, or both:

◆ If neither Animate layers nor Animate pages is checked, each page of the FreeHand file is exported as a separate SWF file. The layers of each page make up a still image for that page.

◆ If only Animate pages is checked, each page is exported as a Flash frame, saving all pages into one SWF file. The layers of each page make up the image for that page (frame).

◆ If only Animate layers is checked, each layer is exported as a Flash frame. FreeHand exports each page as a separate SWF file, with numbered file names to denote the sequence. The layers (frames) for each page are included in the file for that page. Frames of animation are sequenced from the bottom layer to the top layer. The Guides layer and hidden layers (layers that are turned off) are not exported.

◆ If both Animate layers and Animate pages are checked, only one SWF file is exported. All layers of the first page are exported as a sequence of frames, followed by all layers of the second page, and so on. Each page can be used as a scene.

Frame rate

This option specifies the frame rate of the Flash movie in frames per second (fps). As in Flash, choose a frame rate from 0.01 fps to 120 fps, in increments of 0.01. For smooth animations use 12 fps.

Autoplay

If checked, the animation automatically begins playing at the specified frame rate when viewed in the Flash Standalone Player.

If unchecked, the animation stops at frame 1 when viewed in the Flash Standalone Player. Choose Control > Play to start the animation.

Full screen playback

Plays the animation in full-screen. The entire animation will play full-screen until you press Esc.

Although the Flash Standalone Player plays an animation full-screen, this option has no affect on Flash animations played in a web browser.

Compatibility

Choose the Flash version format to which to export the file.

Protect from import

Protects a SWF file exported by FreeHand from being imported by other users.

High quality printing

Each frame in the SWF animation can be printed at high resolution from the Flash 4.x or higher standalone player or browser plug-in. If unchecked, the file will print using the browser's screen resolution.

Supported features

These FreeHand features are supported in the Flash SWF format:

- Basic strokes and fills
- Lens fills (Transparency Lens fills remain transparent upon export)
- Gradient fills
- CMYK or RGB TIFFs and embedded images (JPEG, GIF, PNG)
- Blended paths
- Composite paths, including text converted to paths
- FreeHand-generated clipping paths containing vector paths or image files
- Text blocks
- Arrowheads

For export limitations, see FreeHand Help.

Note: Choose View > Flash Anti-alias to display anti-aliased artwork on the screen as it will appear when exported to Macromedia Flash SWF format.

Placing objects on layers for animation

The Release to Layers Xtra ungroups blends, groups, or objects attached to a path, creates a new layer for each object, and assigns each ungrouped object to a new layer in consecutive order. The Xtra places the first object on the current layer and the last object on the top layer. For best results, design the frames of your movie to animate upwards from the bottom layer to the top layer.

Release to Layers affects the following objects:

- Blends and blends on a path
- Text blocks.
- Text on or in a path
- Inline graphics on or in a path
- Groups

Note: Applying the Release to Layers command to text blocks converts the text to paths.

To ungroup a group of objects to layers, select the group and choose Xtras > Animate > Release to Layers.

When a group of objects is released to layers, the first object in the group remains on the original layer by default. The subsequent objects are placed on layers named New Layer, New Layer-1, New Layer-2, and so on. Display the Layers panel to see how the layers are created and named.

Note: If you include a nested object in a group of objects, it behaves as a single object.

You can choose how objects are released:

Sequence—All objects are released in sequence to separate layers.

Build—All objects are released to layers to create a stacking effect.

Drop—All objects are copied to all layers, except one object is sequentially omitted from each layer.

Trail—All objects are cloned and released to the number of layers specified in the Trail by field.

Creating word effects

When a text block is selected and released to layers, each letter in the text block is converted to paths and released to its own layer.

If you want to include more than one letter on a layer, group them together. For example:

1   Select the letters for the first word and group them.

2   Then, select the letters for the second word and group them.

3   Choose Xtras > Animate > Release to Layers and choose Sequence in the Animate pop-up and click OK.

When played, the two objects are animated as two words flashing.

Importing from CorelDRAW 7 and 8

Using the CorelDRAW 7 and 8 Import Xtra, FreeHand on both Macintosh and Windows can open files saved in the uncompressed CorelDRAW 7 or 8 for Windows file format.

Requirements for opening CorelDRAW files

◆   Files must be saved in uncompressed CorelDRAW 7 or 8 for Windows format.

   CorelDRAW files using either Graphics or Bitmap compression will not import properly.

◆   When opening CorelDRAW files using FreeHand for Macintosh, the CorelDRAW files must have names containing fewer than 32 characters and must have Corel's CDR extension.

For import limitations, see FreeHand Help.

Working with earlier versions of FreeHand

Because FreeHand's features change between versions, some illustration attributes may change or be omitted from a converted illustration. After converting a document to or from an earlier version, be sure it displays and prints properly before deleting the original document.

Converting files from earlier versions

To convert a file from an earlier version, simply open it in FreeHand 9. The converted file's name becomes "<file name> (converted)" (Macintosh) or "<file name>.FH9" (Windows).

Converted FreeHand files appear in FreeHand 9 much as they did in the earlier versions. However, some minor changes occur.

Converting attributes to version 7

These	Change to
PNG files	Not exported to earlier versions.
Lens fills	Paste insides.

To convert a FreeHand 9 document to FreeHand 7, choose File > Export and choose the FreeHand 7 format.

Converting attributes to version 8

To convert a FreeHand 9 document to FreeHand 8, choose File > Export and choose the FreeHand 8 format.

Text on a path

FreeHand 8 and 9 automatically adjust spacing of left-aligned text on a path to avoid overlapping letters due to path curvature. Text on a path in files created in versions of FreeHand earlier than 8 are only adjusted if removed from and re-attached to a path. Likewise, text attached to paths in FreeHand 8 or 9 retain the adjustment when opened in previous versions of FreeHand.

Filled open paths

When opening documents from earlier versions of FreeHand that contain filled, open paths, the fill attributes are present in the Fill inspector; however, the fills may not display. To display the fills, ensure that the Object > "Show fill for new open paths" preference is checked, select the object, and reapply the fill.

Publish as HTML

Use FreeHand's Publish as HTML feature to instantly convert your FreeHand document to a web page. Choose the web page to be viewable with 3.x browsers (converted to HTML tables), 4.x browsers (converted to Dynamic HTML layers).

Choose File > Publish as HTML to open the HTML Output dialog box. Choose settings on the panel, or use the HTML Assistant (Macintosh) or HTML Wizard (Windows) to guide you through the process.

Create multiple HTML settings for the same document. Use them to publish a document to a web page that can be viewed by multiple target browsers or for sites with and without the Flash Standalone Player.

Choose which setting to use when publishing the document as HTML.

Choose whether to publish all pages or a range of pages.

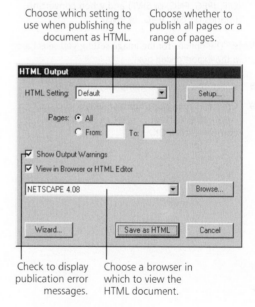

Check to display publication error messages.

Choose a browser in which to view the HTML document.

Creating an HTML setting:

1   Choose File > Publish as HTML to open the HTML Output dialog box.

2   Click Setup to open the HTML Setup dialog box.

3   Click the plus button (+) to open the New HTML Setting dialog box, type a name for the new HTML setting, and click OK.

4   Click the Browse button next to the Document root field, navigate to the destination folder, and click Select or OK.

5   From the Layout pop-up, choose a layout: Positioning with Layers (for viewing in version 4 browsers) or Positioning with Tables (for viewing in version 3 browsers).

6   In most cases, leave Encoding set to the default, Western (Latin 1).

7   In the Export defaults area, choose a default format to be used when converting Vector art (to GIF, JPEG, PNG, or SWF) and when converting Images (as GIF, JPEG, or PNG).

Note: The options for the image setting you select are set in the Export dialog box.

8   When the setting is complete, click Apply.

9   Create as many settings as needed, clicking Apply after each one. After all settings are complete, click OK.

CHAPTER 11
Xtras

. . . .

Managing Xtras

Xtras are plug-in software extensions that expand FreeHand's capabilities. Add or remove Xtra features to meet your specific needs.

With FreeHand's open architecture, many third-party companies develop a wide variety of Xtras to customize your work environment.

Choose Xtras > Xtras Manager to display a list of all Xtras that are installed in the FreeHand Xtras folder. Checked Xtras are turned on. They appear in the Xtras menu and toolbars.

To customize the Xtras menus, turn off Xtras you do not intend to use. Turning off some or all Xtras increases the speed of the application.

To turn on an entire submenu, check the submenu name. To turn off an entire submenu, uncheck the submenu name. To turn on or turn off all Xtras, choose All on or All off from the Options pop-up. Another way to turn on or turn off all Xtras is to hold down Option and click anywhere in the Xtras list (Macintosh) or right-click anywhere in the Xtras list (Windows). Click OK to confirm the changes.

To launch FreeHand without loading Xtras, hold down the Shift key when launching the application. To load Xtras after such a launch, choose Xtras > Xtras Manager and click OK.

After performing an Xtra operation, choose Xtras > Repeat [Xtra name] or press Command-Shift-= (Macintosh) or Control-Alt-Shift-X (Windows) to apply the last performed Xtra operation again.

Installing and removing Xtras

To install an Xtra, drag and drop an Xtra file into the FreeHand 9\English\Xtras folder and restart FreeHand.

To remove an Xtra, drag the Xtra file out of the Xtras folder and restart FreeHand.

Xtras submenus

Xtras with similar features are grouped in submenus. A third-party Xtra may appear in the Xtras menu, the Xtra Tools toolbar, the Xtra Operations toolbar, or in a custom panel, depending on its design and user interface customization.

Submenu	Contains Xtras for
Animate	Creating animations.
Chart	Manipulating charts and pictographs.
Cleanup	Streamlining path manipulation.
Colors	Modifying colors in a document.
Create	Forming new objects.
Delete	Removing objects.
Distort	Altering paths.
Export	Exporting files.
Import	Importing files.
Other	Miscellaneous uses.
Path Operations	Manipulating paths.

Xtras toolbars

The Xtra Tools and Xtra Operations toolbars provide convenient access to some Xtras. If the toolbars are not already visible, choose Window > Toolbar > Xtra Tools or Xtra Operations to display them. All toolbars are

Xtra Tools and Xtra Operations toolbars

customizable and their buttons are interchangeable. For more information on customizing toolbars, see "Customizing your environment" on page 45.

Note: Xtras return to their default toolbar positions after they are deactivated and reactivated or removed and reinstalled.

Select objects before applying Xtras in the Xtra Operations toolbar. To use any Xtra tool, except the Chart Xtra, choose the tool, and then click and drag to apply the Xtra. The Chart Xtra, which appears in both the Xtras menu and the Xtra Tools toolbar, requires additional steps after clicking and dragging the tool.

Some Xtras have dialog boxes that display various options. If a bracket appears in the upper-right corner of an Xtra tool button, double-click it to display the dialog box for that operation.

Xtras at a glance

The following table lists the Xtras currently shipping with FreeHand. For details about these Xtra—including uses, option settings, and examples—see FreeHand Help.

Use Xtra	Location	To
3D Rotation	Xtra Tools toolbar	Apply three-dimensional rotations to two-dimensional objects.
Add Points	Xtras > Distort and Xtra Operations toolbar	Add points halfway between each pair of points on a path.
Arc	Xtra Tools toolbar	Create an open or closed, concave or convex path.
Bend	Xtra Tools toolbar	Create a pinched or bloated look.

Use Xtra	Location	To
Blend	Xtras > Create, Modify > Combine, and Xtra Operations toolbar	Create a smooth transition between two or more paths with respect to shape, stroke, and fill.
Chart	Xtras > Chart and Xtra Tools toolbar	Create charts or pictographs.
Color Control	Xtras > Colors	Adjust the CMYK, RGB, or HLS colors of selected objects.
Convert to Grayscale	Xtras > Convert To Grayscale	Convert colors in the selected objects to grayscale.
Correct Direction	Xtras > Cleanup, Modify > Alter Path, and Xtra Operations toolbar	Alternate the direction of paths in a composite path.
Crop	Xtras > Path Operations, Modify > Combine, and Xtra Operations toolbar	Remove portions of selected, closed paths outside the area of the top closed path.
Darken Colors	Xtras > Colors	Reduce the Lightness color setting by 5%.
Delete Empty Text Blocks	Xtras > Delete	Remove empty text blocks.
Delete Unused Named Colors	Xtras > Delete	Remove unused, named colors from the Color List.
Desaturate Colors	Xtras > Colors	Reduce the Saturation color setting by 5%.
Divide	Xtras > Path Operations, Modify > Combine, and Xtra Operations toolbar	Cut selected paths into sections defined by areas of overlap.
Emboss	Xtras > Create and Xtra Operations toolbar	Create a raised or impressed effect.
Expand Stroke	Xtras > Path Operations, Modify > Alter Path, and Xtra Operations toolbar	Convert an open path to a closed path.

Use Xtra	Location	To
Eyedropper	Xtra Tools toolbar and Toolbox	Extract a color sample from any object—including any imported bitmap image—and apply it to another object.
Fisheye Lens	Xtra Tools toolbar	Create a concave or convex lens effect.
Fractalize	Xtras > Distort and Xtra Operations toolbar	Apply orderly, geometrical transformations to a path.
Graphic Hose	Xtra Tools toolbar	Spray or scatter objects in a specified pattern.
Import RGB Color Table	Xtras > Colors	Load an imported document's colors onto FreeHand's Color List.
Inset Path	Xtras > Path Operations, Modify > Alter Path, and Xtra Operations toolbar	Create a second path with the same contours inside or outside the original path. Positive values yield paths inset from the original; negative values yield paths outlining the original.
Intersect	Xtras > Path Operations, Modify > Combine, and Xtra Operations toolbar	Create a path enclosing the area common to all selected, closed paths.
Lighten Colors	Xtras > Colors	Increase the Lightness color setting by 5%.
Mirror	Xtra Tools toolbar	Create a reflection of an object (Vertical, Horizontal), a 2x2 matrix of reflections of an object (Vertical and Horizontal), a radial group of duplicate objects and their reflections (Multiple with Reflect), or a radial group of duplicate objects (Multiple with Rotate).
Name All Colors	Xtras > Colors	Name all unnamed colors and place them in the Color List.
PICT image (Macintosh only)	Xtras > Create and Xtra Operations toolbar	Convert vector graphics into a bitmap PICT format. Set the number of colors, the image resolution, whether dithering is used, and the extent of anti-aliasing.
Punch	Xtras > Path Operations, Modify > Combine, and Xtra Operations toolbar	Remove portions of selected, closed paths below the top closed path.

Use Xtra	Location	To
Randomize Named Colors	Xtras > Colors	Reassign colors for the entire document.
Release to Layers	Xtras > Animate and Operations toolbar	Ungroup a blend, text block, inline graphic, or group and place each object on its own layer.
Remove Overlap	Xtras > Cleanup, Modify > Alter Path, and Xtra Operations toolbar	Remove overlapping portions of a closed path that crosses over itself.
Reverse Direction	Xtras > Cleanup, Modify > Alter Path, and Xtra Operations toolbar	Switch the direction of any path.
Roughen	Xtra Tools toolbar	Create a hand-drawn look or jagged effect.
Saturate Colors	Xtras > Colors	Increase the Saturation color setting by 5%.
Set Note	Xtras > Other and Xtra Operations toolbar	Attach a non-printing label to an object.
Shadow	Xtra Tools toolbar	Apply drop shadows to vector objects.
Simplify	Xtras > Cleanup, Modify > Alter Path, and Xtra Operations toolbar	Reduce the number of points in a path.
Smudge	Xtra Tools toolbar	Create a variety of effects, including softened edges or drop shadows.
Sort Color List by Name	Xtras > Colors	Sort colors in alphanumeric order.
Spiral	Xtra Tools toolbar and Toolbox	Create an open, spiral-shaped path.

Use Xtra	Location	To
Transparency	Xtras > Path Operations, Modify > Combine, and Xtra Operations toolbar	Create a new path from the area common to two or more closed paths containing Basic fills.
Trap	Xtras > Create and Xtra Operations toolbar	Create spreads and chokes to compensate for misregistration when printing.
Union	Xtras > Path Operations, Modify > Combine, and Xtra Operations toolbar	Combine two or more closed paths into a single path enclosing the entire area of the original paths.
URL Editor	Window > Toolbar > URL Editor	Attach URLs to objects.

INDEX